Death in the Underworld

Betsy Longenbaugh

Kenmore, WA

Epicenter Press Inc.
Alaska Book Adventures

Published by Epicenter Press

Epicenter Press
6524 NE 181st St. Suite 2
Kenmore, WA 98028.
www.Epicenterpress.com
www.Camelpress.com
www.Coffeetownpress.com

For more information go to: www.Epicenterpress.com
Author's website: Truecrimealaska.com

All rights reserved. No part of this book may be reproduced or transmitted in any form or by any means, electronic or mechanical, including photocopying, recording, or any information storage and retrieval system, without permission in writing from the publisher.

Death in the Underworld
Copyright © 2025 by Betsy Longenbaugh

ISBN: 9781684922345 (trade paper)
ISBN: 9781684922352 (ebook)

LOC: 2024940268

Cover photo: Alaska State Library, Photographer Ed Andrews, ASL-P162-125

*To my daughters Maggie and Elizabeth,
who are always there when I need them*

Table of Contents

Chapter 1 1
Chapter 2 7
Chapter 3 16
Chapter 4 23
Chapter 5 26
Chapter 6 35
Chapter 7 40
Chapter 8 48
Chapter 9 53
Chapter 10 58
Chapter 11 62
Chapter 12 67
Chapter 13 76
Chapter 14 79
Chapter 15 87
Chapter 16 95
Chapter 17 101
Chapter 18 108
Chapter 19 115

Chapter 20	125
Chapter 21	144
Chapter 22	150
Chapter 23	155
Chapter 24	164
Chapter 25	169
Chapter 26	179
Chapter 27	186
Chapter 28	192
Chapter 29	199
Chapter 29	203
Chapter 30	213
Chapter 31	219
Chapter 32	224
Chapter 33	231
Chapter 34	237
Chapter 35	244
Chapter 36	251
Epilogue	257
Acknowledgments	261
About the Author	263

Chapter 1

May had worked at the Opera House as a housemaid now for 11 months, three weeks and two days. Her best guess was it would take about 10 months and five days more to save enough for a ticket to Minneapolis, with enough money in her pocket to not be a burden to the family. It was hard work, but she wasn't afraid of hard work. Growing up on a Minnesota farm, she was used to waking up early and working all day. At the Opera House, she also rose early, certainly before the working girls were leaving their beds. She cleaned, washed dirty clothes and linens, and helped in the kitchen if the cook, Mrs. Todd, needed it. It was 1916, and the Treadwell Mine, which kept the Opera House and its workers busy, was still producing enough gold to make it the richest gold mine in the world. Life in Douglas was good – for almost everyone.

Today she pushed the broom down the hallway and paused – there was another of those loathsome small wooden boxes. She picked it up and glanced inside – the condom was not there, which should mean good things for the girl to whom it belonged. She picked it up; it would be taken to the madam and refilled with a reusable rubber casing, lubed and ready for use.

She smiled to herself, "what use was this at an opera?" Glancing out the window at the end of the hall, she spied the sign on the neighboring building – a cigar store and fruit stand. While there was an occasional collection of fruits in the front of the store, it offered little in the way of cigars. Like the well-known Douglas Opera House, the Nenana Cigar Store was a brothel, just on a much smaller scale. Built just a year before, in 1915, the cigar store was another building that appeared as unsubstantial as it undoubtedly was, slapped together after a fire had destroyed most of the block, sparing just the Douglas Opera House. Douglas itself was kind of slapdash – built to offer all the things that the neighboring company town of Treadwell in Alaska couldn't offer – churches, bars, and women.

She knew she had to work, and expected to all her life, and this work wasn't bad, but she missed home so much. She longed to see her mother, father, and the young brothers and sisters she left behind when she and Albert went off on their grand adventure after their wedding. Albert, another Minneapolis farm child, had been her beau since they had made the transition from squabbles during recess to his carrying her books home from school. What had given him the idea that he wanted to leave Minnesota was a mystery to May. She would have been happy to remain near her home, but however much she loved her family, she loved Albert more.

She had loved his long, elegant hands, which contrasted with his burly body hardened by labor. She loved his laugh and was always a little proud when something she said elicited it. When he picked up the fiddle, she thought she could feel her heart leap to the tunes he played. Maybe it was the music that spurred his wanderlust, she thought absently, briskly sweeping wet dirt and sand into the dustpan. She walked down the back stairs to the kitchen, to see if Mrs. Todd had any tasks for her.

She treasured the warmth and dryness of the kitchen, where the cook cooked meals for the house's occupants, and prepared snacks for the Opera House bar – the scotch eggs, bowls of peanuts and pickled herring that helped slow down the fast drunk many of its customers were seeking. Unlike the rest of the building, which often seemed to be fighting a losing battle against the near constant rain of Douglas, Alaska, the kitchen really was dry, despite the wooden rack hung with sodden coats, and the steam coming from the ever-full kettle on the stove. May came into the room as often as her chores allowed and appreciated any opportunity to spend time there.

"Here, child, sit for a cuppa," Mrs. Todd said, nodding to a chair at the table. May smiled to see that her friend, Fannie Miller, was already seated with her own cup of tea and toast. Although Fannie no longer worked at the Opera House, she remained a frequent visitor, and she and May had become close since May had begun her job there.

"May," greeted Fannie with a smile. "I'm so glad to see you. Rosie decided to sleep in today, so I thought I would grace you with my presence."

"You're looking so pretty today," May replied, having learned that while any woman likes compliments, the demimonde thrived on them. Fannie did look good – like any woman in this rainy climate, her skin was not blemished by sun, and her blue eyes sparkled.

"What are your plans for today?" May asked.

"It's Tuesday, so I'll be doing some shopping and errands, but mostly I'm excited because I have an appointment at the photography studio. Mr. Carson asked some of us down the street to come in for some photographs. You know how he has pictures of pretty girls in his store window? Well, he wants some new ones so asked Rosie and me to come by. I'm not sure what I'm going to wear – I'm trying to decide between the dress I have on," she nodded toward the shirtwaist and short jacket, "or an evening gown. The one I was thinking of has that embroidery on the bodice – you know the one I mean?"

"The black one with the red stitching?"

"Yes. I think the photo will be just from the waist up, but I don't know. I'm trying to remember if he ever has photographs showing head to toe. Do you remember? If so, then I also need to think about shoes, and I don't really want to walk a few blocks in my evening slippers, although I suppose I could carry them. But listen to me, I'm going on and on. I guess you can tell I'm excited."

May smiled at her friend's exuberance. Fannie was often excited, or at least the way she spoke would indicate such. That was what had attracted her to Fannie in the first place; May's life right now seemed so predictable and her grief so stubborn that any ray of sunshine was welcomed, even if it came in the form of a working girl. Oh, how her mother would be shocked to know she had become friends with such a person, and May had no intention of ever telling her.

"I'm happy for you. I've often admired those photographs, and know a lot of the miners do too," May said with a smile. "I do remember a couple of full-length photographs – but most are more of the head and shoulders. I think you look lovely in what you have on, but that evening gown is very attractive. Why don't you ask Mr. Carson? Or maybe you and Rosie could wear the same sort of outfit and he could take photographs of the two of you together. Is he going to give you a photograph, or pay you?

"I didn't think to ask, I was so excited," admitted Fannie. "But maybe Rosie will know. She seems so much more experienced in everything, although I think she's about as old as I am."

May considered that. Both Fannie and Rosie looked older in some ways, and younger in others. Their manner of holding themselves, and the lives they had led portrayed a certain sophistication and maturity, but they shared an exuberance and excitement in everyday things that May couldn't help but envy. Her best guess was she and they were about the same age – 23. But she could be off by five, or even more years, she supposed.

Rosie and Fannie had come down from the railway town of Anchorage just a few months before, but all three women had become good friends quickly. Maybe it was that they were all facing new futures, thought May. She had lost Albert and begun working at the Opera House, and Rosie and Fannie had left the brothel to strike out on their own in the little cabins down the road from Front Street in Douglas.

The houses were in the two-block Restricted District, as it was known, so May couldn't visit them there – it was an area where no women but working girls could be seen without there being an assumption they were also working there. May had briefly considered the work – it paid well and no one from home would ever know, but she knew Albert would have been appalled and upset if it came to that. His membership in the Masons had paid for a respectable burial, and the madam had offered her the job of maid.

The pay in the Restricted District was good, though, she thought wistfully. Fannie had told her that she and Rosie had come to Douglas with thousands in savings after working up north. But she had also hinted that getting there had been hard – harder than May could imagine.

She resolutely turned away from that recollection, as she had trained herself to do with so many sad thoughts.

Standing up, she turned to Mrs. Todd. "What can I do for you?" she asked the plump older woman, whose dark dress was covered by a white apron that was much less stained now than it would be by the end of the busy day.

"Well, love, I'm going to start today's baking, so if you can set the tables for breakfast for the girls, that would be helpful," Mrs. Todd replied with a smile. "Although why they persist in calling it breakfast, I don't know. Where I come from in Illinois, this would be dinner time."

May glanced at the kitchen clock and realized it was close to noon; her work was hard but the day did go fast.

Fannie stood, saying, "It's time for me to be off also; I'm going to check on Rosie and see if she ever got up. She would usually be awake by now, but Sadie said she saw a man leaving Rosie's cabin at around 4 this morning, so she must be having a sleep in."

She donned the clogs that helped, at least a little, to keep mud from dirtying the hem of her long skirt and stepped out into the drizzle of the day.

May set a tray with plates and utensils, pushed the swinging door into the small dining room next to the kitchen and began setting the table for the 12 occupants she could hear moving around upstairs as they washed and dressed.

• • •

The meal had ended, but a few women stayed at the table, having another cup of coffee, and talking. May loaded the tray with dirty dishes and pushed the door to the kitchen. She usually enjoyed hearing the women talk about their lives, but today they seemed intent on talking instead about a customer who had insisted on squeezing the throats of the women as he had sex with them. It wasn't that unusual, according to the women, but there was something about this man that made them all a little frightened. He hadn't wanted to stop when they asked, or even pleaded.

May didn't want to hear any more, although the conversation certainly confirmed May's decision to choose making a living with a broom instead of a room.

As she walked into the kitchen, she saw Mrs. Todd standing at the kitchen door to the alley, talking to someone May couldn't see. Although the conversation was low enough that May couldn't make out the words, the tone of Mrs. Todd's voice was alarmed.

She turned and saw May; her face was pale and her lips trembling. "It's murder," she whispered. "Murder."

Chapter 2

"There's been a murder," Deputy Federal Rhys Davies was trying to be quiet, but his words still caused a hush in the restaurant, where Deputy Marshal Frank Leishke was finishing his lunch. The restaurant was located on the ground floor of the Hotel Zynda in downtown Juneau. It had originally served just its residents, but the cook was good enough to bring in other patrons, and the hotel took advantage of its popularity.

"Sit down before you fall down, and whisper, you idiot," Frank hissed at Davies, who looked ready to throw up as he glanced at Frank's corned beef and hash.

The younger deputy marshal set his hat on the table and drew out the chair opposite Frank's, his face pale and sweat evident on his forehead, despite the chill of a March in Juneau. "I just came from there," he spoke in a low voice. "It was the most awful thing I've ever seen. The blood..." he trailed off, turned inward on the memory.

"That is completely useless information," Frank Leishke said with enough bite to bring the man's attention back to the detective.

"Sorry, sir. I ... I just don't know how to describe this."

"I'll tell you what, I'll just ask you questions, then you will not have to describe anything. But let's get out of here. Too many ears," Frank said, gesturing to the other diners, who had remained quiet since the deputy marshal's first words, some even leaning slightly toward their table.

He dropped a 50-cent piece on the table for the 25-cent lunch, grabbed Deputy Marshal Rhys Davies by the elbow, lifted him from the chair, and led him out the door to the hotel lobby, and then to the door leading outside. They both put on their hats as they pushed through the door.

It was a typical spring day in the rainforest of Southeast Alaska, with highs near 40 degrees and rain overhead. The awnings of the downtown stores covered the hats of the two men, but they still needed to dodge corner drains at the end of each storefront. The boardwalk beneath their feet was slippery when wet, and Leishke was again grateful for the tread of his boots.

If you didn't know they were there, you wouldn't see the mountains hovering above Franklin Street, since fog and mist had dropped to the roofs of the collection of clapboard buildings that made up Alaska's territorial capital. Days like today were a bit of a relief to Frank Leishke, who often found the looming mountains a little oppressive. Juneau was built at the bottom of steep mountains that left little room for habitation on their rocky shores, and when Frank took the ferry across the channel from Douglas Island on a clear day, it sometimes appeared to him that Juneau was on the brink of just sliding into the ocean.

Deputy Marshal Leishke dropped the other deputy marshal's arm and walked quickly enough that the shorter Davies had to run a little to keep up with him. They turned onto Front Street and headed up the hill for two blocks to the courthouse, which also housed the police department, the federal marshals, and the jail. It was a steep climb, and both men slowed a little as they reached the courthouse. Davies stepped in front of Leishke and opened the door, ushering him into the hall that faced the central stairwell of the three-story building. To the right was the police office, but the marshal's office was on the second floor, so both men stepped briskly up the stairs. Leishke had just been assigned his own office, which he unlocked and into which he ushered Rhys Davies. He correctly interpreted the quizzical look on the younger marshal's face.

"I'm just in the practice of locking up my office," Leishke said, pointing to a desk piled high with files, a typewriter, loose papers and empty or partially empty coffee cups. "It's easier than trying to keep it clean."

Davies took a few seconds to look at Leishke, who he had met when he joined the marshals last month, but had not worked with. He saw a man in his early 30s, tall and fit, with dark thick hair and a luxurious mustache. He could be perceived as a gentleman except for his hands – they were the hands of a brawler – large fingers and knuckles that looked scarred and permanently swollen.

"Marshal Calhoun told me to fetch you," he said to Leishke.

Calhoun was the Marshal for the First Judicial District of Alaska, the region that encompassed all of Southeast Alaska, the most populous part of the giant land mass that had been purchased from Russia almost fifty years before. He headed the deputy marshal service for the region – the only law enforcement for much of the area, since only a few towns had their own police departments. He was also the man who had hired Leishke, who at the time was a Pinkerton detective, to join the marshal service the year before.

The walk up from the restaurant had apparently calmed the younger man down, which Leishke had anticipated. The upcoming interview would be better held here, and not just to escape nosy locals. He gestured to one of two chairs placed in front of the desk, and took the other, obviously surprising Davies, who glanced at the chair behind the desk.

"Well, young man, let me give you two opportunities in this interview," Frank said, leaning slightly toward Davies, and folding his hands. "I'm going to show you what to ask, and how to behave when you interview a witness. First of all, try to make it friendly. My sitting behind a desk is not friendly, and while that may be a good idea with some conversations, interviewing a witness should include making the witness feel as comfortable as possible. I think you can understand right now how hard it can be knowing you're going to be questioned."

Davies nodded, drawn to Leishke's eyes, which showed both compassion and humor, as did the slight smile on this mouth. He felt himself relaxing slightly, recognized it and realized this was going to be an important skill to learn.

"So, let's start with where and who," instructed Leishke.

"It happened in Douglas in the Restricted District," came the reply. "The victim is a working girl who just moved here a few months ago. Her name is – was – Rosie Brown."

"Good. Now, did anyone see the killing?"

"I don't think so. Her neighbor, another working girl named Fannie Miller, asked a carpenter in the area to break into the house because she was worried about Rosie. I guess the two women have coffee every morning. The two of them found the body and told the Douglas Commissioner, who called us."

The Commissioner of Douglas, John Hensen, was the representative of law enforcement in Douglas as the city had neither police nor sheriff's department. Douglas relied on the neighboring city of Juneau to send over federal marshals when it needed a law enforcement presence. Commissioner Hensen ensured summons and warrants, and called in coroner's juries as needed. With federal marshals a short ferry ride from Juneau, the Douglas City Council had decided against the expense of having its own police department, although Juneau had made the opposite decision. The city of Douglas, however, had been built to serve the thousand miners and staff who worked in the neighboring company town of Treadwell, and consequently, had the churches, pool halls, bars and brothels not allowed in Treadwell. It certainly had enough crime to warrant its own police department and Deputy Marshal Leishke wasn't alone in thinking the council's decision was short sighted. This murder, Leishke thought, might prove it.

"Go ahead," he coaxed his fellow deputy marshal, Davies. "You saw the crime. What did you see?"

This was the hard part; Davies swallowed and then took a deep breath.

"Well, it's a two-room crib, which is bigger than some of the cabins down there," Davies said. "There's a front room and a bedroom in back. The body was in the bedroom, on the floor next to the bed." He froze again, and Leishke felt some impatience.

"So, let's leave it that she was dead," said Leishke. "What killed her?" he asked.

"I don't know – there must have been a knife, but then she also seemed to have been beaten," replied Davies. He added, "Marshal Calhoun has given instruction to leave everything alone, so the Douglas Commissioner can call in the coroner's jury, and he sent me for you."

Leishke gave a sigh and decided to give Davies a break. "I'll just head over there, then," Leishke said, clasping his hat back on his head and heading to the door. Can you please lock it up on your way out?"

Davies nodded, looking a little ashamed (as he should, thought Leishke) and the deputy marshal headed for the stairs.

Leishke hurried down the hill to the ferry dock, taking out his watch to check the time. He had taken the trip often enough, especially when he was investigating the Krause murders last year, to know the schedule. If he hurried, he could catch the next boat, which left every half hour.

Leishke stood on the top deck of the passenger-only ferry as it began the journey across Gastineau Channel to Douglas Island, the home of both Douglas city and Treadwell, which Leishke had been told was the biggest gold mine in the world. Despite the light rain, he chose to stand on the deck, not being overly fond of the low overhead in the boat's cabin.

The deputy marshal stared at the waters of the channel, imagining what lay beneath him, and below the deep channel – miles and miles of tunnels, occupied by hundreds of miners who used hammers and even dynamite to break out the rock they would haul to the surface, pound, and roll into sand, and run through a process to extract the gold.

It was hard to believe that people could actually be working beneath him, Leishke thought, inwardly shuddering at the idea of the miners down there, knowing there were tons of rock and water above them.

The ferry moved toward Douglas, where it would first dock in Treadwell, and then travel about half a mile north to the Douglas dock. As the boat got closer, the noise grew louder. The stamp mills that pounded the big rocks into small rocks were also considered the largest in the world, and they certainly made enough noise to seem world sized. No matter where you were, in Juneau, Douglas or Treadwell, you couldn't escape the thudding, which sounded all day and all night. Frank Leishke had heard that local residents couldn't sleep Christmas night or the night of July Fourth, the only two days the mines shut down, because of the quiet. Although his work had taken him elsewhere on both days this past year, Leishke found the idea easy to believe, surprised at how quickly he had learned to sleep through the sound.

He looked behind the ferry at Juneau, where he spotted the gold mine works there, proving what he had heard might be the case – the gold vein that fueled Treadwell stretched under the channel from Douglas Island and up Mt. Roberts in Juneau. Leishke wondered how far it went – could it travel through the ice fields into Canada, he mused. Although he thought that if it did, the Canadians would have already found that out. Fortunately for him, he thought, he didn't have to rely on gold mining for a job.

The ferry pulled up the dock in Treadwell, where he could see the magnificent mansion that was the residence for the mine's superintendent just a couple of blocks from the end of the dock. The ferry skipper eased the boat to the dock, idled the engine and stepped onto the dock with the mooring rope in one easy movement. Three people stepped off, all of them appearing to be workers at Treadwell, and a couple stepped on. The man held the hand of his partner, helping her make the small but potentially watery step between the dock and boat. They went into the cabin to get out of the rain, but not before Leishke heard the man say to the woman, "you'll feel safer in Juneau."

It shouldn't surprise him that the word was out about the murder, if that was what the man referenced. He had worked in Alaska for the past 18 months, and knew how fast gossip traveled, and how very wrong it could be. Now, he prepared to face a coroner's jury, assuming that Douglas Commissioner Hensen, the man whose job included acting as coroner, had gotten those six men to the scene of the crime as quickly as he was heading there.

The coroner's jury was a tool in common use elsewhere, but

with Alaska being a territory and not a state yet, they were more frequently used here. Frank Leishke's feelings about the juries were mixed – in his role as a Pinkerton detective and now as a deputy marshal, Leishke had seen capable and educated juries, but had also seen men swayed too easily by the authority figures around them. He hoped this jury would be considered and methodical, as he preferred it to be when he investigated a crime.

Coroner's juries were six men – usually chosen from among people known to the authorities and paid a few dollars for their service. Of course, anyone who was Alaska Native, Asian, or otherwise non-white couldn't serve. Leishke didn't envy the jurors the job – they were called to every suspicious death and were expected to view the body at the scene, if possible, and to interview witnesses. Their main task was to determine cause of death, but Leishke had known of coroner's juries who also named the person who killed the victim, or even named the murder as being in self-defense.

Just the year before, a young woman whose estranged husband had tried to strangle her on the street in Juneau had pulled a gun from her pocket and shot him. The one bullet had gone upward through his abdomen and into his heart. She was found to have killed him in self-defense by the coroner's jury, recalled Leishke. Although, he thought, her job as housemaid to one of the more powerful businessmen in town may have nudged the jury toward its decision. Especially when the police had released the woman to her employer, at the employer's request.

Leishke again hoped that today's jury would be composed of men with a responsible outlook. The deputy marshal walked onto the dock in Douglas, right behind the ferry's skipper, who had again brought the boat smoothly to the pier. Leishke tipped his hat to the skipper and walked up the dock, turning right on First Street.

To his left, Leishke passed the Douglas Opera House, a place he had frequented for the beer, but not the female company. Leishke had seen enough violence and venereal disease to be wary of the demimonde. He had sometimes enjoyed the company of a willing widow, but it had been a while since he had spent the night elsewhere and didn't see that changing soon. His detective work, first as a Pinkerton agent, and now as a federal marshal, didn't lend itself to marriage.

He walked down First Street on the broad planked street, passing a cigar store, two pool halls, and a carpenter's shop. The shop was at the end of one block, and the next two blocks were the Restricted District. It was certainly easy to keep this area "restricted," thought Leishke, who noted that the two blocks ended with, somewhat incongruently, a dairy barn, and then, the beach. As he approached No. 7, the cabin belonging to Rosie Brown, he saw a dairy hand herding the cows back into the barn, coming down the steep road from the less developed part of town. He suspected the cows must be taken back and forth each day to find grazing up that hill.

The little cabins, also called cribs, that the prostitutes inhabited, were close together and generally not bigger than one room, although he noted two larger houses that were probably occupied by more than one working girl.

As Deputy Marshal Frank Leishke neared No. 7, he saw another young deputy marshal posted outside, which almost certainly meant the jury was inside. A few other people stood outside the cabin, trying to get a glimpse inside. He realized that having the crime occur in the Restricted District cut down on onlookers, since no respectable person would be seen in the neighborhood, especially during daylight hours.

Leishke greeted the young marshal, a man he knew as Deputy Marshal Matthew McIntyre, and made his way inside. It was tight quarters. He counted eight people – the six jurors, another marshal and a young woman who appeared to be answering questions from jury members. He introduced himself as the deputy marshal assigned to investigate the case, recognizing three of the jurors – two owned stores in Douglas and one was a miner whom Leishke had interviewed during the Krause investigation. They all seemed relieved to see him. Perhaps they thought having a trained detective took some pressure off their decision making, Leishke thought. It wasn't going to work that way.

The young woman was named Fannie Miller, and she was a neighbor of Rosie's, and had found the body. Leishke tried to make himself as inconspicuous as possible and prepared to hear her story. First, he examined the room – the front room of the two-room cabin.

The group was standing in the front room; the door to the back room was shut. Leishke saw a wood stove next to a small stack of wood, a water basin and jug on a washstand, and two chairs and a table. An open cupboard held a few dishes and some cans of food. The table held two half-empty glasses and a bottle of beer. The basin was half filled with pink-tinged water, a towel lying next to it. The white towel had bright red blotches, with some pink areas where someone had apparently wiped wet hands. On the wall behind the washstand, a red handprint stood out against the white paint. Leishke imagined the murderer leaning against the wall to catch his breath before washing his hands in the basin.

Frank Leishke waited to hear Fannie Miller's story.

Chapter 3

May didn't see Fannie until near the end of her workday, for which she was grateful. She collected herself after hearing of Rosie's murder from Mrs. Todd. The typically busy day had been punctuated by the conversations she kept overhearing about the killing. Apparently, poor Fannie had found her, dead in her cabin. After that, May didn't know what to believe. She heard that Rosie had been strangled, beaten, even dismembered. One person swore she had died from strychnine poisoning; certainly, that was believable. May knew strychnine was a favorite choice of those despairing few who killed themselves. It was easy to buy, and certainly deadly enough.

May was getting ready to head home when she poked her head in the kitchen and saw Fannie at the table. Since she had finished her daily tasks, May felt comfortable accepting another cup of tea from Mrs. Todd. Mrs. Todd looked at the two young women, smiled, and said, "I have some things to see to. Can you please keep an eye on the pies?" She left the room, probably to go to her room next to the kitchen.

"Oh, Fannie, I'm so sorry to hear about Rosie. My goodness, that must have been so terrible," May blurted out. Then she caught herself, looking at Fannie's drawn face. Her hands shook as she brought the cup to her lips, and May was taken back to the days after Albert's death. She took a deep breath, and then, more quietly, said, "I am so sorry. I also know you must have been talking about this all day. If you want to talk about it, I'm here, but if you don't, we can just sit here together, or talk about something else."

Fannie also drew a long breath and gave a wan smile. "You're right. It has been a long day of talking about this. First, I had to tell the marshal, then the coroner's jury, and then this detective from the marshal's office. I think it was the same man who helped bring Krause to trial last year. It was exhausting, but…" she trailed off, moving to gaze at her teacup, and began running the tip of her finger around the top of the cup.

May waiting patiently, knowing that grief sometimes meant a friendly presence was the best that could be offered. Her family was large – large enough to have seen its share of lost family members and grief. Farming, while not as dangerous as mining, had its share of tragedies. She had lost an uncle two years ago when his horse threw him, and a cousin had been crippled by a fall in a barn.

"You know," Fannie said, looking up from the cup and into May's eyes, "I do think it would be helpful if I could talk about it. I know more about Rosie's past life than I told anyone today, so maybe you'll believe me when I tell you that I think that past might have caught up with her today."

She closed her eyes, and May saw a tear fall down her cheek. May took a clean handkerchief from her sleeve and passed it to Fannie, suspecting Fannie's handkerchief had been well used today.

"Sadie saw someone leave Rosie's house this morning at around 4," she told May, who remembered that Fannie had mentioned that this morning.

"Sadie described him as having a dark complexion, curly hair and being tall, probably about six feet. That sounds to me like it could have been Rosie's husband."

"But I thought he was in San Francisco," May said. "Isn't that what Rosie said?"

"We did think he was still in San Francisco," replied Fannie, "but you know that Rosie lived in fear that Againsky would find her. When we moved here from Anchorage, she was hoping that she had finally escaped from him. If he tracked her here, he is certain to be the one that killed her."

Fannie paused and looked again at her hand on the teacup. "Whoever killed her, he must have been very angry. I heard the detective say that the murderer had used a knife and a hammer when he killed poor Rosie. There was a lot of blood, that's for certain." She paused again.

May thought about what Fannie had said, and had to ask the obvious, "how do you know what her husband, this Againsky, looks like? I didn't think you had ever seen him."

"Well," Fannie drew out the word. "I know we told you that Rosie and I had met in Anchorage, but actually, we met in San Francisco. It was my idea for us to move to Anchorage. Of course, Againsky knew she was going there. He thought it was a good thing, because he knew she would make a lot of money. After all, a railroad camp in the wilderness with a lot of workers. Bound to be a good place for working girls.

"So, he gave her the money for the ticket and we left. Rosie was so glad to be without Againsky, that I think she would have gone to Timbuktu. Once we got there, though, it was rough. It's mostly just a tent city. Believe it or not, Juneau looks like a big city compared to that place.

"But it was good money, and there were some nice girls there who were friendly. Rosie started believing she may have escaped Againsky and the Warsaw Club altogether. She was learning how to write and had gotten a letter from home. Not the ones that the Club sent to her, but letters she got because she wrote her family."

May wasn't sure what Fannie meant about the Club and letters, but remained silent, letting Fannie tell her story.

"I don't know if you know, but Rosie's real name was Jennie Poplosky. Her family wrote to her that her brother was fighting for Poland in the world war, and that they were worried for him. What really bothered her, though, was they told her that they had gotten her other letters and the money she sent and were so happy that she was living such a good life in America.

"What a story," Fannie said bitterly. "Although I guess it's good now that they will never know the truth. That their 13-year-old Jennie was 'married' to a man who had already claimed five wives, all young Jewish Polish girls. That the America he promised them was Argentina, not the United States. That the riches he promised them was the money they made lying on their backs. That the wonderful lives they were going to lead were lives of misery.

"Those other letters and the money were sent by the Club to keep the family quiet and happy. That way, when another 'rich American' showed up at a Jewish household in Poland, the parents would be happy to let their young daughter marry him. I think there are more than a dozen Againskys – maybe even dozens. These men and the Club are evil. There is no other word for it." Fannie lapsed into silence, gulping her cool tea with a shaking hand, and beginning to weep in earnest.

May stood up to get a fresh cup of tea for her friend, poured it, added a hefty lump of sugar, set the cup in front of her and sat down again. This story seemed to her to be fantastical – a group of men who abducted young Jewish girls into a white slavery ring in Argentina? It didn't seem possible, she thought. Then had to catch herself. Well, last year, it wouldn't have been possible that she would be sitting in the infamous Douglas Opera House. Four years ago, it wouldn't have seemed possible she would be widowed, or in Alaska. Maybe her life had already shown her that the impossible wasn't.

Oh, but the pies. She jumped up to check on them. The three pies in the large kitchen range were perfect. The dried apple slices had plumped up among the raisins and the crust was golden. What luck! Mrs. Todd would have been very upset if they had burnt. She grabbed a dish towel and removed the pastries, setting them on the cloth that Mrs. Todd had put on the nearby counter.

The pie rescue had given Fannie a chance to drink her tea and calm down. The tears had stopped and her color was better. May decided enough had been said for today. She had plenty of questions, but her instinct told her that her friend had endured enough.

She asked Fannie if she had eaten recently, and her friend said no, she didn't think she had eaten anything since a bite in the morning. May prepared a plate of bread and cheese, with some piccalilli that Mrs. Todd put up and May thought was delicious. Fannie must have thought so also, since she had a small taste of the tomato, pepper, and pickle relish, and then spread it lavishly on the cheddar cheese and bread.

Mrs. Todd bustled in, glanced at the pies, and gave May a smile of thanks. She stood behind Fannie, nodding as the young woman ate, and reaching over to fill her teacup again. Mrs. Todd had also come from a large family, but it wasn't as happy as May's had been. The cook had alluded to conflict that made her residence in Alaska a happy one for her.

Fannie had eaten supper with the working girls but was more than happy to take the piece of warm pie that the cook set in front of her, noting she had set a similar piece next to May's plate, which she was rapidly emptying.

"It's good you girls get something in you," said Mrs. Todd. "There is nothing better for a shock than a full stomach. Back home, I would fry up a batch of donuts anytime there was a loss in a family. And they were always welcome."

Donuts wouldn't meet most people's definition of appropriate food for a grieving household, May thought, but also thought they must have been appreciated. She loved the idea of a grief-stricken family member answering the door to Mrs. Todd, who would be standing there, holding a plate of warm donuts. Her imagination worked to clothe Mrs. Todd in this scene. Would she wear an apron? An outdoor coat? Would she have a plate of donuts, or a basket, with a cloth covering the warm fried dough?

May couldn't help but smile, and glanced at Fannie, hoping her friend wouldn't be upset by a moment of levity. Instead, she saw an answering smile, and realized they might be both imagining the same moment. She remembered that this is why she and Fannie were good friends. They shared a sense of humor, and often found themselves both noting the same absurdities.

The two women ate their pie and continued talking with Mrs. Todd. There was no more talk of Rosie, murder or anything called a Warsaw Club.

After half an hour, May and Fannie donned their coats and left together. It was dark now, and May was glad she didn't have far to go. Fannie turned right toward the Restricted District, and May turned left, after giving her friend a fierce hug and kiss on the cheek.

May walked down Front Street, up a slight incline and then turned left again to follow St. Ann's Avenue toward St. Ann's Hospital. She lived with another miner's widow in a house a few blocks down the street, near the hospital, which was run by the Sisters of St. Ann. The block that held the hospital also housed a Catholic school and the house of the parish priest.

May greeted her landlady, Edith, as she walked into the front room of the house. Mrs. E.L. Starling had opened the small boarding house after her husband's death in the mine. May found solace with Edith, who understood the sadness and confusion of losing a husband who was healthy and hearty one day and gone the next.

"I heard there was a murder down at the Restricted District," Edith said to May. The widow was about a decade older than May. She had two children, ages 8 and 10, both of whom seemed well behaved and quiet to May, who nonetheless was grateful that Albert had not left behind children. She had grieved during her marriage as her courses came each month, but now she was alone, she was glad to not have the additional burden. She honestly did not know how she would have coped if she had children and faced supporting herself and them.

However close she and Edith had become, May had never told her about her friendship with Fannie. It was bad enough that she worked at a brothel, if Edith knew she had become friendly with a working girl, she could imagine that Edith would evict her. She was careful in her response to Edith's comment.

"Yes, I heard that too. But I don't know anything else. There was a lot of talk and speculation, but I didn't hear anything that I could say without doubt was true. Just that someone died. I am sure someone will be caught soon. After all, Edward Krause was caught, and no one thought that would happen."

Edith nodded, and May made her way up the stairs to her bedroom. The room was small but had everything May needed. There was a single bed with a warm blanket, her trunk at the foot of it. A dresser and wardrobe held her four dresses, under linens and night dresses. A washstand held a basin and pitcher, with a hand towel on a hook next to them. The small table next to the bed held the treasured photo of her and Albert on their wedding day. He was so handsome, and she looked so happy. She had felt pretty and treasured, and looking at the photo, May couldn't recall another day filled with such happiness and anticipation. She had just known she would have a wonderful life with Albert. They would have children, a home of their own, and a farm of their own once Albert was able to put together enough cash to buy land.

She pulled her gaze from the photo and looked out the window next to her bed. It was dark, but the rain had ended, and she thought she saw some stars in the clearing sky, way up high, above the peak of Mt. Roberts. The lights of Juneau shone like bright stars of their own across the dark expanse of Gastineau Channel, and she could see the house lights and streetlights of the Douglas Indian Village below her, filling the beach between St. Ann's Avenue and the ocean.

She began preparing for bed. Tomorrow was another long day and she needed her rest.

Chapter 4

It was about 8:30 a.m. when Deputy Marshal Frank Leishke stood next to the metal table in the morgue at the Carson Undertakers in Douglas. He had decided to begin his investigative day by examining the body. Leishke had worked with the undertaker before, and Michael Carson had led the deputy marshal to the small room where Carson prepared bodies for burial. Carson had then returned to the front of his store, whose importance to the community placed it on the town's main thoroughfare, Front Street. In a community serving a major gold mine, fatalities were frequent enough to warrant front-page advertisement for undertaking services in the local newspaper.

The back room fit just one body on a table; a metal three-tiered shelf against the wall could hold three additional bodies if needed. Leishke remembered an explosion the previous March that had killed five miners. Those shelves had likely been filled that day, he thought to himself.

Leishke looked down at the naked body of Rosie Brown. She had been washed by the undertaker, so her wounds were easier to see today than the day before, when her clothes and the blood had made it difficult to discern the cuts and gashes.

A knife wound ran across her throat, deep enough that Frank could see the white of the bone in the center of the cut. The killer had also drawn the knife upward through her face, moving from the center of her throat to her nose, slicing through her mouth and left nostril. Removing the blood had made this wound particularly shocking to witness. It was a cut not intended to kill, but to maim, and Leishke thought it indicated the need of the murderer to do more than just get rid of a witness to theft. There were also two depressions in her skull, one just above her left hairline, and the other above the left ear, as if either she or the murderer had turned slightly between one hammer swing and the next. Frank knew it was a hammer because he had found it, still covered with blood and gore, dropped behind the trunk in Rosie's bedroom. He had been unable to find the knife, although he and the other deputy marshal at the scene, Matthew McIntyre, had done a thorough search. Leishke had directed McIntyre to put items back into place after moving them during the search, in hopes of keeping the scene as much as possible as the murderer had left it.

The search had revealed the theft, which was not the typical theft that Frank Leishke had seen at the scenes of other such murders. In his experience, a house theft typically meant disarray in the residence – clothes on the floor, dressers open, the kitchen ransacked. In Rosie's bedroom, a coin purse in the trunk had its bottom cut out and emptied, and Leishke could find no other cash, but all the items had been in their proper place. Even the coin purse had been put back in the victim's trunk, which had held letters and other personal effects.

Frank Leishke continued examining the body. It was never easy to look at the victim of brutality, and when the victim was young and had been beautiful, it was harder. Rosie had thick blonde hair, had dyed her carefully shaped eyebrows dark, and her big blue eyes stared vacantly at him. She had a full figure – a lush bosom and hips that showed bruises where large fingers had dug in. It was impossible to tell if she had been raped, and Frank wasn't sure if a working girl could ever even be considered to be raped, but he thought she had had sex the night she died. Although clothed when found, she was wearing a chemise and nothing else, and he thought he had seen a white fluid on her thighs. That had also been washed away by the undertaker.

Frank Leishke picked up her left hand. There was a depression around the base of the ring finger, but no ring. A similar depression on the middle finger of her other hand indicated the removal of at least two rings. One may have been a wedding ring. It wasn't usual for prostitutes to wear wedding rings, but it also wasn't unusual – some were forced into the life by ne'er-do-well, or simply greedy, husbands. The fingernails were torn on both hands. This didn't surprise Leishke. The scene of the killing had indicated that Rosie had fought, however futilely. She had thrown a bed pillow at the killer, with about as much effect as one would expect, thought the deputy marshal, but the bruised knuckles and torn nails showed she had fought as hard as she could.

Frank Leishke stepped back from the table where the body lay and looked again at the wounds. They had all occurred while the killer was standing in front of Rosie. There were no hits on the back of her head and even the knife wound on her throat most likely took place as she looked at her killer's face. This, Leishke thought, told him something else about this killer. Whoever killed Rosie Brown wasn't someone who shied away from death, even when it involved a lovely young woman with whom he had just recently had relations. It seemed likely to Frank that this man had killed before. The careful and thorough search and the theft of all valuables, down to the rings on the woman's hands, also portrayed a killer who was able to control the rage he had displayed in the killing.

What had killed her? Was it the knife or the hammer? Deputy Marshal Frank Leishke wasn't sure it mattered but suspected from the amount of blood at the scene, that her heart had still been pumping when her throat was cut. He imagined the killer hitting her unconscious with the hammer, and then using the knife to finish the kill and maim her face. It was a ferocious attack – Leishke was convinced of that, and probably very personal. This was someone who was very angry.

Chapter 5

Looking at the body before him, and thinking about her killer, Deputy Marshal Leishke felt chilled. Did he have another depraved killer like Krause on his hands? Did the killer see each victim as simply someone standing between him and money? At least Krause had not killed women, so far as Leishke had been able to determine.

Frank Leishke decided to go for a walk to clear his head. It was a rare sunny day in Douglas, Alaska, and spring was advanced far enough to give the sun real warmth. He had worn his winter woolen overcoat for the brisk ferry ride from Juneau but thought he might come to regret it as he began walking toward Treadwell. Leishke followed Tlinket Avenue through the Douglas Indian Village, admiring the carved canoes pulled up on the beach, and noting two Native women sitting outside their homes, surrounded by hand-woven baskets they were hoping to sell. The homes on the downhill side were on pilings to prevent the twice-daily high tide from flooding them, and the tide was coming in, so there was low water beneath the homes on that side of the street. Leishke wondered what this neighborhood was like in the winter, when the Taku winds wailed directly off Mt. Roberts and onto the beach. He suspected it was miserable; he had heard the winds were sometimes clocked at more than 100 miles an hour.

It was too early for the tourists who would begin coming in May, but the miners and their wives often came to the village to look at the wares. They had money to spend, and many of them expected to be in Alaska for just a short time before heading back to their homes in the south.

Although Leishke noticed the women and their baskets, they didn't draw his interest. Instead, he found himself recalling the Krause investigation, most likely because it had begun here, in Douglas and Treadwell.

Two years before, Frank Leishke had been hired by two fraternal organizations in Douglas – the Masons and the Odd Fellows – to investigate the disappearance of two of their members. Jim Plunkett and William Christie had both been seen in the company of a third man, Edward Krause, before they disappeared. Krause was a big, burly 48-year-old with a mysterious past. He was German, and still spoke with a faint accent.

At the time, Frank Leishke was a Pinkerton detective. He had just wrapped up a political investigation in Idaho, where, in 1905, a pro-union member had assassinated the former governor of the state, Frank Steunenberg. Leishke wasn't the lead investigator on the case, so wasn't needed for the trial, and was ready for a new assignment. Although he had spent most of his time with the Pinkertons working in the Northwest, he hadn't made it to Alaska, so when the opportunity presented itself, he jumped at the chance.

Leishke arrived in Juneau just two weeks after the second of the two men had disappeared. William Christie was an amalgamator with the Treadwell mine – a responsible job given to men the company trusted not to steal the pure gold that was being created during the amalgamation process. That's why his disappearance had been so quickly noticed. He was also newly married – another anomaly for Krause's victims, who Leishke believed were chosen in part because of their lack of close family.

Krause more commonly chose itinerant workers – fishermen, or the two young men working as caretakers at a remote mine. None had immediate family nearby, and all could be missing for some time before someone noticed. Jim Plunkett had also fit the bill – he was a charter boat skipper who could be gone for days or even weeks without anyone taking note. Most importantly, they had money or assets. The two fishermen linked to Krause had owned their boats, the two young caretakers had just received

$1,000 for putting together a log raft, and another of his victims had owned property in Washington State.

Although Plunkett and then Christie hadn't been missing long and Krause had already been arrested, without bodies or direct evidence, Leishke had his work cut out for him. He dove into the investigation ferociously, more and more convinced that Edward Krause could be the most dangerous person he had ever known.

Krause had earned a reputation in Petersburg as being head of a "murder gang," a group of men who ended up with thousands of dollars' worth of fox furs without owning a fox farm, men who took other men fishing or hunting, and their "guests" were never seen again. Petersburg, the little fishing village in Southeast Alaska settled by Norwegian fishermen, didn't have much in the way of law enforcement, and thought the safest way to deal with Krause and his confederates was to ignore them.

Krause was also a compelling man who had a way with a story, Leishke had discovered. He was a favorite with Petersburg ladies for his Shakespeare readings, and conversation. He was also a Socialist and had even run as such for the Territorial Legislature but was not elected.

In addition to agreeing to spend the money to hire a Pinkerton detective, the Odd Fellows and Masons had also agreed to offer a $500 reward for anyone whose information led to Krause's arrest. Because their members were convinced that both Christie and Plunkett had been murdered and their bodies thrown into Gastineau Channel, they had paid to have the channel dragged.

That was one of the first things Leishke saw when he arrived in Alaska on that day in early November, 1914, the barge in the channel methodically dragging the bottom. Leishke had never believed any remains would be found. He knew enough of tidal action to know that the narrow channel between Juneau and Douglas Island ran fast and furious during the twice-daily tide changes and a body was not going to be resting on the bottom waiting for discovery.

Now, two years later, Leishke also knew that any organic material in the channel would be quickly stripped of flesh by the bottom-feeding fish and other sea creatures, most notably the crabs. He had also learned that, while gases in decomposing bodies floated them to the surface in warmer climates, in cold-water Alaska, the bodies remained on the bottom.

Krause had apparently come to Alaska from Seattle, where he had lived in the fishing community of Ballard, and where he had built his distinctive boat, the Cecelia. The Cecelia wasn't a typical fishing boat, although Krause had occasionally used it for commercial fishing. It was more a liveaboard boat – it had a commodious main cabin and wheelhouse, with built-in bookcases, and distinctive windows. Oval in shape, instead of the more typical round portholes, they had also made it easy for eyewitnesses to track the boat's comings and goings. That had not worked in Krause's favor, thought Leishke.

Leishke's walk had now taken him across the boundary between Douglas and Treadwell, entering the company town. It was not an attractive place. The immediate area was treeless – due to a combination of logging for the wood needed to build the town and the chlorine emitted by part of the mining process. The gas had killed off whatever trees remained after the initial logging. The main road into town was lined on both sides with mine works – on Leishke's right, the huge building that housed hundreds of stamp mills, and to his left, the generator building that held the giant oil boilers supplying power to the town, the mines, and the residents. The noise was deafening; he felt the stamp mill pounding jarring his skull and thought he could feel it vibrating down his spine and into his feet.

Maybe not the best place to come for a quiet think, Leishke smiled to himself, but knew in a few blocks, it would be quieter. He walked a little faster. The deputy marshal was now at the town plaza, which was defined on one side by the three-story superintendent's mansion, on the other side by the assistant superintendent's more modest house. Again, the lack of trees made the area seem raw and unfinished, but he noted that both homes had some raspberry bushes and small gardens, which gave the area some welcome greenery. The plaza itself was just dirt with some tufts of grass and a bit of very low rock wall surrounding it – enough of a wall to contain the water that was poured into the area each winter to make an ice-skating rink. Now, though, a pathway through the plaza led to the grocery and Treadwell offices that shared a concrete building painted yellow.

Leishke continued walking, heading uphill toward the Seven Hundred Mine, one of the four mines in the Treadwell complex. This was the mine where Krause's last victim, William Christie, had worked. Leishke realized he was walking the same path that Christie and Krause walked on the last day anyone saw Christie. Krause had appeared at the mine, posing as a federal marshal named Miller, and saying that Christie was being summoned to appear before the marshals in Juneau. The killer made it sound routine, and Christie's supervisor was fine with sending the two away together. As they walked down the path, they ran into Christie's new sister-in-law, the sister of Cecelia Geskus, who Christie had married just two weeks before. She knew both men and greeted them, but not by name. For the hundredth time, Leishke wondered what Christie would have done if he realized he was being taken to the dock by the infamous Edward Krause, and not by a deputy marshal Miller.

Other witnesses saw the two men enter the distinctive Cecelia, Krause's boat, and noted as it left Treadwell and headed north, but it didn't dock at Thane, or Juneau. It anchored instead off of North Douglas, a few miles from Juneau, and was there until at least 10 p.m. It was gone in the morning, and Christie was never seen again.

Leishke had already passed the boarding house where the newly married couple had been living at the time of Christie's disappearance. He heard that last year, after the trial, Mrs. Christie and the two children she had with her first husband had moved to Sitka. He hoped she had found some happiness. She remembered Mrs. Christie as an attractive woman who was understandably grief stricken by the loss of her new husband.

There had been plenty of talk about her relationship with Krause at the time. Her first husband, John Geskus, had been friendly with Krause. Leishke had heard that Krause frequently ate dinner with the Geskus family when they all lived in Petersburg. Geskus took a job at Treadwell, and his family moved to be with him. Then Geskus died, under somewhat suspicious circumstances – he accidentally shot himself in the head while on a solo hunting trip on Douglas Island. Leishke didn't really know what to make of this. He had found letters that Mrs. Geskus had written to Krause, when he searched Krause's boat, and they were friendly, but not romantic or intimate.

Would Krause have killed Geskus? Yes, Leishke had no doubt that Krause would kill him. He had also noted the coincidence that Krause's boat was named for Cecilia Geskus, and it was a fishing tradition to name your boat for your sweetheart. Mrs. Christie, as she was now known, claimed to have never been wooed by Krause, even during her year-long widowhood. She also professed utter shock that he would have had anything to do with her new husband's disappearance, and only reluctantly concluded he must have had after talking to her sister and Leishke.

Mrs. Christie had expected her new husband home by 3:30 a.m. the day after he left the mineworks with Krause, since he was working a 12-hour shift beginning at 3 p.m. When he hadn't come home, she had gone downstairs and found a note that was supposed to be from him and stated that he was called to Seattle unexpectedly and would return as soon as possible. Not only did she not recognize his signature, but the letter was also typed, and he could neither type nor had access to a typewriter.

Unlike other men who had disappeared in Krause's vicinity, Christie was immediately missed, by the mine supervisor and his wife. By daylight, police and marshals were looking for Krause and Christie, and had discovered that Plunkett had also last been seen in Krause's company.

In the end, it was a traveling salesman who located Krause. He was in Juneau when the $500 reward was offered, and since he was headed south anyway, he thought he would look for the fugitive. The steamship's first stop after Juneau was Ketchikan, and the salesman heard in a bar there that someone who appeared to answer Krause's description had been seen in town. He hurried back to his steamship and stood near the gangplank as the passengers embarked. The last man who came aboard, just before the ship pulled away, looked like Krause, the salesman thought. He told the purser, who told him that there was no passenger by the name of Krause on his manifest. The purser must have continued thinking about it, though, because he contacted police and Krause was met by police officers and arrested at the Seattle dock.

Leishke had heard the story of the traveling salesman from a federal marshal and had thought it too bad that the fraternal groups had decided to give the $500 reward to the Seattle police officers, and not the salesman. He thought Juneau authorities were a little miffed by that also – they probably wanted the reward as much as anyone. It was true the Seattle police had found deeds and bank books belonging to eight different men, and a typewriter, when they searched Krause. Luckily, they had recognized the importance of the evidence, and kept it all carefully cataloged, including the typewriter.

But, Leishke thought with satisfaction, he was the one who connected it all. He was the person who discovered that all the men whose bank statements and other documents in Krause's possession were missing. He had found the boat belonging to the Juneau charter boat skipper -- hidden in a cove near Krause's cabin near Petersburg. He had compared the typewritten letter to Mrs. Christie, and typewritten letters to insurance companies and banks claiming the possessions of other victims and found a match with the typewriter found in Krause's belongings. He had even gone from watch repair shop to watch repair shop in Seattle until he had traced the original owner of the watch that Krause had been wearing at the time of his arrest. It matched the serial number of a watch owned by a Seattle-area fisherman named Ole Moe, who had last been seen fishing with Edward Krause.

During the months of painstaking investigative work, Leishke had continued to be paid by the Odd Fellows and Masons, but after Krause had been convicted of impersonating a federal marshal and sentenced to 10 years in prison, the fraternal groups told the federal marshals that couldn't bear the cost of keeping Leishke on the payroll any longer. The federal marshals knew that Leishke was finding the evidence they needed to try Krause for both kidnapping Christie and killing Plunkett – the indictments being sought by the federal prosecutor. They telegraphed authorities in Washington, D.C., saying they wanted to take over the Pinkerton contract. They were told that was impossible.

The Pinkerton Detective Agency had its own political baggage. It had become associated with union-busting activities by large mining concerns and other corporate interests. President Woodrow Wilson and his administration was not eager to be seen supporting the Pinkertons. So, Leishke obligingly gave up his career as a Pinkerton, and became a federal deputy marshal. He found it an easy decision – the Krause case had consumed him for more than a year by this time, and he wanted to see the bastard get his comeuppance.

He had. Krause was easily convicted of kidnapping Christie, and then found guilty of killing Plunkett. It was the first time a jury had been sequestered in the Territory of Alaska, and the first time in Alaska that a man had been convicted of first-degree murder without a body as part of the evidence. The prosecutor had used federal maritime law to frame the conviction, since that law allowed for a first-degree murder absent a body. The prosecutor had then used the evidence found by Leishke to weave an intricate web of circumstantial evidence, making even Krause's most fervent advocates believe him guilty.

Leishke had gone down to the jail to interview Krause after the conviction. He was due to be hanged in less than four months, and Leishke thought Krause might finally be ready to confess. He was not. He had hinted he might reconsider if the sentence could be commuted from hanging to life in prison, but Frank knew that would be a lost cause. There was no way anyone would come out against the hanging – Krause was too feared and hated.

Well, he was gone now – after a failed jail escape. He had succeeded in escaping (which later resulted in all three jailers losing their jobs) but was shot three days later by a homesteader on an island south of Juneau. Leishke had attended the hastily arranged and unpublicized burial – in an unmarked grave in Juneau's city cemetery. A fitting end, he thought.

As Leishke continued to review the case that brought him to Juneau, he found his feet retracing his steps back to Douglas. Past the machinery and that damned racket of the stamp mills, through the Douglas Indian Village and back to Front Street in Douglas, where the undertaker's building was located. It was next to the Carson Photo Studio, which had come in handy once or twice when a family wanted a photo of their deceased relative as a keepsake. Leishke doubted that would be the case with Rosie Brown.

Leishke headed to the ferry dock, but passed the Douglas Opera House, and the sign advertising five-cent beer drew him in.

Chapter 6

As usual, there were a few men on the porch, maybe even a few more than usual, given the sunny weather. They greeted Leishke – most knew him from his work on the Krause trial. Others were probably just demonstrating the friendliness of an Alaska town, Frank Leishke thought. Inside the bar, he was surprised to see some sunshine had made its way through what appeared to him to be unusually clean windows. In fact, he thought as he looked around, the whole bar seemed cleaner than usual. The floor was mostly clear of peanut shells, and the long bar counter, which took up almost the entire width of the room, was practically shining.

It wasn't crowded; it was only 2 p.m., so the current mining shift didn't end for another hour. Experienced Treadwell workers knew better than to imbibe before heading to work, so the few men sitting at the bar were more likely habitués than regular miners. Leishke automatically scanned his surroundings and saw a few of the working girls who lived and worked upstairs. They were easy to spot – only working girls would be seen in such a space, and they were certainly not dressed as respectable women. Most wore wrappers over their chemises, especially since many of them had probably just arisen from their beds, thought Frank. They sat at a few tables, and all had one or more men for company. The girls at the Opera House were known to be congenial, experienced and, perhaps most importantly for some clients, received regular health check-ups.

Frank Leishke glanced through the open door of the kitchen and saw a young woman who was working – but not at the job for which the Opera House was known. The woman was wearing a dark-colored skirt and white blouse, mostly covered by an apron, and was briskly washing windows. There was something about her that Frank found unusually appealing – she had a mass of dark hair anchored in a serviceable bun, a slender form and moved quickly and easily. Her back was to him, but as she continued scrubbing at the windows, she turned her head to talk to the cook, and gave a quick laugh. Her smile made him catch his breath. He couldn't remember the last time he had been so drawn to a female. Frank even found himself turning toward the kitchen, as if to approach her, but he caught himself, walked up to the bar and ordered the drink he had been seeking when he came into the building.

The beer was good – Leishke had heard the Opera House was buying its beer from a local brewery that had actually used a cold fermenting process, with casks stored in a mining adit. He downed half of it in one waft and held up a finger to the bartender for another. Two beers were typically his limit; Frank had discovered long ago that drinking and investigating were not a good mix. He also realized he was hungry and was glad to see a bowl of pickled herring and plates on the bar. He ate a few bites, and found his gaze drifting back to the kitchen, but the door was firmly shut and he didn't see the maid again before he left.

"Where to go now?" Leishke asked himself. He had done a pretty good search of Rosie Brown's cabin but thought it wouldn't hurt to check it out again, especially since he was already in Douglas. He had drunk the second beer and eaten a few more snacks, so felt a wave of renewed energy. Yes, he decided he would go back to the cabin.

Leishke walked the few blocks down Front Street to Rosie's crib. The sun continued to shine, and he saw, on the hill above First Street, laundry on lines. He heard children's voices from above – First Street ran along the base of a hill on one side, with the beach at the bottom of the hill. The voices he heard came from Second Street on the hill to his left. The hill made a natural division between the scandalous First Street and the rest of Douglas, with only one wooden planked road leading up the hill at the far end. It allowed the cows from the dairy barn at the end of the street to travel to higher ground for grass. Leishke took off his hat for a moment to revel in the warm sunshine, and thought that, perhaps, his renewed energy was from a rare sunny day, and not beer and snacks. The tide had risen since he had walked on Tlinket Avenue, and a passing steamship had created a wake that was now splashing rhythmically against the beach on his right. Seagulls cried out, and the wind had picked up slightly, so he clamped his hat a little firmer to his head.

As Deputy Marshal Leishke walked the few steps from the street to the cabin door, he remembered locking the door yesterday, and checked his pocket. The key, which he had found yesterday on an inside nail next to the door, was still in his pocket. As he reached for the knob to insert the key, however, he found the door unlocked. He looked closely at the handle, and saw scratches indicating the cheap, poorly constructed lock had been picked. Leishke walked inside, bracing himself for a ransacked cabin. Instead, he found that it looked, so far as he recalled, the same as when he had left it yesterday. That surprised him.

Leishke walked into the bedroom, noting again the disarray he had seen yesterday. The bedclothes were a jumble, the pillow on the far side of the room where he believed it had been thrown by Rosie. The pillow had a blood stain on it, and he thought it may have been used to wipe the killer's knife, based on the stain pattern.

He saw blood stains around the bed, where Leishke thought the initial attack with the hammer had occurred. Blood had splattered on the walls, and he glanced up and saw splatter on the ceiling. Next to the bed, where Rosie Brown's body was found, the pool of blood had congealed, but was deep enough to still be liquid in the center. Leishke kept looking, searching for anything out of place from the day before. He didn't find it initially, but then looked more closely at a stain between the bloody pool next to the bed and the door that opened to the front room. Was that a footprint? He looked more closely, bending down while trying not to step in blood himself. Yes, he decided, he could see a boot tread. He knew that he and the other marshal had been careful to watch where they stepped, and he was convinced he had not seen the tread mark yesterday. But Leishke also knew the coroner's jury members had all likely stepped into the room as part of their investigation. He decided he would ask Deputy Marshal McIntyre if he remembered the stain. In the meantime, he measured it, and using his pocket notebook, made a quick sketch of the tread marks, which seemed to have a missing bit in the middle of one tread. He measured that gap also – about half an inch.

Putting the notebook back in his pocket, Leishke continued looking around the room. Rosie's trunk had been pushed against the wall. Such trunks were a necessary piece of furniture for almost anyone in Alaska, at least anyone who had moved there as an adult. They were often the main piece of luggage for travelers and were then adapted as places to hold pretty much anything found in a household, from blankets to dishes. Leishke had quickly gone through it the day before – that was where the empty coin purse was discovered. He moved over to it and opened it again.

Oh, Leishke thought, that's what the intruder had been doing. Yesterday, Leishke had seen a blanket at the bottom of the chest. On top of that were a primer, some underclothes, a small collection of letters tied with a ribbon, and a man's watch. Leishke had taken the watch – surprised to find anything of value left in the cabin. When he looked at it later, back in the office, he discovered it wasn't working. Now, the trunk appeared to hold everything he had left in it yesterday, except for the letters.

The deputy marshal hadn't looked at them closely the day before but had noted they weren't in English. That hadn't surprised him, since Fannie had told the coroner's jury that Rosie had been from Russia originally. Now, though, he wondered what was so important about these letters that someone, and he suspected the killer, had returned to the cabin to take them. Leishke knelt before the trunk, again working to avoid blood splatters, and began a careful search. He placed each object on a clear space on the floor as he removed it – the clothing, the primer, and the blanket.

Leishke stopped and leafed through the book. The primer was one that would be typically used by a young child – it focused on the alphabet and beginning words. Fannie had also told the jury members that Rosie had been learning to read – like many young immigrants, she had been illiterate. Leishke could see where Rosie had lightly underlined words and phrases with a pencil – "home" and "money." He set it aside and picked up the blanket. As he unfolded it, one letter fell out. It appeared to be in the same language he had noted in the letters yesterday. He wasn't sure, but he thought it was addressed to someone named Jenny Poplosky. He wondered if Fannie could read, and if she could, whether she could read this letter. Fannie had a slight accent that Leishke couldn't place but sounded Eastern European. "Perhaps that's how the two girls became such good friends," he mused as he tucked the letter into his inner breast pocket.

Leishke looked around the small cabin for a while longer but couldn't find anything else of interest. Yesterday, he had pretty quickly found the machinist's hammer that had been used against Rosie, and he had hoped to find the knife today. It didn't appear to be anywhere here. Maybe, and he knew it was unlikely, they would find the knife still in the possession of whoever they ended up arresting for the murder. Frank Leishke left the cabin, again locking the door, for what good that might do, and headed to the dock to ferry across the channel.

Chapter 7

May finished washing the kitchen windows – washing windows was one of her favorite chores. It gave her the opportunity to stand in as much light as the typical Southeast Alaska clouds let into the buildings below, and the chore was usually quick and easy. It always did leave her with smudged hands – the effect of the newspapers she used to wipe the windows. That was easily solved, she thought, washing up at the kitchen sink.

What was next on her list, she wondered for a moment. The bar was as clean as it could get, the hallways swept, the windows washed and dishes clean until supper. There was always laundry, and the day was nice enough she could try drying outside. During the winter and rainy days, of which there were so many, she and the other maid, Lily, relied on the racks in the basement. She didn't like going down there – it was damp and she was convinced there were rats, although Lily and Mrs. Todd swore they were mice. If they were mice, May thought with a grin, they were Alaska-sized mice.

She headed upstairs to grab the laundry from the baskets in the hall closet – the working girls were instructed to put their linens and clothes into those baskets, and they always seemed overflowing. She didn't like the basement, but that's where the laundry tub was, so she envisioned spending the rest of the afternoon in the damp.

May kept hard at work until 6 p.m., when she made her way to the kitchen for a bite of supper. She was finishing up the simple meal of soup and bread when Fannie slipped in the back door.

"Oh, it's so good to see you," May exclaimed, rushing over to give her friend a hug. "I've been thinking of you all day."

"Thanks, May," said Fannie, who looked tired.

"What have you done today?" asked May, before catching herself. None of the working girls ever wanted to answer that question.

Fannie replied. "I've spent most of the day answering questions," she said. "All the other girls in the district had question after question. They're frightened, which I suppose we should be. I really do think that Rosie was chosen specifically. I think the rest of us don't have anything to fear, at least from the man who killed her. I didn't see any customers last night – I was too tired. And sad. Tonight, I really need to work. So, I thought I would come visit you before heading back to work. I also might find a customer or two down this end of town."

"I'm glad you came to see me," said May, noting that Fannie was not going to want to answer any questions. May felt as if she was bursting with them. She had thought about what Fannie had told her today and wanted to know so much more. Could Rosie's husband really have come to Douglas? What was that about the Warsaw Club? What would happen now? Was Rosie's body going to be buried here? May thought that Rosie had told her she was Jewish, and May had the vague idea that Jewish people buried their bodies differently than Christians.

But she looked again at Fannie's tired face, and bit her tongue. It was most important right now that she was a good friend to Fannie, not that she found out more about Rosie. Rosie was beyond worry now, May thought reflectively. She reached over the table where they both sat and clasped Fannie's hand.

"Well, it sounds as if it's been quite a day. Catch your breath and have a cup of tea." Sure enough, Mrs. Todd had entered the kitchen while they spoke and set cups of tea in front of both girls, adding a bowl of sugar and a pitcher of milk.

"Thank you," Fannie gave Mrs. Todd a smile and gave May's hand a squeeze. Adding sugar and milk to her tea, she smiled, a trifle wanly. "I know I told the girls they shouldn't be frightened. I really do think that Rosie was killed by her husband, Againsky, and I don't think there's any reason he would kill them. But … I'm a little afraid for myself. I'm the only one here who knows what he looks like, and I think he may remember what I look like. I only met him once, and he is very distinctive looking. He didn't pay me much attention, but I'm still worried. I should probably have told the deputy marshals about him, but I'm not sure I trust them."

"What makes you think you can't trust them?" asked May.

"Well, I've heard that a lot of the Juneau police take advantage of the girls over there," said Fannie. "They don't just expect to visit them for free, but they even demand money from them sometimes."

"That's awful," said May. "But you said detective Leishke is involved in this, and he isn't a Juneau police officer. He's a federal marshal."

"What's the difference?" asked Fannie. "Their offices are in the same building, and they must talk to each other. If Leishke told the wrong person, I could be in real trouble."

"Well," said May slowly, thinking. "I think you need to tell someone, or at least write it down. You'll feel better getting it off your chest, and you might even decide it's nothing to worry about."

"You could be right," said Fannie. She paused, taking a sip of tea, and staring out the window.

"I know," she said decisively, looking at May. "I'm going to tell you everything. Then you can tell this marshal, and no one will know who the information came from. No one is going to expect you to even know me or Rosie, so I don't think anyone will suspect the truth."

May was not as convinced of the wisdom of this plan but couldn't think of a better idea. After all, she's the one who had suggested Fannie tell someone. She looked behind Fannie and saw Mrs. Todd working on the dough that would rest overnight for the morning bread. She seemed occupied with her task but May knew that the cook could make bread in her sleep, so could certainly listen to a conversation while she did it.

"I have to check on the laundry," she said, rising to stand and trying to give Fannie a meaningful look. "Why don't you come with me?"

"Laundry? I thought we were going to...oh," said Fannie, looking at the cook, who appeared to be studiously ignoring them both. "I'll come with you. Maybe you could use another pair of hands."

The two young women opened the door on the other side of the kitchen from the bar and walked down the creaky wooden steps to the basement.

"I can't believe I suggested this place," May confessed in a whisper to Fannie. "I hate it down here. But I couldn't take you to my room, or go to your cabin, so I guess we're stuck with this." The basement held the women's underthings, strung on clothes lines throughout. Mrs. Todd and the madam would not have wanted them out on the line with the sheets, towels, and dresses. May reminded herself to check on the outside line – the other wash should be dry by now. The day had continued fine, and it would be daylight for another hour or so.

The two perched on a couple of stools that had been brought down here to allow maids to do exactly what they were doing – taking a break. May looked at Fannie expectedly.

"Rosie and I met in San Francisco, like I told you," said Fannie. "But I knew all about where she had come from because I had made the same journey. I was just luckier than she was.

"We both grew up as Polish and Jewish. But, just like now, there was no longer a country called Poland – just a people. Poland had been divided among Russia, Austria, and Germany. My family was in Germany; Rosie's was in Russia. You have no idea how hard it was for the Jewish people back in the old country. We would settle in a town or city, and then get chased out. People despised the Jews – they blamed every misfortune on us. If the crops didn't come in, if a child fell ill, if the cow stopped giving milk – it was our fault. And every effort our fathers made to scrape out a living was yanked away. A storekeeper would be shut down, a farmer would have his land stolen. As a child, all I knew was poverty and all I saw was unhappiness, and bitterness. Our faith helped – our rabbi did all he could to remind us that we will rise higher in the afterlife, but that is hard for a child to understand."

"So, when a young man who said he was from America, was Polish and Jewish, and was interested in your daughter's hand, it was the dream for every parent. And every daughter," Fannie added softly.

"That's what happened to both of us. We didn't know each other, but we were both wooed by men who were part of the Warsaw Club. These evil men had created this group in Argentina, but...I'm getting ahead of myself.

"Anyway, my beau's name was Bolek Nowak and we met at synagogue. I had heard others saying there was a rich American man who was visiting relatives in town and then I saw him. I had just turned 14, and I knew that my parents had begun looking for a husband for me. When he smiled at me, I felt butterflies. He was a slender man, very nicely dressed with a trim beard and mustache and dark hair. He seemed to me to be everything that was perfect, and when my parents said he was interested in me, I couldn't believe my luck."

May looked at her friend. She thought that whoever this Nowak character was, he should have been considered the lucky one. Fannie had a lovely figure, big blue eyes, thick blonde hair with enough curl to always look lovely, and a contagious smile. May didn't say anything, though, she didn't want to interrupt the story that Fannie was telling.

Fannie continued. "We got married and he told me we were leaving in just a few days for his home in America. We left on the steamship from England because tickets to North America were cheaper from there, rather than from Germany. It was aboard the steamship that I began learning the truth. First, I hadn't known what men wanted from women when I was 14, and now, with the experience I've had, I realize that Bolek did nothing to make it better for me. In fact, it was as painful as it could be, and it continued to hurt so long as the marital relations went on." Fannie raised her eyebrows and gave a small smile. To May, it didn't seem at all funny, but her own marital experience had been vastly different, and apparently better.

Fannie continued. "I also found out on the ship that I was one of three girls that Bolek had so-called married. They were like me, and like Rosie, as I found out – poor Jewish girls whose families were happy to give us in marriage to a young rich American. We three girls spent a lot of time crying on that voyage. None of us could read or write, and it quickly became clear that the ship's crew was not only uninterested in our plight. They were probably being paid to keep their mouths shut.

"That became even clearer when we reached Buenos Aires. All three of us tried to tell immigration officials about what happened to us, and even those we thought understood our language, they acted as if we weren't standing there, three young girls in tears, pleading with them. One of us, Rywka, ran to the police that first week, and what happened to her taught us all. The first thing the police did was call Bolek, who arrived and said his wife was disobedient and needed to return home. He took her from the police station, brought her back to the house where we all worked, and beat her. He then sent her away – we were told by the house's madam that she went to a much lower-class brothel in a really bad part of town. We didn't see her again.

"I was in despair, and then I found out I was pregnant, and it was even worse. Bolek seemed happy about it at first; I think he saw it as another way to stop me from leaving. But when I began showing, he started becoming more abusive. And one beating meant I lost the baby. He didn't call anyone to help me, but one of the other women knew something of childbirth. She told me it was unlikely I would ever have a baby again, and she was right." This time, the incongruous little smile was tempered by the tears in her eyes. May reached over and squeezed her hands, now clasped tightly together in Fannie's lap.

"After a few years, Bolek came to me and said that he was taking me and two other girls to San Francisco. Business was still good in Argentina, but I think Bolek had...what is called itchy feet. Anyway, he took the three of us there and set us up in business.

"Things were different in San Francisco. I'm not sure how to explain it. The Warsaw Club had everyone on their side in Buenos Aires. In San Francisco, it made me feel that I might have a chance to escape. But I didn't know how – Bolek kept all our money, of course. But all three of us began talking about a way to leave him. Then, in April of 1906, our chance came. It was early in the morning, but two of us hadn't yet gone to bed, and were at a bar near our house looking for customers. Everything started moving. At first, it was kind of a gentle swaying, but then it grew bigger and bigger, and things started falling. The mirror above the bar and the glass bottles hit the floor. It was loud and ... terrifying." Fannie's fingers were turning white as she clutched them even tighter, and May saw a shudder engulf her frame.

"Ada and I crawled under a table, and then just watched. The giant chandelier dropped from the ceiling, but the quick-thinking bartender threw two pitchers of water on it before it could catch the building on fire. He saw us under the table and dragged us out. We didn't want to go, and both of us yelled and tried to escape him, but he just clung tighter and pulled us out into the street. It didn't feel any safer there, but it was. The earth was still shaking, and we saw the roof of the bar fall into the room we had just been in. A crack opened in the street, and we watched horses and their riders fall into it. The bartender started running up the hill, pulling us along. Fires were beginning in some of the buildings, people were screaming, and others ran with us. A few times, we were almost hit by bricks from collapsing buildings, but God was watching over us. We made it to safety in the park, where there were no buildings to fall on us.

"We stayed there for a few days; people set up tents, and others began fetching food and water. It wasn't easy, but the bartender – his name was Joseph – stayed with us and made sure we were all right." Fannie gave a little laugh, and May saw her briefly relax. "He was in love with Ada. They are still together, I think. I get letters from her sometimes. They don't live in San Francisco anymore; they moved south to Los Angeles and Joseph quickly found work. They even got married and have two children now. Ada is so happy and I'm happy for her."

Now that Fannie had stopped talking for a moment, May realized that it was getting late, and darker. In fact, she realized she couldn't see very well in the dark of the basement. "I think there's a candle here somewhere. Let me look," she said, slipping off the stool and turning around. Fannie grabbed her skirt before she could walk away, and she heard something at the same time.

There were footsteps coming down the stairs, and they were heavy – definitely the footsteps of a large man with boots. She could easily hear them over the sound of the nearby furnace. She was getting ready to call out when Fannie pulled her close and whispered. "We need to get out of here. Is there a cellar door?"

May froze for a moment, her mind searching for her knowledge of the basement. There wasn't a cellar door. The only access was the stairs from the basement. The basement held shelves for preserves, beer kegs for the bar, a laundry tub and clothes racks and the coal furnace that heated the building. "A coal furnace," she whispered back to Fannie. "There's a coal chute."

Chapter 8

After taking the ferry back to Juneau, Leishke went back to the office to type up his notes. He then walked the four blocks to the small cabin he rented on Fourth Street. It had been a long day but a productive one. He washed up and headed back down the street to find a meal. The City Cafe, a restaurant owned and run by a local Japanese family, was open on Front Street. Front Street was called that because it fronted onto the ocean. The water side of the street held stores and businesses on pilings, hovering above Gastineau Channel. The other side of the street was further up the slope from what used to be a beach, and backed onto the steep hill that defined the downtown of Juneau, Alaska. The City Cafe was always open – it was the only restaurant in town that operated all day and all night long. The food was good. It was filling and cheap, although some Juneau residents thought it tasted too foreign. Leishke liked the liberal use of soy sauce, and he really liked the way the vegetables were cooked – they were still crisp and fresh tasting on his plate, unlike the usual fare of overcooked carrots and green beans.

Frank Leishke had a pan-fried steak, rice, and broccoli, followed by a piece of pie. He thought, as he ate his last bite of pie, that he had practically wolfed down the food. He had been starving. He cast his mind back and realized that other than the bar snacks at the Opera House, he hadn't eaten since breakfast. His big frame and active life meant at least three full meals a day, and often more. It was always an indication that he was investigating a case when he missed a meal or two. He nodded at the waiter, who had come by with a coffee pot, and the waiter obligingly refilled his cup to the brim.

Frank leaned back in the booth. The cafe was sparsely populated, but he noticed a couple of men pointedly avoiding eye contact as he glanced around. One he recognized as a suspect in a local burglary ring. Just as he had recognized him, he suspected the maybe-burglar knew Leishke, and wanted nothing to do with him. "That was fine for now," thought Leishke. He would prefer a quiet mealtime anyway.

He didn't think he had seen the second man before and he noted his facial features so he would recognize him again. He was tall, blonde haired with a somewhat elaborate handlebar mustache and trim beard. As he looked closer, Leishke realized he did look faintly familiar. but he couldn't place him. He let the question of the man's identity drift away, content with knowing it would come to him, but not if he focused on it.

He pulled out his notebook, to go over what he had learned from Rosie Brown's cabin earlier in the day. The first thing he noted as he flipped through pages was his sketch of the boot print. "Well, no time like the present," he thought, pulling out his tape measure. He lifted his right foot onto his left knee and measured the bottom of his boot. Ten and three-quarters inches – he wore a size 10 and a half shoe. The boot print had been a little smaller; he guessed a size 10. He jotted that down next to the sketch. He turned to a blank page and began making a list of tasks. First, the boot print. He needed to ask Deputy Marshal McIntyre, the fellow officer who had helped him observe the cabin the yesterday, if he had noticed the boot print yesterday. Then, he needed to find out if McIntyre or the six coroner's jury members, or the doctor, or that other marshal – the younger one – wore size 10 boots.

Next came the hammer; it had looked new to him. He knew that, with the number of miners and gold mines in the area, finding a place that remembered selling a mining hammer, much less who it was sold to, was looking for a needle in a haystack ("or a hammer in a gold mining town," he thought ruefully), but he would still check with all the hardware stores. Leishke had learned years ago that detective work was walking work. "What else?" he thought, after jotting down these tasks.

"Oh, the letter." He needed to find someone who could translate it. He decided he would begin with Fannie Miller; if she couldn't read it, she might know someone else who could. He wanted to talk to her again, anyway, and the letter gave him a good excuse to go see her. He had listened closely to what she had told the coroner's jury yesterday, and he suspected she either had more to say, or hadn't been truthful about what she had said, or possibly both. She had claimed not to know Rosie well but had also noticed the window curtains being closed longer than usual.

She also seemed to know a lot about this woman she said she barely knew. She had told the jury members that Rosie was from Russia, had arrived in Juneau the previous fall, and was 25 years old. Her obvious grief over Rosie's death also gave lie to her claim of not knowing her well. Leishke had talked to enough prostitutes to know that the troubles in their lives meant they were all used to sad events. They usually were less likely to feel such events as keenly as women whose lives had been made easier.

But Fannie was obviously deeply shaken by Rosie's death. Leishke considered this further. She was very upset, but she had, after all, seen a woman she knew dreadfully maimed and dead. That would be enough to shake anyone, even a hardened prostitute. The six coroner's jury members had also expressed their shock at the state of Rosie Brown's body, and Leishke knew three of them had viewed other scenes of death while serving on previous juries.

There was something else about Fannie's testimony and reaction to the scene. Frank tried to grab hold of it. What had he seen in her face as she spoke? Grief, certainly. Shock. And fear. That was what he had seen. She was frightened, very frightened. She had tried to cover it up, talking quickly about her relationship with Rosie, and her decision to ask a passerby to help her into the cabin. He thought the hands she had clutched in front of her hid their shaking. Her face was pale enough that he feared she was going to faint. What could have been so frightening? Of course, all the women of the district would be scared after hearing of the murder, but Fannie had seemed absolutely terrified. He jotted at the top of his written list – talk to Fannie.

Putting notebook and pen back in his pocket, Leishke drew out cash for the meal and grabbed his hat. Standing up, he glanced around and realized that during his reverie, the two men he had noticed before had left. Instead, Frank caught the eye of a pretty young woman who, he suspected, was a working girl. Although not as obvious as the women he had seen earlier in the day at the Opera House, her smile at him told the same story that those women had told with their state of undress.

Frank Leishke smiled back, politely, but donned his hat and quickly took his leave. Walking back up the hill to Fourth Street, he passed the mayor of Juneau, Emory Valentine, leaving the building he had built that contained the Valentine Jewelry Store. Leishke tipped his hat at the mayor, who he knew had campaigned on a platform of law and order, but who had little success actually changing much. The Line, as Juneau's Restricted District was known, was as popular in Juneau as its companion neighborhood was in Douglas.

City officials could complain all they liked about the red-light districts, but there were too many businesses and men dependent on them. Leishke remembered that, until a few years ago, the women of Juneau's Line had actually paid the salaries of the local police. It had been a pretty dramatic move for the city council to move that expense to local property owners. Valentine's pleas to close the Line had fallen on not just deaf ears, but ears listening to something else.

Frank continued on up the hill, entered his little house, and washed again. His wash basin stood on its stand next to the kitchen sink. The cabin, he realized as he undressed, was quite similar in layout to Rosie Brown's. It had two rooms – the front room with a table, chairs, an easy chair, wood cooking stove, kitchen sink and water pump. The back room held Leishke's bed, trunk, and a dresser. His bed was large – and the one luxury he insisted on wherever he lived. His height made many beds too short, and a single bed not only couldn't accommodate his length but didn't allow for his restlessness. Leishke had not slept well for most of his adult life, haunted by the tragedies that made up his past, and unable to set aside his usual physical restlessness when asleep. This bed was, as usual, specially made to accommodate a bigger mattress – one he had had the Juneau furniture store manufacture for him.

The ocean spray from his ferry rides to and from Douglas, and the walk into the Treadwell mine complex had left a mix of salt, sand and dirt on his face and hands. Frank scrubbed up, stripped to his long johns, and crawled into bed. He turned off the bedside light and fell deeply asleep within minutes.

Chapter 9

May's thoughts frantically searched for a way out of the basement. The fading outdoor light and lack of windows made the basement pretty hard to navigate but May knew it well from the hours she had spent working there.

She grabbed Fannie's hand and pulled her close. "Follow me," she breathed into Fannie's ear and gave her hand a squeeze. Fannie, whose quick breaths had turned raspy with fright, calmed, and squeezed back.

May led Fannie silently toward the basement stairs; she felt Fannie's instinctive tug away, but held fast and moved quickly, dodging the clothes racks, buckets, brooms, and other impediments. May realized she knew the way so well because she was always so anxious to get out of the basement, she usually negotiated her way in the space without a light.

The footsteps had stopped at what sounded like the bottom of the stairs. May peered around a cupboard that stood between her and the stairs and saw a figure, lit behind by the light of the open doorway. He was tall and not heavily built, but substantial enough to clearly be male. He didn't carry a light, for which May was very grateful. As she watched, he held out a lantern and appeared ready to light it. May knew she had to move fast.

She quietly opened the cupboard, pulling out a plate, since the cupboard held extra dishes, which is why Mrs. Todd had placed it near the bottom of the stairs. May didn't hesitate – she threw the plate as hard as she could in front of her, listening with satisfaction as it hit the wall on the opposite side of the basement.

The intruder swore and turned toward the sound. He had lit the lantern by now and held it in front of him as he strode away from May and Fannie. May knew the distraction gave them little time to react. Holding Fannie's hand in a firm grasp, she ran toward the stairs and up them. Their footsteps seemed to ring out on the wooden stairs and, out of the corner of her eye, she saw the man's lantern turn as he swung toward them.

Just two steps from the top, Fannie slipped, almost dragging May down with her. The intruder had stumbled over a coal bucket, on his way to the stairs, and the women were still out of his reach. May pulled Fannie as hard as she could and dragged her over the last two steps and behind the basement door, which she slammed shut.

There was no lock on the door, since the basement held little of value to thieves, which May took a moment to regret, as she dragged a kitchen chair to put under the knob. It was a flimsy chair and May suspected it offered just a little time for Fannie and her to escape.

Fannie had reclaimed her footing and grabbed her coat. She was out the door before May could say a word, and although May ran to the door to call after her, she had already disappeared into the night, which had now fully swallowed the daylight. May knew it was futile to look for her – she may have fled to the Restricted District or gone to the Juneau ferry and May didn't think she could find her. She hoped that meant the man temporarily trapped in the basement couldn't find her either.

May heard the man begin pushing the door and knew it wouldn't hold long. She wasn't sure what to do. She didn't think he had gotten a good look at either woman but hesitated to rely on it. She didn't see Mrs. Todd, and all May wanted to do was run to her bed in the boarding house, but the laundry was still on the line, and May just couldn't leave it out.

While the stranger continued to pound on the door, she grabbed the laundry basket she had conveniently left near the back door and went outside to gather the dry clothing and linens. As she walked out, she was relieved to hear the bartender from in front of the building yell toward the kitchen, "What's going on in there? Does someone need help?"

She knew he would be back by the basement door soon and felt safer finishing up the day's tasks. As she gathered the laundry from the line, the door to the kitchen was suddenly flung open and she saw a figure run out. This time, the light from the door and window next to it allowed her to discern the man's features. She knew she hadn't seen him before but would know him again. His complexion was dark, his dark hair curly. He had a strong nose and a large but not overly groomed mustache. He didn't carry anything – she guessed he had left the lantern behind – but she saw the handle of a pistol poking out of the back of his waistband as his jacket lifted momentarily as he ran.

He must have assumed that both May and Fannie had left, since he didn't look around him at all, just began walking quickly toward the Restricted District. May prayed that Fannie hadn't gone in the same direction.

• • •

Fannie ran to the ferry dock, deciding against heading toward the district – she didn't know any of the women there well enough to ask for shelter, especially with a man she believed a killer almost certainly looking for her in the Restricted District.

She was in luck; the ferry's skipper was holding his cast-off rope in hand as she ran down the dock. He waited for her and even leant her a hand as she stepped from the dock to the moving boat. She recognized him and suspected he knew her also, but he didn't take liberties, unlike other ferry crew she had met in the past. She slipped past him and ducked into the cabin. Lined on each side with wooden seats, the cabin was full as workers in Douglas headed to their homes in Juneau, or perhaps to a favorite eating place.

She sat down, squeezing between two women who looked like housemaids to Fannie. One was an Alaska Native and the other looked Scandinavian. No one made eye contact with her, and she suspected that, just as she made guesses about their occupation, they had guessed hers.

She took a slow, deliberate breath, knowing she had the short ferry ride to come up with a plan of action. She had rejected the district because she didn't know her neighbors there well enough to either count on their discretion or risk putting them in danger. There was a woman in Juneau she could rely upon, she thought, another working girl who was clever and trustworthy. Unfortunately, though, she didn't have a house. She worked instead at a local hotel. She was Alaska Native, and Native girls weren't welcome in the restricted areas or brothels where the non-Natives worked. One of her customers paid for her room at the hotel since it was convenient for him. It wouldn't really work for Fannie to stay there, though. It was, after all, just a single room without accommodation for another person.

Maybe Selena would have some suggestions about what Fannie should do next. Fannie's own instincts were to pack up her belongings as soon as possible and leave on the next steamship. Two things prevented her. She hadn't finished telling May the whole story about Rosie, and Fannie still wanted to do all she could, without putting herself in direct danger, to seek justice for Rosie. She also suspected that Againsky would keep looking for her and would probably have the steamship docks watched.

The Warsaw Club relied on bribes to keep its wheels oiled – it bribed judges, police, immigration officials and possible witnesses. With the fortune it had from the work of women like Fannie and Rosie, the payoff expenses were a drop in the bucket. Fannie knew that Againsky would have the resources to hire people to help him look for her, and she had to be calm and clever to escape his notice.

The boat docked in Juneau – Fannie was grateful that it must have already stopped in Treadwell before she boarded. She stepped off the dock, glad for the darkness now that she was out of the shelter and safety of the boat. She quickly walked toward the Circle City Hotel, where Selena lived, knowing her purposeful gait was the opposite of the slow and suggestive walk she often used when in downtown Douglas.

It was somewhat busier downtown than was usual, as the lovely spring day had brought out residents as if from a winter's sleep. Shedding the thick coats, scarves, and gloves that they had depended on since October, Juneau's citizens strolled down the streets, smiling at each other, and stopping in small groups to exchange gossip and talk about the warmer weather. Many businesses were still open, even as it approached 9 p.m., since the gold mine that operated near town operated all night. May knew the next shift got off at midnight and many restaurants and other businesses stayed open to catch the shift change.

She headed up South Franklin Street to North Franklin. The Circle City Hotel was to the left-hand side of Franklin. Franklin wasn't the main street in Juneau – that title went to Main Street – but it had more businesses and traffic than Main Street, which paralleled it nearer the channel. Franklin Street started one block to the left and above the courthouse and made its purposeful way straight downhill to the ferry dock. Fannie's brisk walk faltered during the last steep block to the hotel; the fright that had fueled her escape from the Opera House seemed to have used up all her body's energy, and she thought she could feel it seeping from her fashionable walking boots.

Fannie stepped into the hotel lobby, suddenly so tired she just longed to drop onto a lobby chair. Instead, she pulled her coat collar up around her jaw and stepped to the hotel's desk. A young man she didn't know lifted his gaze from a book and looked at her inquiringly. She was the only one in the lobby, she realized, glancing around.

"I'm looking for Selena Dowling," she said. The man said, "Room 23" and gestured toward the stairs. "Second floor." He dropped his eyes back to the book and Fannie headed for the stairs. "Oh, good," she thought, "more uphill."

Outside Room 23, she leaned toward the door, listening for any sound that would indicate that Selena had a visitor. She heard nothing, but still chose to tap lightly, in case the room's occupant or occupants were sleeping. She let out a sigh of relief when the door opened quickly to Selena, whose face betrayed her surprise at seeing Fannie.

Chapter 10

Leishke stepped into the courthouse and up the stairs to his office. He held a cup of coffee in his hand. The City Cafe staff, where he usually ate breakfast, had grown accustomed to his unusual request for coffee to go, and so long as he provided the cup, were happy to fill it on his way out the door. During the winter, it was too cold for the coffee to make the walk to his work and still remain even tepid, but with the day again starting out sunny, he took the chance.

The deputy marshal set the cup on his desk and hung his hat and coat on the rack. He didn't expect to spend much time in the office. He knew he couldn't really proceed with an investigation while sitting in the courthouse. There were more people to interview, including his fellow marshal, McIntyre. He always started the day here, if he could, to get his thoughts in order and ensure that the Federal Marshal who oversaw the deputy marshals knew what he was doing.

Leishke also took the time each morning to type notes from the day before, if he hadn't done so then. These notes were invaluable resources for him, both during the investigations and when he testified on the witness stand.

Leishke opened his pocket notebook and reviewed his notes from the evening before. There, at the top of the page, was "Fannie Miller." That would be his priority today, he decided. He also wanted to talk to some of the other working girls in Douglas, which would necessitate another visit to the Opera House. Maybe he would see that housemaid again, he thought, and then caught himself. "No time for thinking of women," he said to himself, even as he thought again of her laugh, abundant hair, and graceful figure.

Leishke finished his coffee in a couple of gulps – it had certainly cooled down but was perfectly drinkable. Frank preferred his coffee to be a little cooler; this cup was perfect. He decided to check in with the U.S. Marshal for the First Judicial District of the Territory of Alaska before typing his notes. It was usually easiest to track down the Marshal earlier in the day.

Marshal Calhoun, as befitted his position, had a corner office with views down Main Street to Gastineau Channel. The spacious office held his imposing desk, a table, and chairs for meeting with his staff, and two bookshelves. Calhoun himself looked larger than life, and his presence seemed to fill out to fit the large office. He was sitting at his desk, feet upon it, while chatting with two deputy marshals who stood before him.

It was typical that he hadn't asked them to sit, thought Leishke. Upon his entering the room, the two other deputies left, obeying the unspoken message from Calhoun, who had turned his attention solely to Leishke. Leishke sat, deliberately choosing the one chair in the room that wasn't designed to ensure its users sat below the level of Calhoun's desk chair. He had discovered this within a few days of meeting Calhoun, and later found it was the chair that Calhoun would pull up to the table when he had more formal meetings.

"I wanted to ensure you are aware of the state of the investigation into the murder of the Douglas prostitute," he told Calhoun.

"I'm aware you've gone into this with your usual enthusiasm," said the Marshal with a smile. "We can always count on you to move quickly. I'm again grateful that you took me up on joining the force. With three major gold mines now in the immediate vicinity, I'm afraid crime will not be slowing down anytime soon."

"What can you tell me about this case?" Calhoun asked.

Leishke filled him in, describing the footprint, and his plan to continue talking to witnesses. He concluded by describing the vicious nature of the murder.

"Poor thing," said Calhoun absently. He tapped a pencil on his desk, the eraser end bouncing off the polished wood. Leishke knew this was a tell – Calhoun had more to say but was considering how to say it.

"I don't want to discourage you from investigating this thoroughly," Calhoun said. "But I have to tell you I'm concerned about the impact of this murder on the reputation of our office, and that concern is shared by authorities in Douglas. I've already heard from the mayor over there that the city council is considering shutting down the entire Restricted District. I know that will make some officials happy, but it will just make matters here in Juneau harder, as the customers won't stop seeing working girls. There will just be more of them coming over here."

He continued. "We want answers, but we want them quietly. And remember," he looked Leishke in the eye. "This woman was not an innocent victim. She chose to live a life that put her in danger. And she was experienced. She should have known better."

Leishke nodded and got up to leave. As he walked back to his office, he couldn't shake the impression that Calhoun had known Rosie Brown as more than a name that crossed his desk.

Frank was just finishing up typing his notes from the day before when Deputy Marshal Davies came into his office. Davies, hat still on head, looked flustered and, thought Leishke, remarkably similar to how he had appeared when he saw him at lunch the previous day. He soon learned why.

"There's been another murder," Davies blurted out. He then caught the look Leishke shot at him, and caught his breath, let it out in a long exhale and sat down on a chair. He took his hat off his head and set it on his lap.

Leishke was impressed – it appeared that Davies had taken yesterday's lessons to heart. He waited silently for the younger man to collect himself.

Davies took one more deep breath and then spoke. "I was in Douglas meeting with Douglas Commissioner Hensen. He has been having trouble lately with some of the Treadwell miners selling liquor to the Natives there. He wanted me to serve some warrants at Treadwell, which is always difficult. The management there doesn't like anyone coming on their property to serve summons or warrants." Davies caught Leishke's eye and stopped. Then he continued.

"Anyway, a man called from the Opera House and said that they found a body there. I think it was the bartender who called. He was pretty upset, and said the victim was the cook, a Mrs. Todd. He said the body was found by the house maid when she came to work this morning. I got there as quick as I could. The body had been moved to her bedroom, which is near the kitchen, and put on the bed. Apparently, it was found sort of wedged in between the stove and wall. The housemaid said the victim was still wearing her clothes and apron from the day before."

Leishke sighed and decided to continue his tutoring of Davies.

"It's been my experience that we should always ask that bodies not be moved unless it's absolutely necessary. Sometimes, you can find clues from the scene that don't appear later," Leishke said. "It's too bad that that didn't happen this time. I'm guessing the killing wasn't as bloody as Rosie Brown's."

"You're right," said Davies, looking impressed. "She had been strangled, and there wasn't any blood. Not that it didn't look pretty horrible, but it was like that suicide last month. I'd seen it before, so that's why I think it was strangulation. That...and the rope around her neck. They hadn't removed that. I told them to leave everything alone until you had seen it."

"They've already called for the coroner's jury, of course. But I think we may just beat them there this time," Davies said.

"Good. Let's get to it then," replied Leishke

Leishke stood up, grabbed his hat and jacket, and hurried out, ensuring his door was locked behind Davies. The two men quickly descended the stairs and headed downtown toward the ferry dock.

Chapter 11

Fannie softly knocked on Selena's door; her room adjoined Selena's which meant she didn't have to risk being seen in the hall. Still, she tapped quietly; the sounds from next door last night had certainly indicated that Selena had not been able to go to sleep until late.

Selena answered the door, looking as tired as Fannie felt, and dressed in a wrapper. It was a lovely one, Fannie took the time to note. She thought it might be silk, and it had an exotic oriental pattern.

"How are you this morning?" Selena asked with a yawn. "I hope you got some sleep."

"I did. Thank you. And I hope you thanked your friend for getting me the room."

"Oh, I thanked him all right. He got lots of my appreciation last night," said Selena with a sly smile.

"How long can I stay here?" asked Fannie. "I have money, but I think it's best if I don't go anywhere in public for a few days, including the bank. I also need to figure out some way to get my clothes and other things from the cabin."

"If you give me a key, I can ask my brother to get them," said Selena. "Brown boys are invisible to white people. He could go there in the broad daylight and no one would even notice him." She looked at Fannie's face. "But don't worry. I'll send him at night. He can pack up your trunk and get it over to us tonight. I can't help you with the bank, though. You'll need to go there."

"I know. But do you think your friend can keep paying for the room for a few more days?"

"I think I can persuade him to do that, yes," Selena replied.

"I also need to figure out some way to talk to my friend, May," said Fannie. "As I told you yesterday, I don't want anyone else to know how I got in this fix. I don't want anyone else to be threatened. May is an innocent – no one will even suspect she knows me, so no one will expect I've told her anything. And I told her I would tell her all of it, so she can tell the detective. But I can't ask her to come here and I can't go there."

Selena paused before replying. "Hmm. Well, I've got a couple of ideas about that. We need to find a place she and you can both go, but it won't be noticed or commented on, right?"

"Right."

"How about the Indian Village in Douglas?" Selena asked. "My brothers still live there, and you know that anyone who marries an Indian has to live there. It's not too unusual for white women to go there, even if it's just to look at baskets. I think that might work, but it could take a while for me to set it up. I'll see what I can do."

"That sounds like a good possibility," said Fannie. "I just don't want to put anyone else in danger. But I think May's boarding house is just a block or two from the village, so she may be able to slip down there safely. It might be a little trickier for me to get there. But so long as it's dark and I judge the ferry times correctly, I could slip back and forth."

"I'll let you know what will work after I have a chance to talk to Eli and Matt, my brothers," said Selena. "Right now, come inside. I always have coffee and rolls delivered to my room in the morning and they should be here soon. It's almost 11."

Fannie, who was also wearing a wrapper she had borrowed from Selena – of a more serviceable flannel -- came in and sat on the end of the unmade bed. The state of the bed reflected the noises she had heard last night – pillows were on the floor and the blankets and sheets were hanging from the bed. It had definitely been a busy night for Selena. Fannie knew better than to comment. Instead, the sight reminded her again of her current inability to earn a living. She had to get back to work as soon as possible, and with any luck, it would not be anywhere in the vicinity of Douglas.

Fannie looked at her friend, who had washed her face and was now going through the wardrobe to pick out her clothes for the day. Selena was younger – Fannie guessed she could have been less than 18. But she was a lovely girl – half Native and half white, her father had been a well-known and well-respected prospector until he had turned to drink. Selena, like the other Alaska Native girls who had become working girls, wasn't allowed in the areas where the white women were. After her father deserted her family, Selena became well known in Douglas and Juneau for her beauty, and that led to a number of local businessmen being interested in cultivating a relationship.

A 'relationship,' scoffed Fannie to herself. Really, it meant that Selena was being kept in style at a downtown hotel by her customers. It was an unusual arrangement but seemed to be working for the girl.

Fannie had met Selena shortly after Fannie moved to Douglas. Selena had come to the Opera House looking for work, but as a housemaid, not as a working girl. She was turned away since May had the job, but Fannie had felt sorry for the girl and had slipped her a few coins. This was very much out of character for Fannie, but there was something about Selena that Fannie recognized in the desperation she had felt in Argentina. Selena had been very grateful, and continued to seek Fannie out as much as a Native girl could. So, the two women had chatted on the street when they saw each other, and occasionally met for a quick meal in downtown Douglas.

Fannie knew of Selena's involvement with, and subsequent employment by, the Juneau businessmen. She had counseled her on safety and health, including introducing her to the reusable rubber condoms and telling her about the necessity to wash her clients' private parts before sexual congress. These were the things that Fannie had learned from more experienced prostitutes in Buenos Aires, and they had worked. So far, Fannie had stayed healthy, and prayed she would remain so.

Selena had now dressed in a day dress and was just finishing with her cuffs when a knock on the door drew her that way. She silently nodded at Fannie, indicating a recess between the wall and the large wardrobe. Fannie slipped into the area, knowing it would hide her from the view of anyone in the hall. The wardrobe wasn't flush against the wall, however, and through the narrow gap, she could see the door and the interaction there.

"Here's your breakfast, Miss Dowling," the teenage waiter said, handing Selena a tray. She took it and stepped back, preparatory to closing the door, but the waiter said something and she stopped with her foot holding the door.

"Do you know the woman in the room next to you?" the waiter asked. "There was a man looking for someone who sounded like it might be her this morning. He said he owed her some money."

"No. I don't know anyone on this floor," said Selena shortly. "What did he look like? Maybe I know him."

The waiter didn't seem nonplussed by Selena's confusing claim. "He's tall with dark hair and a mustache. Nothing really different about him, except for his accent. He doesn't speak English very good. I think he might be Russian, or German, or something like that."

"Oh, that doesn't sound like anyone I know," said Selena. "Sorry to take your time."

Setting the tray on the table next to the bed, she picked up a coin from a small pile on the dresser and pressed it into the boy's hand. "Thanks." She closed the door on him, and turned to Fannie, who stepped back into the room. She raised an eyebrow, and Fannie nodded.

"Sounds like the man who I'm hiding from," she admitted. "Can you trust the people who work here not to tell him I'm here?"

"I certainly couldn't trust them to hide you out of the kindness of their hearts," Selena replied, walking to the dresser, and pulling out a small purse. "But there are different ways to earn trust," she said, talking out some coins and bills. "I'll take care of it."

"Oh, I don't want to ask any more of you," Fannie protested.

"It wouldn't make sense for me to go to the trouble of hiding you here if a maid or house boy let it spill," said Selena. "Let me take care of it," she repeated.

Fannie nodded. Selena was right. If she was committed to hiding from Againsky, she needed to do what was necessary to successfully hide. "I'll pay you back as soon as I can," she told Selena. "Keep track of how much this costs you."

"I'm not concerned about the cost," replied Selena. "I'm concerned about you. And I know," her voice dropped, "you would do the same for me. You already have."

Fannie knew what Selena was talking about – when they first met, Selena had been the victim of a man in her neighborhood. As she had become older, his attentions had moved from friendly neighbor to interested suitor. One evening, after he had too much to drink, his interest in her had led him to taking liberties. The kind of liberties that left a teenage girl with a shattered reputation and fewer choices for her future. That had led to where Selena was now.

The two friends smiled at each other. After the light breakfast, Selena left, saying she had some errands to run, but suggested Fannie remain in her room. Fannie readily agreed, and sat on the bed, where she quickly found herself drifting asleep.

Chapter 12

May had been the one to discover the body of Mrs. Todd, crammed between the stove and the wall.

May had come into the kitchen, hanging up her coat on the hook by the door and was surprised to realize the stove was off, and no coffee yet begun. Initially, she thought the cook must be ill. She couldn't remember a time when Mrs. Todd wasn't the first one in the kitchen, and the last one to go home at night. But May then realized she hadn't seen Mrs. Todd the previous evening either; after finishing the laundry and placing the clean clothes and linens in the upstairs linen closet, she had gone into the kitchen just to grab her coat and hurry home.

She hadn't slept well, disturbed by thoughts of the man in the basement, the tale told by Fannie, and the very real fear she had felt. She had been looking forward to that cup of coffee and felt more than a little disappointed that it wasn't ready for her. "Oh, well," she thought. "It wasn't as if I didn't know how to make coffee."

She grabbed some wood from the pile by the door and went to the stove to begin the fire. That's when she saw the body. The wood fell from her arms as she stood, staring at Mrs. Todd, whose protruding eyes and tongue seemed to be silently screaming for help.

May couldn't remember what happened next, but she must have gone into the bar to fetch the bartender, who had also just arrived at work. Together, the two returned to the kitchen. May couldn't bear to see that face again, so pointed toward it, noticing absently how her outstretched arm trembled.

"She's there. I think she must be dead."

The bartender's face blanched at the sight of the cook. Made of sterner stuff than May, or perhaps reluctant for her to see his own fear, he knelt, feeling for a pulse.

"Well, I think the first thing is to move her," he stated firmly. "Let's lay her out on her bed."

The cook's room was next to the kitchen but May knew she wasn't going to be able to help with this task. What to do?

"Let me see if there's anyone on the porch who can help," she said. She went through the bar to the front door and opened it. There were three of what May thought of the Usuals, leaning on the rail, talking in a desultory manner, and waiting for the bar to open.

"Hey, you three," said May. "We need your help."

All three men followed her with alacrity, probably hoping a favor might lead to a free drink or two. Their enthusiasm for the job faltered once they saw the body but, unwilling to lose face with each other, they helped drag Mrs. Todd from her cramped resting place and carried her to her bed. May followed behind, picking up the keys that fell from the body's pockets, and feeling both useless and grateful not to be participating.

Once the body was laid on the bed, one of the Usuals took off for the Douglas Commissioner's office, and May sat down to think about what should happen next. She again found herself craving coffee and realized that was the next thing to do.

The working girls would soon be up and expect breakfast. May went into the kitchen, started the stove up and began preparing breakfast. The task kept her body and mind busy enough to let her somewhat escape from thinking of Mrs. Todd, but not completely.

"Who killed her? Was it the man from the night before? It must have been, but why? Did he want to ensure that no one knew what he looked like? Had he really meant to kill Fannie and May in the basement?"

As she began the coffee and took out the dough that Mrs. Todd had left to rise in the warming compartment of the stove, May realized that her fears of the night before were justified, but what should she do now? She really didn't think the man had seen her last night, but had Mrs. Todd told him that Fannie was in the basement with her friend, May, or with the housemaid? Or had her presence even been noted?

Automatically, her hands began shaping the dough into cinnamon rolls – once they came downstairs and heard the news, the girls would appreciate the comfort of the warm, sweet rolls. As she thought of this, she remembered Mrs. Todd's story of delivering donuts to grieving families. Her hands stopped, and a tear rolled down her cheek. Mrs. Todd was going to be very much missed.

Frank Leishke and Deputy Marshal Davies stepped off the dock and headed toward the Opera House. The weather had reverted to form; the sun was replaced by a low-hanging fog and misty rain. The rain dampened Frank's coat and hat, but the temperatures stayed warm, and he wasn't sorry that he had left his gloves behind.

As they approached the building, Leishke began feeling the energy that he had frequently observed around the scene of a murder. A few more men than usual stood on the porch, and as Leishke and Davies approached, their talking came to a halt.

"We heard there's been another murder," one man said; Leishke thought he may have been chosen by the others to do the speaking since everyone else had crowded behind him and were listening intently. Leishke thought for a moment. What would be the best way to respond?

"Yes," he decided to reply, circling around the knot of men, and headed for the front door.

"Just a minute," the spokesman said loudly. "Some of us have wives and children who live here. What are you doing to catch this mad man and keep our families safe?"

"My job," said Leishke. "And you're stopping me from doing it."

He heard the angry muttering as he moved through the main door and stepped inside. He waited for Davies to come in behind him and then closed and locked the door, pulling the blind down over the door's window.

"Hey, what do you think you're doing?" yelled the bartender, who briskly walked to the open end of the bar and headed toward them.

Leishke looked around; the room was only about half full with mostly working girls and a few patrons. He turned toward the angry looking bartender and saw the moment when the man recognized Leishke.

"You're Tom, right?" said Leishke to the young man.

"Tom Moore," the young man replied with a nod.

"I really need to get anyone who doesn't live here out the door," Leishke told him.

"I'm not sure I can do that without getting the OK from Mrs. Montgomery," Tom told him, referring to the Opera House's madam.

"That's fine – do you want to ask her, or do you want us to?" asked Leishke.

"I'll do it, but perhaps you should come also?"

Leishke was struggling with impatience. He really wanted to begin his investigation. He turned to Davies. "You go with Tom," he said. "Tell her we need some time to talk to the witnesses and look at the scene without interruptions. We also expect the coroner's jury members very soon, and they will want to meet without the place being open. I don't expect it to take longer than a few hours."

He turned again to Tom. "Where's the body? I would like to examine it before the coroner's jury, if possible."

Tom led him through a door into the kitchen. There, he saw the house maid he had seen the day before. She was slicing a roll of cinnamon rolls into a pan. She glanced at him, looked back to her work and then back again at him.

"Can I help you?" she asked. She had finished putting the rolls into the pan and, after wiping her hands on her apron, put the pan in the oven and turned back to him.

"I-I," he stammered, and realized he might actually be blushing. "What the hell," he thought. He didn't stammer or blush. "I'm Deputy Marshal Frank Leishke," he said, realizing he might actually be blurting it out.

"Oh, you must be here about Mrs. Todd. I found her this morning. That's why I'm cooking breakfast," the young woman said. Frank was relieved to see she also sounded flustered, but realized it was more likely shock and grief than feeling some kind of attraction to him. He tried smiling at her, hoping to help her feel more comfortable.

"I'm May Svenson," the woman said. "I can show you where I found her, if you like." He nodded.

She walked over to the recess between the stove and wall. "She was sort of crammed into this space," May said. Her eyes were filling with tears, and Frank realized he felt bad for asking her anything. He couldn't remember the last time he had felt this guilty about questioning a witness.

"Thanks for showing me," he said gently. "Can you point out the room where the body is?"

May showed him to the bedroom door, and then returned to the kitchen.

Leishke stepped next to bed and looked at the body. Rigor mortis had come and gone, he thought, most likely because her body had been next to the hot stove, which would speed up the process. He also saw that one side of her clothes appeared scorched, and her left hand and lower arm, which were unclothed, looked red and burned. "It was a lucky thing the clothes hadn't caught fire," he thought. If it had, the building would probably have burnt down and there would be no evidence left.

As it was, clues were scant. The cord around her neck might provide some clue. He bent over to examine it more closely. It appeared to be a sash cord from a window; each end had been cut recently with a sharp blade. He reached down and put his hands in the apron pockets and the pockets sewn into the woman's skirt. Nothing. He couldn't tell if that meant she had been robbed, or if she usually carried nothing in the pockets.

He left the room and re-entered the kitchen, where May now appeared to be cracking eggs into a bowl. In a nearby room, he heard women's voices, and realized the working girls were gathering for breakfast. He said to May, "I have a couple of questions. I know you're working, but I think you can answer these pretty easily."

May nodded and glanced up at him. He kept his gaze on the windows, looking for one with a missing sash.

"Go ahead," she said. "I'll see if I can answer you."

"Did the cook – Mrs. Todd – keep anything in her pockets? Any valuables?"

"No, just her keys. And I found them when they carried her into her bedroom. They're right here if you need them." May dug into her apron pocket and showed him a bundle of keys.

"I don't need them. You can give them to Mrs. Montgomery. I also wanted to look at your windows."

Leishke walked to the wall next to the oven and noted that one of the windows was missing its sash cord. He turned to May.

"Did you notice anything out of place this morning?" he asked.

"You mean other than the body of my friend?" replied May, feeling, and sounding irritated. She knew this was the deputy marshal she was going to tell Fannie's story to, but he seemed completely unmoved by what had been for her one of the worst experiences of her life.

"Sorry." Frank realized he had not looked May in the eye since he entered the room. He was trying to keep his focus on the investigation and didn't want to risk giving her his attention, but her question demanded his response.

He turned to her and looked in her face. It was his first opportunity to study it. May had thick, well-shaped brows above dark brown eyes. Her mouth was set in a grim line as she stared at him. Her lips were full, but she appeared to have a slight overbite. The hair he had noticed yesterday was already disheveled from her busy morning; a hairpin was falling out above her left ear, and a dark curl was brushing her forehead.

Frank noticed her mouth had changed from a grim look to one that was slightly puzzled and realized he had been staring too long.

"Um," he stuttered. "I ... I mean I'm sorry if I wasn't being respectful about the cook. Were you two close?"

"Yes," said May. She was the one who now averted her eyes from his. "We have worked together every day I've been here. We visited over coffee or tea at least twice a day, and ... I think she may be one of my best friends here in Douglas."

"Well," said Frank. He found himself struggling for what to do next. He said, "Why don't we sit down and talk about her? Do you have time now?"

"Yes," said May. She had finished the rolls and the coffee was on. "The girls will be down in about half an hour for breakfast, and I'll need to cook eggs and bacon then, but I have a few minutes now. Do you want coffee?"

"Yes." Frank walked over to the table but waited to sit until after May had handed him a cup, placed milk and sugar on the table, taken a cup for herself and sat down. He pulled out a chair so was sitting kitty corner from her.

"I am sorry about your loss," he said. "Can you tell me what you know about her?"

"Well, she was like me. She came here with her husband, who was a miner. But he was killed shortly after they moved here, and she didn't have the money to leave, so she took a job here. I think she enjoyed it. She liked cooking and was old enough to sort of become the mother of all the girls. I mean, I know that Mrs. Montgomery gives the girls lots of help and advice, but Mrs. Todd would listen to them. If someone had bad news from home, or was worried about...something, then Mrs. Todd would be there to help. She couldn't do much, but she was a good listener. I know I've told her more than I've told pretty much anyone about my situation here, even my family back in Minnesota." May stopped, looking at her hands, still marked with flour and a little cinnamon.

She smiled suddenly – and Frank found himself shaken again. She had two dimples and although the smile was small, he spied them. Her teeth were white, but one eye tooth was a little crooked, and that imperfection seemed to make the rest of her face even more beautiful. He stared at her, not realizing how intent he had become until the smile slipped away and she again looked at her hands.

"She was a good friend – to all of us. But you were asking about her, not about me," she said. "She was childless, so far as I knew. Her family was back in Illinois. She had a sister, brother-in-law, a brother, and his family there. She wrote them regularly but had decided a year or so ago to remain in Douglas. She liked the work and the pay was good. She sent money back to the family regularly – I think she was helping a nephew with school. She also was setting money aside so she would buy her own boarding house. She wanted to open one in Juneau, because she is hearing what we're all hearing here – the Treadwell mines are playing out. When they're gone, Douglas will go with them. There will be nothing to keep people here."

Leishke had also heard these rumors and had to agree. The reason for Douglas's existence was the thriving network of gold mines next to the town. Once those were gone, Douglas would probably fade from existence. Fortunately for Douglas inhabitants, Juneau's gold mining operations would be able to absorb some of the Treadwell miners, and store owners and others would probably just move across the channel. He also doubted the predictions of the mines failing soon. He had been in the west long enough to know that it could take years for mines to completely play out.

"You may be right," he told May. "But let's talk about why you think she was killed. Had anyone threatened her, or did she know something that could put her in danger?" He watched May closely, knowing these were the questions that lay at the heart of the murder. Did May know something?

May hesitated. She needed to tread carefully. She was convinced that Mrs. Todd had been killed by the man who had tried to find her and Fannie last night. She also knew that Fannie's story had been interrupted by that same man. May glanced at Leishke's unsmiling face, and decided she wanted to be able to tell him the whole story at one time. She needed to find Fannie, hear the rest of the story, and then go to Leischke and tell him what she knew. If she talked now, she was afraid that Leishke would try to find Fannie, and May now believed that could result in Fannie's death.

"I don't know of anyone threatening her, or of anything she knew that might put her in danger," said May. She then remembered something she could use as a red herring. "But...the girls here were talking about a man – a customer – who liked...." May wasn't sure how to end the sentence. "Well, he liked...he liked to put his hands around the girls' necks when he was..."

"When he was having relations with them?" asked Frank softly.

"Yes. Maybe one of them told Mrs. Todd, and she decided to confront him. I think she would do something like that. She was brave enough, and she was strong. Not just physically, but also mentally. What if that man decided to kill her? She was strangled, right?"

"Hmm," said Leishke, thinking. If this man had been challenged by Mrs. Todd, would he kill her? It seemed unlikely; Leishke suspected the man was as uncaring about the staff at the Opera House as he was about the women who worked there. He also knew that just because a man throttled a woman with whom he was having sex, he wouldn't necessarily kill someone that way but it was worth pursuing.

May didn't wait for his signaling the end of the questions but left the table to begin cooking the remainder of the breakfast. Frank stood up when she did, and then sat again. He took out his notebook to go over his notes for the day and took a sip of his coffee. He also glanced at May, who was laying out bacon on a griddle on the stove. She wasn't looking at him, and the longer he stared at her, the more he became convinced that she was deliberately avoiding his gaze. He wondered if she had left something out – she had ended the interview quickly, and he wondered if she had something more to say.

He glanced at his notebook and saw Fannie Miller's name underlined.

"One more question," he told May. "Do you know Fannie Miller?"

Chapter 13

Fannie woke up about 3 p.m., having fallen into a deep sleep after Selena had left her in the room. She was a little surprised that Selena hadn't returned but was feeling so much better after the long sleep that her natural optimism had returned. The world didn't look as dark as it had the night before. She had escaped Againsky and made it to a friend's door. The friend had already helped her and was planning to arrange one more meeting with May. Then, once the full story was told, she would get her belongings, again with the help of Selena, and make her way out of Juneau. It was a solid plan, and she felt confident all would be well. She would not only escape Juneau but help bring Jennie's killer to justice.

She stretched, stood up and opened the door that led into her room. She had locked it before going to sleep, but the other side remained unlocked. She stepped inside her room; the daylight was fading into twilight, but she still saw enough to know that someone had been in her room while she slept, and it wasn't the hotel maid. The person who had searched the room had done so after maid service; the bed was neatly made up and a fresh towel was next to the wash basin, but her dress and jacket had been pulled off their hangers from the hook on the wall and lay crumpled on the floor. The pockets were inside out and empty. She thought hard, struggling past the paralyzing fright, and didn't recall leaving anything in them. She moved to the bed, looking down at it, and saw the indent on the pillow, matching an indent on the bedspread at the foot of the bed. Whoever had searched her room had then laid down on the bed. Had he been waiting for her? Had she slept next door as her would-be killer slept on this bed?

It was a chilling thought. She shivered, grabbed her dress, jacket, and shoes, and quickly returned to Selena's room. The searcher hadn't even considered she could be next door, she thought. That was lucky, but she wasn't sure that luck would last. She would wait for Selena, then must move to another location. But where?

• • •

May kept frying bacon, focusing on the mundane task so she could collect her thoughts before answering Leishke.

"I do know her. She was working here when I began, but she and her friend, Rosie Brown, decided to move to their own places a few weeks after I began here." She left it to Leishke to assume she didn't know them well. "They were friendly girls, and I think they continued to visit Mrs. Todd now and again, but I was usually too busy to talk with them when they came by. I was very sorry to hear about Rosie's death. But wait ... do you think her death has something to do with what happened to Mrs. Todd?"

Even to her ears, her question sounded stilted, and she knew that Leishke must have heard it also. She threw him a glance and saw him looking at her. She turned the bacon, staring at the meat as if it might leap off the skillet by itself.

"Mrs. Svenson," said Frank. He glanced at her left hand and noticed again the bright gold band. When he had first noticed it, his heart had sunk, but after he heard her say that, like her, Mrs. Todd had come here with a miner husband who died, he found himself hoping that the husbands were both dead, as well as both being miners. He also found it hard to believe that any husband would want his wife working in a brothel, even as a house maid.

"I have a feeling that you might know something you're not telling me," said Frank, surprising both of them with his frankness. "Are you certain there's no one else you suspect?"

May hesitated, pulling the bacon off the griddle, and setting it in a pan to stay warm on the back of the stove. She reached for the carton of eggs, using the cooking tasks to give her time to form an answer.

"There may be something else I can tell you, but I don't know the whole story. I want to wait until I know more to tell you. Can you wait?"

"I'm afraid, given what has been happening here this week, that waiting could put you, and maybe others, in danger," said Frank, baldly. "Why don't you tell me what you know now and the rest when you find it out?"

"I can't," said May, realizing that she had said too much. How was she going to convince the detective to wait until she had the whole story? "The little I know now doesn't even make sense. I need to wait." She reached for a bowl and began cracking eggs into it.

"What might not make sense to you could make sense to me," argued Frank. "Can you just trust me to use the information wisely, and not get anyone else hurt, or even killed?"

May stirred the eggs with a fork, adding salt, pepper, and some cream, hearing increasing noise from the dining room as the girls came in for the meal.

"No. I can't. I have to wait. But I can promise I will tell you as soon as I have a complete picture. I'm hoping that will be very soon. Maybe even in the next day or two."

Frank's response was visceral, and very unlike him. "I don't think I can live with that," he said harshly. "This person may have already killed twice. What makes you think he won't kill you too?"

Chapter 14

May met with Mrs. Montgomery after breakfast was served and she had cleaned up. The coroner's jury had arrived, she had been questioned briefly about finding the body, and then excused. She thought that Frank Leishke was still with the jury. May knew that Leishke was unhappy with her decision, but she wasn't prepared to tell him what she knew because she didn't have key parts of Fannie's story. How had she and Rosie ended up in Alaska, and how had Againsky found her? She also found herself wanting to avoid Leishke. For some reason she couldn't identify, he made her uncomfortable. When he looked at her, she felt his gaze as almost a physical touch. She blamed his profession on his intense attention to her, but it still made her uneasy.

She and Mrs. Montgomery discussed how she was going to fill in for Mrs. Todd. Mrs. Montgomery also told her that Lily, the other house maid, had quit her job that morning after hearing about the murdered cook. May had already told her boss she didn't want the job of cook; it required living at the Opera House, which she didn't want, especially after the frightening experience in the basement and, of course, Mrs. Todd's death.

Fortunately for Mrs. Montgomery (although not as fortunately for the young widows), there were usually a number of women in Douglas who had lost husbands to the dangerous job of mining. Like Albert, some had been blown up during explosions to loosen rock. Others slipped to their deaths from the steep slopes of the mining pit or had fallen prey to a number of the almost monthly accidents that caused fatalities. It was no problem finding women who needed employment. It was more difficult finding one who was willing to put her reputation (and that of her children) on the line to work at the Opera House, and to find one with sufficient experience to become a full-time cook was also a challenge.

Mrs. Montgomery told May it would likely take a few days to bring someone on as cook, but she anticipated quickly finding a housemaid to replace Lily, who had taken the job as a temporary post before she returned to her hometown in Idaho. Mrs. Montgomery told May that the brothel was busy enough that a second housemaid could become a permanent post, while assuring May that her job would continue to be full-time also.

"I'm realizing, now that you're doing such a good job cleaning, that our previous maids didn't have the same attention to detail. I also know that you are regularly leaving late, so hiring another maid will help you, but will also allow us to continue to enjoy clean windows and floors," the older woman said with a smile.

May liked Mrs. Montgomery. She had attained the position of madam after almost three decades as a working girl. May knew that many of the working girls at the Opera House hoped to earn the wealth and stability enjoyed by Mrs. Montgomery but suspected that it was a rare success story. Although now in her 50s, the madam was still very attractive, usually cheerful and had a friendly demeanor. May knew she could also be a harsh taskmaster. May knew enough about the work at the brothel to know it was hard and sometimes dangerous work. Mrs. Montgomery's job was to ensure that the working girls protected themselves, but also earned enough to pay for their room and board, as well as bring a steady profit to Mrs. Montgomery.

That profit, as was common with all the women May knew at the brothel, was displayed on Mrs. Montgomery in part through expensive and showy jewelry. Gold chains, pearl drop earrings and a number of gem-encrusted rings were part of Mrs. Montgomery's daily adornment. Such obvious wealth also made working girls a target for thieves. In Juneau and Douglas, the residents of the Restricted Districts had protected themselves in part by befriending police, who were usually more than willing to be so befriended. That was one of the reasons that Fannie had been so reluctant to tell the police her story. She had seen too many officers leaving cribs early in the morning – and usually without paying.

Beneath her usual charm and friendliness, May could see that Mrs. Montgomery was worried. She had not just lost a cook, but lost her to murder, and on the premises. This was not good – not just for the reputation of the brothel but May knew that the madam also worried for her girls. May decided to probe a little bit.

"I heard the girls talking about a customer who would put his hands around their necks," she commented. "Do you think that's the person who did this?" May hoped that by approaching the topic this way, it would keep Fannie out of the discussion altogether.

"It certainly could be. I've talked to the three girls he patronized, and they told me he gave each of them a different name. I need to ask around and see if anyone knows his real name."

"What does he look like?" asked May.

"He's tall, dark-haired and large, so I'm guessing he is accustomed to doing a lot of physical labor," the madam replied. "I've seen him but didn't pay close attention. I told Deputy Marshal Leishke about him and he said he would ask around."

"Is there anyone else you suspect?" asked May.

"Not really. I think that Leishke is also investigating Rosie Brown's death, and it's hard not to think the two killings related, but I guess they don't have to be." Suddenly, Mrs. Montgomery looked tired and a little anxious. "I keep thinking about that case over in Juneau last year. I knew the woman who was killed – not well because she was so new to town – but I did know her. That was an awful thing. It was good police work that led to his arrest, so I'm hoping that we'll have the same luck."

May thought about that murder – a working girl in Juneau had been killed in her crib in an isolated spot at the end of The Line, as they called the Restricted District in Juneau. She had also been robbed. May wasn't sure about the good police work – the killer had been found after a steamship purser noticed his bag had contained a lot of women's clothes and possessions. The killer's story explaining the stolen items was ridiculous, and the marshals had acted quickly to arrest him. He was now serving a life sentence for the killing.

May knew such a quick resolution in this case was unlikely – it was already a couple of days since Rosie's murder, and the marshals didn't seem any closer to finding a suspect. She wasn't sure what else she could ask Mrs. Montgomery; it appeared that May already knew more than she did. She stood up, and said, "I better get back to work. I was going to prepare some snacks for the bar and then it will be time to cook dinner. I hope we can get that other housemaid soon – I am definitely not keeping up with my regular chores."

"Don't worry, my dear," said Mrs. Montgomery. "I have two women coming by today who are interested...and I haven't forgotten how to wash a load of laundry either."

...

Leishke had decided to return to the Restricted District. He had met with the coroner's jury, who had determined that Mrs. Todd was killed by someone unknown. He had charged Deputy Marshal Davies with talking to some of the women at the Opera House about the client who liked to throttle women with whom he had sex. He had also asked Davies to begin talking to store owners about anyone recently buying a miner's hammer.

He wanted to talk to Fannie again, and he also wanted to talk to some of the other women who lived there. Since it was about 2 p.m., he was in hopes that the women down the street would be awake and not yet occupied. His first stops were the houses next door to Rosie Brown's – Fannie had lived on one side and a woman named Sadie lived on the other side.

After no answer at Fannie's crib, he knocked on Sadie's door, and it was promptly answered by an attractive woman still wearing her morning wrapper and holding a cup of coffee. She gave him a flirtatious smile, and stood aside, gesturing with her coffee cup for him to enter.

Leishke stepped inside, taking off his hat as he did so. The layout was the same as Rosie's crib – two rooms with the front room containing a small kitchen, table and two chairs and one padded chair next to a small table. A plate with what appeared to be the remains of breakfast was on the table. A curtain covered the doorway between this room and the back bedroom. Sadie, her blonde curls cascading down her back, stepped over to the table to move the dirty plate to the sink. She turned toward him.

"I know who you are, Deputy Marshal. I'm surprised I haven't seen you before now. After all, I think I could be called a witness."

Leishke could tell she was trying to provoke and played along. "Oh. Well, I'm sorry I didn't get here sooner. It's been a pretty busy couple of days. I am certainly interested in whatever you can tell me. You're Sadie Jones, right?"

Sadie nodded and pulled a chair from the table, placing it slightly facing the upholstered chair, gesturing for him to sit. He did so, taking the less comfortable chair and moving it a little further from the other chair. Sadie smiled and sat down, ensuring her wrapper dropped open just enough to show a shapely calf.

"Well, I knew Rosie pretty well, you know," she said. "In fact, she might have considered me her closest friend. I knew she was from Russia, and also knew her husband just moved here."

Leishke pulled out his notebook and pencil, indicating he wanted to hear more, without showing her the level of interest he was feeling. He had the sense that she enjoyed drama, and he didn't want to encourage her to further embellish any information she had.

"I didn't know her husband was here," he said. "Did he live with her?" He knew that was unlikely. While it wasn't uncommon for working girls to be married, their husbands were smart enough (and mercenary enough) to not let their presence discourage customers.

"Oh no, he lived in Juneau. I think he worked at the mine over there…if he worked at all," Sadie said somewhat derisively. "He just got here – I think he arrived this week. I had seen Rosie that night – the night she was killed – and she said that her husband had just come to town. She seemed very unhappy about it."

"Do you know his name? I had heard it was Poplosky," replied Leishke, lying through his teeth. This was the first he had heard of any husband.

"No, his name is Againsky," said Sadie. "I don't know where you heard the name Poplosky. Maybe a boyfriend or something."

"Did she have a husband and a boyfriend?" asked Leishke.

"No," Sadie said. "I was surprised to find out she even had a husband. She wasn't very attractive and certainly wasn't young. Most of her customers went to her because I was already occupied."

Leishke was a little startled at this open criticism of a woman that Sadie claimed as a close friend. He also wondered if she hadn't recognized the name Poplosky. He began to think his initial instinct had been correct, and that Sadie was more interested in his attention than in helping find Jennie Poplosky's killer.

"Have you ever seen this husband?"

"That's what I wanted to tell you. I'm pretty sure I saw him the night of the murder. I was expecting a customer that night, and heard something outside, so I peeked through the curtains. I saw a man who I'm almost sure was Againsky coming out of Rosie's house."

"What time was it?"

"I think around 4 in the morning. I had said goodnight to an earlier customer at around 2:30 – he was starting work at the 3 a.m. shift. My next customer was supposed to show up when he got off work at 3, but never arrived. He came the next day, so I think I just got the date wrong. Anyway, that's why I was looking out the window and saw Againsky. I'm sure it was him now that I'm telling you about it. Rosie had told me to watch for him – she said he was dark with curly black hair and a mustache. She said he was tall but slender. And the man I saw that night had the same build and coloring."

"Did he see you?" Leishke was worried; it appeared that Rosie's killer didn't hesitate to kill, and here was a woman who may have just named herself as a potential victim.

"No, he didn't," she replied. "I asked around, and no one else saw him that night. Although I suppose Fannie might have. I haven't seen her for a couple of days, so I'm not sure. But I suppose you've already talked to her. I heard the coroner's jury questioned her. I think they should have talked to me."

"I think you're correct," agreed Leishke. "I really appreciate you telling me this."

"You might want to ask Fannie about him also," said Sadie reluctantly. "I think that Fannie was from the same place as Rosie, so they had coffee together every morning." She looked at Leishke. "They usually asked me to join them, but I have a strict list of things I do every morning to keep my complexion fresh. I think it works very well. Don't you?" she again smiled at Leishke.

He answered her smile with one of his own and tried to marshal his thoughts. Sadie had just presented him with the lead suspect in the case, but he wanted to be sure she didn't know something more. He decided to play on her weakness for drama.

"I can tell you are a very observant person," he told her. It was not the type of compliment she was hoping for, but Sadie took it happily.

"I am very good at noticing things," she agreed. "For example, I could tell that Fannie and Rosie had some sort of secret. I often found them talking in some language I didn't understand and when I asked them what it was, they said it was Hebrew. I'm not sure what country speaks that language, but wherever it is, they aren't very friendly people. I also think they're Jewish." This last statement was a whisper, as if someone could overhear them.

"And you know that that means," she added.

Leishke looked at her, not sure how to respond, but she didn't need any encouragement.

"I've heard Jews drink the blood of babies," she again whispered.

Leishke agreed with Sadie that the women speaking in Hebrew did probably mean they were Jewish but didn't want to encourage any more speculation. "That's unlikely," he stated.

"So, you're telling me that Fannie and Rosie were close friends, were probably both Jewish and may have had a secret," he said. "Do you know if Fannie knew about Againsky's arrival?" He was thinking that might explain her disappearing act.

"I don't know," said Sadie, somewhat petulantly, obviously upset that Leishke hadn't responded the way she hoped to her shocking comment. "All I know is what Rosie told me; I don't remember if I saw Fannie again after that."

She could tell that Leishke was planning to conclude their conversation; he was lifting his hat to his head when she blurted out, "you should talk to that Selena Dowling. I believe she would know where Fannie is – those two girls were very close."

The ploy worked. Leishke set his hat back on his lap and looked at her. "Who is Selena Dowling?"

"She's an Indian girl – a working girl. We don't want her kind down here in the district, so last I heard, she was working in Juneau. But she was friendly with Fannie – I saw them together a couple of times. You should look her up."

"Thanks for the information. I appreciate your time," Leishke told her.

He stood up and headed toward the door. He knew he had to find Fannie Miller and this man Againsky as quickly as he could. It was clear that Fannie Miller had not been candid with him when they had spoken. It was also likely she was another woman in danger. This case felt as if it was getting away from him.

"You don't have to leave yet, do you?" asked Sadie plaintively. "I'm sure there are other things I know that would be helpful."

"You've been very helpful today," said Leishke as he opened the door. "We'll be talking again, I'm sure. Thanks for your time." He tipped his hat to her, stepped out the door and decided to try Fannie's door again, although her cabin looked as empty as it had before. He needed to decide where to go next if she wasn't home – was it more important to find her or to find Againsky?

Chapter 15

Fannie had dressed and decided to wait for Selena's return before leaving the hotel. Her first instinct had been to flee, preferably to the steamship dock and out of town, but she knew that Againsky would also certainly have the place watched. The Warsaw Club was an expert at closing all avenues that a desperate woman would choose. She had learned that in Buenos Aires, and while Againsky was working alone, she knew he would have the money he needed for bribes and hiring help. Juneau, like Douglas, was home to plenty of men who wouldn't look too closely at anyone who was open-handed with their funds.

She was getting increasingly anxious as the time ticked by, and when Selena finally returned at 5:30 p.m., Fannie felt ready to run past her through the door. Drawing on the control that had saved her life more than once, she clutched her hands together and stood as Selena came into the room.

"Oh, I'm so glad to see you," she exclaimed. "He was here. I went into my room a couple of hours ago and he had been there. He had searched the place and didn't even care if I knew. In fact, he had lain on the bed – I think he knew I would see the mark on the pillow and know. I am so frightened."

"My goodness," Selena saw, divesting herself of her jacket, hat, and purse. She moved slowly and thoughtfully, and Fannie found herself calming a little as she watched her. "I'm sorry I was gone so long, but my gentleman caller sometimes likes me to spend the day with him at his house, and this was one of those days."

Selena continued. "I did have a chance to ask around a little about this man, however. He apparently arrived in Juneau on the steamship four days ago. I was going to look," she paused, going through a pile of newspapers on the bedside table. "Oh, here it is. Let me see." She shook the paper open and looked at the bottom of the third page. "Yes, he's listed here as an incoming passenger. Harry Againsky. I'm a little surprised he used his real name."

Fannie was also but guessed that he thought he wouldn't find Rosie in Juneau, but in Anchorage, since that was the last place he knew she was living. So, it wouldn't matter if the Juneau steamship company had his real name.

"I'm guessing you were too busy to talk to your brother or arrange for a meeting in the Indian Village," she asked Selena. "I really think I need to leave Juneau as soon as I can arrange it, but I need to tell May the rest of the story first."

Selena had asked Fannie to tell her the story of Rosie and Fannie, but Fannie was already feeling guilty putting May in danger. She was not going to do the same with Selena.

"I did talk to my brother and visited my cousin in the Juneau Indian Village. I think she would be fine if you wanted to stay there for a couple of days while you put things in order to leave town. I can also get word to May to meet you there if you need me to. I think it would be safer to meet here, rather than over in Douglas."

"That would be wonderful," said Fannie. She was worried for both Selena and May, but it didn't appear that Againsky had realized she and Selena knew each other, since he certainly would have come into Selena's room if he had known. She had had a narrow escape and knew it.

"I think it would be best if I left here tonight," she told Selena. Selena nodded. She pulled out a small valise and packed a nightgown, hairbrush and clean under linens. Fannie protested, but Selena insisted she take it, along with a few dollars. It wouldn't be dark until almost 8 p.m., so the two women decided to wait until then to leave. Selena ordered dinner for one, but asked for a full meal, so enough soup, beef and vegetables arrived for both of them. Fannie again hid next to the wardrobe when the food was delivered.

After eating, Selena lay down for a quick nap, and Fannie sat quietly, thinking over the events of the past few days, and trying to put together a plan of escape. At about 8 p.m., Selena woke and washed quickly. She had told Fannie she didn't expect her gentlemen callers (as she referred to them) tonight after her active day. She left the room, wearing dark-colored garments, and carrying a purse that Fannie knew held a gun.

Fannie waited a few minutes and then picked up the valise. She looked carefully into the hall, saw it was vacant, and moved swiftly to the far end, where a set of backstairs led to the kitchen and was used by hotel staff. She slipped quickly down the steep stairs, and coached by Selena, turned immediately to the left at the bottom of the stairs, entered a short corridor and went out the back entrance to the hotel. Standing in the alley near the refuse cans, she remembered Selena's instructions.

She quickly wrapped a scarf around her hat and then her mouth, leaving only her eyes visible. It was the same hat and scarf arrangement that Selena had when she had left earlier. From a few feet in the dark, the women would have appeared very similar.

Fannie walked through the alley, entering Franklin Street. Now on a wooden sidewalk, she found herself quickly part of a crowd of men and women, exiting and entering the many restaurants and saloons facing the street. She didn't look around; she knew that would be too obvious. Instead, she looked at reflections in the many storefront windows. It didn't appear that she was being followed, but she felt exposed and frightened. As she crossed from Franklin Street to the less populous Front Street, she became even more uncomfortable. Front Street crossed Main Street, and she saw Selena standing on the Main Street sidewalk, waiting for her. She walked toward her quickly, and the two women, without speaking, began walking together toward the ocean channel at the base of the street. Shortly before reaching it, they turned right and started toward the Village. They had walked about two blocks, so fast they were almost running, when they heard footsteps behind them.

"Hey, you two girls," someone yelled.

They looked at each other and again, without talking, began running. The footsteps quickened but didn't break into a run. It appeared that their pursuer didn't want the attention a man running after two women might attract but he was getting closer; he must be tall because his stride was significant. They ran past a Native family group – parents and three older children. Fannie thought Selena said something to the male of the group. She and Selena ran around the family.

"Get out of my way, squaw," their pursuer said to the family. She heard one thud, followed by another. She took the time to glance behind her and saw the entire family stepping calmly over a man lying on the ground. She saw enough to know he wasn't Againsky; this man was blonde with an elaborate mustache now marred by the blood flowing from his nose. He appeared unconscious. She looked at Selena, and both women slowed back to a brisk walk.

"That white man should have known better than to be chasing Indian girls in the Village," said Selena. "He was lucky it was a fist and not a knife."

She took Fannie's hand and pulled her down a narrow dark alley. After passing three of the houses, which were built so close to each other that it would have been difficult to squeeze between them, Selena opened a door and pushed Fannie inside. Selena looked carefully in each direction before closing the door behind them.

Fannie found herself in another kitchen – she recognized the stove, wash basin and table and chairs but there was a lot that was unfamiliar. First was the smell –it smelled of fish, cooking oil and something else, more elusive. Fannie gave another sniff and recognized it was yarrow, a white flowered weed that was hanging upside down in bunches from the ceiling. She knew yarrow had medicinal properties, and it appeared the residents of the house knew that also. Against one wall was a multi-level rack, covered with drying salmon. What was most puzzling to her was the large basket on the table, which appeared to hold spruce boughs covered with something white. From a distance, it resembled snow, but she looked closer and realized it was actually clutches of tiny eggs.

"Oh, this is wonderful," said Selena, who had also been gazing about her, but with much more familiarity than had Fannie. "I'm just in time for some herring eggs." She glanced at Fannie and smiled, unwinding her scarf and removing it, as well her hat and jacket. She hung all three on a hook on the back of the door and gestured to Fannie to do the same.

"Herring eggs are a spring delicacy," Selena explained. "We put the spruce boughs out in the water, and the herring lay their eggs on the boughs." She looked again at Fannie. "Well, you may not appreciate them as much as we do, but I think you should try." She added, more quietly, "if you don't have some, it would insult my cousin."

"Well, then of course I'll have some," replied Fannie, reminding herself that caviar was also fish eggs.

"Selena, it is so nice to see you," said a voice behind Fannie. She turned to see a woman, probably in her thirties, standing in the doorway to the rest of the house. She was almost as lovely as Selena, with shiny black hair and warm, expressive brown eyes. She was introduced as Jane, although when Selena greeted her in Tlinget, she seemed to call her something else. Fannie wondered if she had a Tlinget name also.

"Fannie," said Selena. "Jane says she would be happy to let you stay for a few days. She will try to be sure that your presence here is secret, but you should know, there are few secrets in the Village. However, it's unlikely that anyone who lives here will be telling anyone outside the Village that you are here. It won't be the first time we have hidden someone."

Jane listened to Selena, and then added, "You need to know that if someone from the law comes here to look for you, we won't be able to hide you. It's too dangerous for us to harbor someone the marshals or police want."

"That is more than fair," said Fannie. "I can assure you," she told Jane, "no one from law enforcement is looking for me." As she said that, however, Fannie wondered if it was true. If Leishke had found out that she knew more than she had told him, she knew he would be looking for her.

Jane made tea for all of them and set out a plate of herring eggs. Fannie found them not unpleasant – salty with a little bite of fish taste. They were rich, but good.

Over the snack, Fannie learned more about Jane. She was the daughter of Selena's mother's older sister. Their parents had moved about 25 years ago from Auk Village north of Juneau, as the mines opened and jobs became available. Jane had married another Tlinget, a miner in Juneau, and had three children, all visiting an aunt and uncle in the neighborhood right now. As was customary, Jane's mother had helped raise Selena, even though she was mixed race. Fannie learned that aunts and uncles played a big role in raising their nieces and nephews, sometimes taking on a bigger parental role even than the parents. Selena's white father, however, had limited his children's interactions with their Native mother's family. Fannie realized that Selena didn't have the same close relationships with this side of her family as Jane enjoyed. She also saw a genuine fondness between the cousins and noted some physical resemblances and mannerisms they had in common.

It felt good to her to be around such close family members; it had been years since she had left her extended family and she cherished the warmth between Jane and Selena. After about an hour of visiting, the kitchen door was flung open and the children entered. They weren't little children, probably of ages between 10 and 16, guessed Fannie. In a way, that was too bad. It was clear that Fannie's presence was going to need a good explanation. She waited to see how Jane would describe her visit.

"Harry, George, and Sally, this is a friend of your cousin. Her name is Lizzie and she's going to be staying with us for a few days. You remember when your cousin stayed here last year? She had that bad man looking for her? That is the same situation for Lizzie. Let's keep it in the family that she's here, all right?"

The three children nodded, glancing at Fannie, who had been a little startled to be christened Lizzie but she knew it was a smart move on Jane's part; if something did slip out, it wasn't going to be the name Fannie. She also wondered about the other woman that Jane's family had sheltered – was Jane someone who routinely helped people in distress? Fannie knew that there was certainly enough need out there – if there had been a Jane in Buenos Argentina, she would have been kept busy.

The children were told by their mother to fetch their schoolwork, which prompted Selena to prepare to leave. Fannie realized that the kitchen table where they had been visiting was also the center for schoolwork. She told Jane she would walk Selena out to the main road and slipped out the door with her friend.

The two women didn't walk toward the road, however. They had wordlessly agreed to hold their conversation in the darkness of the alley.

"Thank you so much for bringing me here, and I hope you can find that family who knocked down that man who was chasing us. They should be thanked also," Fannie told Selena.

"Oh, I'm sure that just knocking him down was thanks enough," Selena said with a little laugh. "I told you that I talked to my brother about getting your trunk. He'll go there tonight; I gave him your key. I will also get word to May about coming over here to meet you. I knew we had talked about you seeing her in the Douglas Indian Village, but I think, especially after being chased tonight, that the less you leave this house, the better."

"I agree," said Fannie. "But I wish there was something I could do to help you. And I still need to figure out how to get my funds from the bank. Do you have any ideas about that?" Fannie realized that Selena had now taken on the role of caring for Fannie, instead of being cared for by Fannie. There seemed to be something about being in the Village, among other Alaska Natives, that gave Selena a confidence and gravity that wasn't as evident elsewhere.

"I do have some ideas about that, but I need to work on it."

"What can I do to help while I'm here?"

"I'm not sure there is anything to help me, but I know that Jane can always use a hand. Raising that handful of kids, especially those boys, takes a lot of work and patience. Her husband is a good man, but he works long hours, so she's on her own a lot. She would probably welcome some help. But you'll need to be persistent asking her; she will want to treat you as an honored guest," said Selena.

"An honored guest," replied Fannie. "I don't think I've been one of those before. But I do know how to clean and cook and can help her with that."

"Just keep asking her to let you help," advised Selena. "I better go. I don't want anyone to see you out here." The two women exchanged hugs and parted.

Fannie returned to the kitchen, and Jane. There, she found her bed would be daughter Sally's bed. Fannie protested, insisting she take the pallet on the floor that Sally would have taken. After a brief argument, Jane agreed to let the two share the bed. Fannie hoped that Jane would let her help with housework in the future. Exhausted by the day's events, especially the anxious hours awaiting Selena's return to the hotel, Fannie changed into a nightgown and gratefully crawled into bed, appreciating the warmth that Sally offered.

Chapter 16

Leishke entered his office, again carrying a cup of rapidly cooling coffee from the City Cafe. As he walked in, he had seen Davies, and asked him to join him. The two men hung up coats and hats and sat. Leishke had typed up yesterday's events last night, working until almost midnight to capture his first impressions of the new murder site, and detailing his conversations with witnesses. He now wanted to hear what Davies had discovered the day before.

Davies, possibly sensing Leishke's desire to begin the day, began his accounting.

"I had no luck with the hammer," Rhys Davies said flatly. "I went to the Treadwell store, and the two stores in Douglas that sell such items. I then checked over here in Juneau; there are three stores that sell miner's hammers. The Treadwell store accounts for all their sales by name because purchases there are taken out of paychecks."

Leishke nodded; this was standard practice for company towns. He had seen many places where such accounting always seemed to come out to the company's advantage, but he had heard few complaints about Treadwell stores. He nodded encouragingly toward the younger deputy marshal, who continued.

"Anyway, they keep track. But there were no hammers purchased there in the past two months. At the other stores, it's cash only for mining equipment. I think the store owners have learned that prospectors are more numerous than gold claims, and are more cautious granting credit," Davies commented. "Altogether, they've sold 12 in the past two months, but can't remember to whom they were sold."

"What about in the past week?" asked Leishke, remembering that Sadie said Againsky had just arrived.

Davies opened a notebook that was identical to that used by Leishke. The older detective hid a grin; he had to get those notebooks from a stationary shop in Juneau because the marshals' notebooks weren't small enough to fit in his jacket pocket. Davies had obviously taken the trouble to track down the same stationary shop for his brand-new notebook.

"I wrote that there were three purchased in the past week, with only one sold in Douglas," said Llewlyn. "The storekeeper didn't remember the purchaser. He said the day he sold it was an unusually busy day." He looked up at Leishke. "I think the nice spring weather probably prompted a lot of men here to decide to take up prospecting."

Leishke agreed; a warm spring day in Alaska tended to encourage new endeavors by pretty much everybody.

"What about your conversations with the women at the Opera House?" he asked Davies.

"I talked to five women, but only three had encountered the man you mentioned," he said. "They all agreed that he had frightened them, and it wasn't until they talked amongst themselves that they realized he had given each of them a different name. He had visited them all last week. Two of them hadn't seen him before, but the third thought she had. She couldn't remember where, though, just that he looked familiar."

The comment reminded Leishke of the man he had also thought he recalled, two days ago as he dined at the City Cafe. The man's name still hadn't come to him, but he was confident it would eventually. He hoped the same would happen with this witness and told Davies as much.

"I suggest you return in a day or two to check back with her," Leishke said. "You should also ask the other women about him. Did you ask them to call here if they see him again?"

"Yes, but I'm not sure that will happen," Davies replied. "They weren't very happy talking to me, and I don't think they would have, but Mrs. Montgomery stayed with me during the interviews."

This wasn't ideal; it was certainly possible that Mrs. Montgomery was guiding the women's responses, but Leishke thought it could also be working to their advantage. He nodded, thanked Davies, and gave him some new assignments. He knew it wouldn't be long before Marshal Calhoun demanded results or shut down the investigation. They needed to work fast.

"I'm hoping you can help me track down Fannie Miller," Leishke told Davies. "Could you ask around at The Line here in Juneau, and the steamship dock? I'm going to be focused on hotels here and Douglas. I think she is avoiding me and I think it's because she knows something important."

He also described the person that the witness Sadie had thought was Againsky to Davies and added inquiries about him to the deputy marshal's list for the day. Leishke had already confirmed the day Againsky had arrived, according to the passenger list in the Daily Empire. His plan was to check for both Againsky and Fannie at hotels. Leishke was also going to be looking for Againsky at local watering holes. Juneau and Douglas were bustling communities filled with transient men, but they were both still small towns and Leishke knew that women weren't the only gossips in any community.

Both deputy marshals prepared to leave the building to begin their inquiries, but as they were donning hats and jackets, a secretary knocked on the door and told Leishke that Marshal Calhoun wanted to speak to him. Davies took the stairs to the front door, while Leishke accompanied the secretary to Calhoun's office.

Calhoun glanced up from his desk as Leishke entered the room. "What the hell is going on over in Douglas?" he demanded. Leishke was taken aback by this greeting from the usually affable marshal but covered his surprise.

"I'm guessing you're referring to the second murder," Leishke replied.

"Yes. I just read your report from yesterday. What is going on? Do we have another Krause on our hands? You have got to get a handle on this. The Douglas Commissioner is calling me almost every hour asking for updates. And..." Calhoun lifted up Leishke's typewritten report and then dropped it back to the desk, "this has nothing."

"I share your frustration with the case," Leishke said. "I am turning over every rock I can find, and Davies is doing an exemplary job assisting me, but this is a complex and difficult case."

Calhoun looked at him. Leishke grabbed his preferred chair and pulled it near the desk. He sat down.

"Originally, it appeared that this was a case similar to the one in Juneau last year – a prostitute murdered by a thief. And it's certainly true that valuables and cash were stolen. But ... the viciousness of the attack indicates it was more personal than just an opportunistic thief. And as I noted in my report, a man called her husband apparently arrived in Juneau shortly before her death. If he's the killer, I'm not sure why he would have also killed the Opera House cook. So, I have to keep in mind it could be an unusual coincidence that both women were killed within two days in Douglas. It is still possible that the cook could have been killed by someone else, and Davies is helping me explore that theory.

"However, I believe it was the same killer," Leishke continued. "I'll be spending the day looking for this husband, Againsky, and looking for Fannie Miller, the other working girl I suspect may know more about the entire situation."

As he updated Calhoun, Leishke realized that he had avoided mentioning the Opera House maid, May Svenson. He had also left out her name from the written report. She was one witness who definitely had more to tell him, and he was going to talk to her again today, but for some reason, he had chosen not to reveal her existence to anyone else.

"I know you did a good job for us catching Krause, but I need you to give that same dedication to this case," Calhoun told Leishke. "The other deputies are busy, and while I can give you Davies for another day or two, his assistance isn't indefinite."

Leishke nodded agreement but was realizing that Calhoun was asking for results with one hand, but denying the help that was needed to get the results with his other hand. In his Pinkerton days, Leishke had often investigated alone, but he knew the benefits of more officers looking at a case. He had an idea for a way to persuade Calhoun to keep Davies helping him.

"You know, sir, that most of the deputies here haven't had the benefit of training as investigators," he said. This was a diplomatic way to point out that deputy marshals, and police officers, were typically patronage jobs doled out as thanks for political support or to placate a family member. It wasn't a surprise that the mayor's nephew was on the police force. Training was on the job and depended on the skill and integrity of the training officer. At its worst, such hiring practices resulted in law enforcement officers who took bribes, covered up crimes as favors, or even committed crimes themselves. Even those officers trying to do their best didn't usually receive adequate training, especially in investigation. It wasn't a coincidence that it had taken a Pinkerton detective to gather the evidence to convict Krause, who had been killing with impunity for years.

"I have already begun training Davies in investigative procedures," Leishke continued. "Think how useful it would be to have two trained detectives on your staff. He could then continue to train more officers if my investigative duties make it difficult for me to do so. You could end up with the best-trained, most productive deputy marshals in Alaska."

Calhoun liked the idea. He smiled, settled back in his chair, and began the pencil eraser thumping.

"Hmmm. That would be a serious feather in my cap," he mused. But he then looked again at the report on his desk.

"I still want these murders solved as soon as possible," he stated. "And if you can find this Againsky fellow, I think he is the killer. I expect to see him in the basement tonight." He gestured downward, referring to the prison cells in the basement of the courthouse.

Leishke signed inwardly – trying to anticipate Marshal Calhoun was a bit of a job all on its own. He stood, saying, "I'll do my best, sir. Thanks for your assistance."

The deputy marshal left the courthouse, satisfied that he hadn't made any firm commitment to arresting Againsky, or anyone else. He decided to begin the day with a ferry ride to Douglas and headed toward the ferry dock.

Chapter 17

May had gone to bed the night before after enduring another round of questions from her landlord about the latest murder. She had a difficult night, haunted by her discovery of the body and the interview with the detective. She admitted that his interest in solving the case seemed genuine, and he certainly seemed capable, but his intense interest in her was concerning. Did he suspect her of being involved somehow?

She had hoped that she would have heard from Fannie during the day but had not. If she didn't today, she would have to go to Juneau and begin cautiously asking for her. Although she had tried to keep an eye on activity in the bar at the Opera House the day before, she had not seen the man who had been in the basement. The bar's occupants and the working girls were definitely showing the stress of Mrs. Todd's murder. The level of talking and alcohol use had increased, and she suspected she would be preparing a very late breakfast today. That could work in her favor, because she wanted to make a quick trip down to the Restricted District before work.

May dressed hurriedly and slipped out the door before Edith, her landlady, had come downstairs to begin preparing breakfast for her boarders. The weather was in her favor; low-hanging clouds covered the sun and a light rain fell steadily. She put up her umbrella, grateful for the lack of wind. The wind was often high enough to make umbrellas worse than useless.

She decided to enter the Restricted District from the other end of First Street, so headed down Second Street, turning off to the steep hill that led down to the dairy barn near the cribs and brothels. As she came down the hill, walking carefully on the rain-slicked wooden planks of the path, she saw the dairy herd walking up the hill, led by a teenage boy holding one cow's halter. The herd was followed by another teenager with a stick he used to prod cows who stopped to munch some spring greens on the side of the path. The herd would be taken up to Second Street and then walked to some open grassland for feed.

May stepped off the path for the dozen or so milk cows to travel by, trying to avoid the numerous cow patties along the side of the path. The teenagers must just knock them off the wooden walkway because there were so many. She also noted, absently, that they were obviously great fertilizer; the spring grass flourished along the path, at least where it hadn't been suffocated by manure. Behind the grass, in the marshy ground that abounded in this wet climate, she saw the first bright yellow buds of the giant skunk cabbage that would grow throughout the summer, some spreading into a circumference the size of a wagon wheel.

After the cows had passed her, she proceeded back down the hill to First Street. Once there, it was only a few steps to Fannie's cabin. It didn't appear to be occupied, and no one responded to her knocking. She paused, wondering whether to leave a note. She decided against it and turned to go to work. As she did so, she realized she was being watched. Down the street, near the carpenter's shop that, along with the dairy, made up the other legitimate business on the street, stood a man. He was not making any attempt to hide his interest in her. A tall blonde man with an overly elaborate mustache, he smiled at her. It was not a friendly smile.

Although May had intended to walk to the Opera House along Front Street, she quickly decided against it. She did not want this man to know where she worked, and the Opera House was at the other end of First Street. She began walking, as quickly as she could, back up the hill to Second Street.

She heard a shout from behind her, and realized her watcher was trying to catch her attention. She ignored him, and continued up the hill, as quickly as the slippery wooden planks would allow. She could hear him behind her, and realized he was trying to run up the hill, but faced the same difficulty on the wet wood as she did. He was still gaining on her, however, and would certainly catch her if something didn't stop him. Thinking swiftly, she folded her umbrella and dropped it to the ground, giving it a push with the top of her boot. The umbrella obligingly began rolling down the wooden walkway toward her pursuer. He was close enough now to see he had a somewhat swollen and bruised face. It appeared he had been in a fight. He was also close enough that he had little time to avoid the closed umbrella rolling toward his feet. Trying to kick it out of the way, his foot slipped and he fell to one knee, dropping that knee directly onto the umbrella.

He cursed, and May winced in sympathy, but she took the few seconds of his dilemma to reach Second Street, turn to the left and walk, as quickly as she could, toward the next intersection, which would take her back down to First Street and the Opera House. As she turned to go downhill again, she looked behind her and saw the man. He was now noticeably limping and had slowed considerably.

She made it to the Opera House before the man had reached the intersection, so she knew he didn't see where she had gone. She removed her damp jacket and wet hat, which she was afraid might not recover from the loss of the umbrella. Tying on an apron, she began the day's chores.

She had been working for about an hour, and was giving the bar a quick lick and polish when Leishke came in. May surprised herself at the pleasure she felt seeing him. As he had yesterday, he immediately saw her, and gave her his full attention. He also smiled, a quick gesture that felt like a kick in the chest. It was the first time she had seen such a spontaneous smile, almost a grin, on his stern face, and it suddenly made him very attractive. She caught her breath but succeeded in smiling back.

"It's good to see you," he said unreservedly as he walked toward her, removing his damp hat.

May glanced around at the few occupants in the bar, all of whom seemed very interested in their exchange. She suggested to the deputy marshal that they go into the kitchen to talk.

Once there, she offered the detective coffee, which he accepted and they then sat down at the table. It felt to May that this man, who she had just met yesterday under very trying circumstances, had suddenly become a friend. She thought it was perhaps because, although her decision against talking to him had angered him, he had respected her enough to stop pushing her. His reluctance to force her to talk yesterday was clearly gone today.

"I hope you are going to tell me that you reconsidered your decision to keep information from me," Frank said. "I think a night's reflection should be enough for you to realize that I am best suited to deal with whatever you have found out."

"I haven't changed my thoughts on this subject," replied May. "As soon as I can, I will tell you whatever information I think would be of assistance."

Frank looked at her, his admiration for her steadfastness overwhelmed by exasperation and continued fear for her safety. He took a deep breath and called upon his expertise. Sometimes, he knew, a witness opened up if he or she thought there might be something in return. He decided to offer her some information.

"After we spoke yesterday, I talked to a friend of Rosie's, a woman named Sadie," he said, watching May closely for any reaction. "She told me that Rosie had told her that her husband had just arrived in Juneau." He couldn't miss the small gasp that May made, even as she tried to school her face to show no reaction. May, he now knew, was aware of something about this husband.

"I know you said you didn't know Rosie well, but had you heard anything about a husband?" he asked, thinking he may have finally broken the walls that May had so successfully erected. He was to be disappointed.

Despite her reaction to his revelation, May refused to tell him anything, saying again that she needed to learn more before confiding in him. He again warned her about the consequences of keeping her counsel, and then left.

Her refusal was infuriating, and he realized he was also taking it personally. "After all, what had he done to make her not trust him?" he thought. He was walking down Front Street to begin his questioning at hotels and saloons when he remembered that he didn't take things personally. A large part of his success as a detective lay with his ability to remain objective; to look at facts with a clear and unbiased eye. What had this woman done to him?

After serving the late breakfast she had anticipated to a number of subdued and clearly hung-over women, May went to Mrs. Montgomery's office to check in. Mrs. Montgomery welcomed her warmly and said she had hired both a new housemaid and a cook. The housemaid was going to come in the afternoon so May could begin training her. The cook would begin in two days. This meant that May's opportunities to look for Fannie were going to remain limited for a few more days. It was frustrating and worrying. She returned to her household duties feeling unsettled. She also decided to try to remain as out of sight as possible, given her job. Since she had cleaned the bar earlier, she planned to remain in the less public spaces of the Opera House as much as possible. She now had two men to avoid – the man who she had last seen after the basement encounter, and the blonde man of this morning.

It was mid-afternoon, as she made bread in the kitchen, when a young Alaska Native boy came to the door. He knocked tentatively, and she wiped her flour-laden hands before opening it, and inviting him in. He stood indecisively, staring at the floor. May had been around Alaska Native people in Douglas long enough to know that eye contact was considered rude, so she went back to baking bread, in hopes of easing his discomfort.

"Do you want a snack?" She knew that Mrs. Todd was in the habit of slipping buns and bar snacks to children who came to the kitchen but didn't remember seeing this boy before. He was about 10, dressed slightly better than the children who usually frequented the Opera House – his pants and jacket showed no holes and his shoes were in good repair.

"I have a message for you," the boy said in a low voice. "Your friend in Juneau wants to meet with you at the Indian Village."

"Oh, you mean Fannie?"

The boy looked puzzled. "No, a woman named Lizzie."

May wasn't sure how to respond. She didn't know anyone named Lizzie, at least here in Alaska. but perhaps Fannie was going by another name. She thought for a few seconds, then asked the boy, "Did she tell you anything else?"

"You mean, other than about the meeting?" the boy asked. "Yes. She said that she wanted to talk to you about your friend, Jennie."

May remembered that was Rosie's real name. She looked again at the boy. "Of course, Lizzie. I remember now that she wanted to meet with me."

It was not a very believable lie, and the child's face said as much, but he nodded.

"She wants to meet you tonight in Juneau at my house in the Village. She wants you to come at about 8 p.m. Can you do it?" asked the boy.

"Tonight, and in Juneau? I don't know. I am working extra hours here, but I should be off work by then," said May, thinking about how to make this work. "Yes, I'll be there. Where do I go?"

She had already met with the new housemaid, who was right now cleaning rooms upstairs, so May thought that getting to Juneau by 8 p.m. would be possible. She would need to tell her landlady she'd be out late and would miss dinner but should have time to do that before she caught the ferry to Juneau.

As she thought out the plan, the boy had taken a piece of paper from his pocket and was now handing it to her.

"This is a map to my house," he said. "It can be kind of confusing to look for house numbers, so we decided to draw you a picture instead."

It was a good map, clearly describing a route from the ferry dock in Juneau to a house in Village. May took it with thanks and tucked it into her pocket.

"Oh," the boy said. "Lizzie said to be careful with that map. No one knows where she is and she wants to be sure it stays that way."

"Of course," said May.

The boy left clutching a bun from May, and May continued cooking, knowing she still had several hours of work ahead of her.

As the boy, Jane's son George, left the kitchen, he didn't notice the dark-haired man with the mustache watching him, even as the man casually began following him to the ferry dock.

Chapter 18

Leishke's day was not going well. After his unsatisfactory encounter with May, he had struck out on his inquiries for Againsky anywhere in Douglas. Fannie was still not at home, and Sadie was also not at home. He had thought of questioning her again, in the absence of anything else. As he took the short ferry ride to Juneau, he pulled out his notebook and reviewed his list of leads. It was short – too short. Without any cooperation from May, and unable to find either Fannie or Againsky, he had a shoe size, an unknown person buying a hammer and nothing else. He flipped the notebook pages and noticed something. The letter – the one he was going to have Fannie translate. Certainly, there was someone else in this multinational town who could translate a letter.

He looked up and noticed a tall blonde man staring at him from across the deck. Leishke had again made the unpopular choice to stand outside the small passenger cabin. The rain had ceased momentarily, but it was still chilly and the deck was slippery with rain. This man, who Leishke noticed was favoring one leg, had also chosen to wait outside. The man's gaze quickly slid past him, and he turned to face the town of Juneau as the ferry approached the dock.

Leishke searched his memory, which had been teased by the man's appearance, and remembered seeing him at the City Cafe. He had seemed familiar then also, but Leishke still couldn't recall why. The boat had docked, and the blonde man had left the boat. Leishke watched as he headed toward the steamship dock and office, located a few blocks from the much smaller ferry dock. The man didn't look back.

Feeling a renewed sense of energy, Leishke headed up the hill to his office. He would look for a translator and then go back to the task of canvassing hotels and saloons.

• • •

"I'm honestly not sure what language this is," said the bookstore owner. On his way up the hill, Leishke decided to see if the bookstore proprietor might be able to help out his search. The owner, an older man whose small store was not well frequented by locals, had been delighted when Leishke came in. He was less thrilled now as he examined the letter carefully.

"I suspect it's a Slavic language, and that is good news for you," he told the detective. Leishke agreed – he knew, as did the bookstore owner – that many people working at the gold mines in Juneau and Douglas were Slavic. There was even a Slavic cemetery in Douglas – a testament to the many workers from the Eastern European countries.

The bookseller continued. "I think the best thing for you to do is to take the letter to church."

Leishke raised his eyebrows.

"The priest at the Serbian church in Douglas is a well-educated man and I know often helps his parishioners with letters home. I think he may very well be able to assist."

Leishke thanked the man and left. He appreciated the advice but was not enthusiastic about another trip to Douglas. He decided to complete his canvassing in Juneau and see if he still had time after that to go to Douglas, especially given Marshal Calhoun's edict from the morning. He decided to start at the Circle City Hotel. This hotel, built by a pair of enterprising brothers, was named for a town up north.

It wasn't uncommon for hotels in Alaska to be named for different communities in the territory, but it could certainly be confusing. Juneau had an Arctic Hotel and an Alaskan Hotel, as well as four others with more traditional names. Leishke just hoped that Againsky had booked a room at a hotel, and that he used his real name. Leishke didn't have a good physical description of the man and perhaps none at all, if that Douglas woman, Sadie, wasn't correct about the man she saw. Dark hair and a mustache weren't much to go on. And, if Againsky had decided against going to a hotel, he could also find room and board at the multitude of such places throughout both Douglas and Juneau. A search of those locations, especially with such a limited description, would be extremely time-consuming and it would still be possible to miss a home that may just take in one or two boarders.

The Circle City Hotel had an impressive front featuring two large bow windows. Leishke opened the hotel's door in time to hold it for a young woman who was leaving. She was Alaska Native, dressed fashionably, and very attractive. She glanced up at Leishke with a practiced smile that dimmed as she saw his face. She cast her gaze down to her shoes, murmured "thank you" and walked briskly down the street. Leishke wasn't sure what had prompted her response; he was accustomed to flirtatious looks, but not looks of shock.

"Except ... could be she was someone who recognized him as law enforcement," Leishke thought. He decided to file another face away for examination later. He walked up to the desk.

"Who was the young woman who just left? I think we have met in the past, but I can't recall her name," Leishke asked the young clerk. The clerk was young, but old enough to suspect the question. He also was aware of Selena's occupation and saw no need to protect her privacy. The man in front of him could end up being one of her loyal customers, although he didn't have the prosperous appearance of her other visitors.

"That's Selena Dowling. She lives here. She's a very ... friendly young woman," said the clerk.

Leishke understood the context behind the comment. He introduced himself and inquired for both Againsky and Fannie. Againsky hadn't checked in, nor had any single man recently off a steamship. When it came to Fannie, however, the clerk thought she might have been the woman who had inquired for Miss Dowling one evening this past week. She didn't have a room at the hotel, however, and the clerk hadn't seen her since that one evening.

Leishke left for the next hotel. If true, that certainly explained Miss Dowling's reaction to seeing him at the door, thought Leishke.

• • •

George had an uneasy feeling. Since he was a very young child, he had been taught to be wary of strangers, especially white strangers. The dark-haired man with the mustache had been staring at him since the ferry left the dock. George had tried to make himself small and inconspicuous, but when he glanced at the man's way, it was to see his gaze again upon him. He knew that his mom was worried about letting people know Lizzie was staying with him, so he thought carefully about what to do next.

When the ferry pulled near the dock, George made a jump for the dock before the skipper had tied up. It meant he was yelled at for the stunt. But it gave him a head start on the white man, and he headed to the Village as quickly as he could, without running. A running Native boy in Juneau was suspicious all by itself. He glanced behind him and saw his early exit from the boat had not lost his pursuer. The man was walking calmly and quickly, keeping a close eye on George. George would need to come up with another plan of avoidance.

His mind working quickly, George was near the Village when he saw help. His cousin, Joe, was hanging on the beach with a couple of his friends. Joe was only a few months younger so they were in the same school grade. The cousins looked alike; it created constant confusion at school, to the delight of the boys. Now, George saw a way it would pay off.

The Village was built along Gastineau Channel, in part so its residents could pull their canoes up to their houses, just as they did in Douglas. As in Juneau, the first street on the water had its houses built on pilings. When the tide was up, the water lapped beneath the houses, but it was low tide now, so it was a prime place for children to play. Joe and his friends seemed to be throwing rocks, so George thought they were probably playing a favorite game – war.

He began climbing down the rocky bank to the beach. He was not wearing play-approved clothing, but he thought his mother would forgive him. She was pretty easy going, and he thought he would like his plan to be sure the man didn't follow him home. As he reached the beach, he yelled at Joe and ran to the boys.

"Hey, Joe," he said. "Do you see that man up on the road? The white man with the dark hair and mustache? He's been following me, and I had a great idea to fool him. Are you willing to help?"

"Sure," said his cousin. Good old Joe, he was always ready for anything. He told him the plan and then the boys got back to the important job of saving the world from the Germans.

• • •

Againsky was getting angrier and angrier. This whole situation was Jennie's fault. Jennie, who he had thought really loved him and would do whatever he wanted. He should have known better than to trust a bitch, especially one who sold her body. When she stopped sending money and letters, he knew he had to come find her. If the Club had found out one of his women had escaped without consequences, he would lose his standing, his money, and his women.

The plan had been to go to Anchorage, where he knew she still lived. She was too dumb to be able to figure out how to travel on her own, and she could barely read or write. He had wondered if that other bitch, Fannie, had persuaded her to stop sending money, but Fannie was just as dumb as Jennie – they were really two peas in a pod, he thought.

It was a surprise to find the women in Juneau, and a stroke of luck. It was going to take a couple of days of waiting before he could get a steamship north – a ship had gone aground near Juneau and had been re-floated but affected the ship's schedule. He was fine with that. He wasn't a good sailor and had too many times needed to take the ships between England and Argentina to enjoy being at sea. The trip up to Alaska had been hair raising, in his opinion. After crossing the open sea between San Francisco and Ketchikan, the boat had been moving through the Inside

Passage, which seemed designed to put ships on rocks, or run into islands. He would be glad to leave this territory.

He had headed over to Douglas, attracted by the notion of a town that served a large company town of miners. He smelled opportunity in such a setting. Instead, he had found Jennie. He had gone into the Opera House for a beer and been approached by a blonde-haired slut whose name was Sadie. He could tell she was breaking house rules because she didn't live at the brothel, but came there, looking for customers. He was willing, and even idly wondered if he could persuade her to marry him and join his women in Argentina.

That speculation was quickly put to rest when he realized how unpleasant she was. She had spent the walk to her crib criticizing the other women in the neighborhood, taking particular aim at two newcomers, Fannie, and Rosie. He couldn't believe his ears. Jennie had used the name Rosie Brown when she worked in San Francisco and Anchorage, and here she was, practically falling in his lap. What a stupid slut she was.

After a quick visit with Sadie that had cost more than he expected, he stepped over to Rosie's crib. It was next door – he spied her through the window. What were the chances? He wasn't the type of idiot these two women had been. He just talked to Rosie during that first visit, trying to persuade her that he missed her, and was so happy to see her.

She had given him some cash and pretended to be delighted that he was there but he knew differently. He knew she was going to leave without him just as soon as she could. He kissed her and told her that he wouldn't be back for a few days. He told her that Douglas seemed like a good place to settle down for a while, and it would take some time to get established. He left, convinced that she believed she had some breathing room, and that she would act soon. She had told him that Fannie had her own crib next to Rosie's, so he carefully planned his return visit.

After taking care of Rosie, he realized that he didn't have time to deal with Fannie. His work with Rosie had taken longer than he expected, and he wanted to take his time with Fannie in the same way. He realized now that was a mistake.

He had now spent two fruitless days looking for Fannie; he had sent that idiot Lars after her, and Lars was the one who said he thought she had gone to the Village with an Indian girl. Againsky had chosen to watch the Opera House, convinced that Fannie would be in the vicinity, since that's the last place he had seen her. Instead, he had seen that Indian boy, and decided to follow him.

So here he was, watching a bunch of Indian brats play on a beach. He was about to give up and find a saloon, when the boy headed back up the rocks. He knew him from the jacket – it had a beaded symbol on one shoulder. He headed toward the boy, but the little jerk ran across the street and headed for a large building about a block away. Its sign said it was the meeting place of the Alaska Native Brotherhood.

Againsky followed, keeping a close eye on that jacket, and steadily gaining. Just as the boy grasped the door to the large hall, he grabbed him by the arm.

"Ow," yelled the boy, turning toward Againsky.

At the same time, he realized this boy was not the boy he had seen on the ferry, the door opened and a large Indian man stood there. "What are you doing with my son?" asked the man menacingly.

"Nothing," said Againsky. "I ... I thought it was someone else. Sorry."

He left quickly, headed back to the beach where all the kids had been. They were gone.

Chapter 19

By the time May had returned to her boarding house and told Edith she was meeting a friend for dinner, she was exhausted from the lack of sleep the night before and from worrying all day about getting to the Juneau Indian Village without being seen. She was also nursing a small amount of hope – once she had talked to Fannie, she would be able to turn the whole thing over to Deputy Marshal Frank Leishke. He made her feel uncomfortable, but she also trusted him.

May washed up, replacing her working skirt and blouse with a dark walking dress, and put on her jacket and hat. Before she left her room, she studied the map that the boy had given her. She knew the light would be dim or nonexistent between the boarding house and her meeting with Fannie, so she wanted to memorize the map if she could. The rain had continued on and off all day, but there was still little wind, so she borrowed an umbrella from Edith and left for the ferry.

The trip was uneventful, for which she was grateful. She had kept a close eye out for both men she suspected, but there was no sign of either. Once in Juneau, she tried to walk confidently toward the village. It wouldn't be a good idea to pull out the map or appear to not know where she was going. Fortunately, her memory, and the map, were excellent. She reached the house a little before 8 p.m. and knocked softly. No one. She knocked a little louder. Still no answer. She could hear activity in the house, so knocked even louder.

This time, the door was answered, by the same boy she had seen earlier. He opened the door wide, and said, "Hello. I'm George. Come on in."

She stepped into a busy scene, and one that explained why no one had heard her knocking. Three children, including George, were playing a rousing card game with a Native man who appeared to be their father. An attractive Native woman stood at the stove, stirring a pot of what smelled like hot chocolate. Fannie, who had been standing near the woman, ran to May and hugged her.

May looked at her; she looked relaxed and happy. She also looked oddly at home in this warm family scene. May realized she had never seen Fannie with children, and felt a pang of sadness, remembering that Fannie had told her she couldn't conceive.

"I'm so glad you made it here safely," Fannie said. "When Selena brought me here, we were followed by this tall blonde man. Luckily, he got knocked down by another man, and we got here safely."

"Oh, my," said May. "I believe that blonde man may have been the same person who followed me this morning." She described her morning's trip to Fannie's cabin, and her narrow escape. The two women looked at each other and burst into laughter. "He had such a swollen nose and face," May exclaimed, laughing.

"And now he's got a limp too," added Fannie with a grin.

They had been joined by the other woman, who Fannie introduced as Jane, and were then introduced to the other children and their father, Frank.

"It's time to finish that game. I have hot chocolate for you all before bedtime," said Jane.

Her announcement was greeted with an amusing combination of excitement about hot chocolate and dismay about bedtime. While Fannie and May quietly talked to catch up with the events that had happened since they last spoke, the children finished the game, drank their hot chocolate, and left for bed. Jane and Frank said they would step out for a bit to give the two women an opportunity to speak privately. Fannie and May thanked them and said they would be happy to listen for the children. Fannie told May, however, that her experience the night before was they were solid sleepers.

Fannie had not heard of Mrs. Todd's murder before May told her. Unsurprisingly, she was shocked and saddened. She also felt to blame for bringing a killer into the Opera House. May tried to reassure her, but not very successfully, since she also felt guilty about her friend's death.

"I think Jane must have known about it, but she's been trying to give me a relaxing day," said Fannie. It was Saturday, and after breakfast, Jane had sent George to Douglas with the message for May. The rain had not stopped the children from spending most of the day outside or with friends. In the afternoon, the family had gone to the Alaska Native Brotherhood Hall for an entertainment that included a short film and performances by some local residents. During the family's absences, Fannie had done some cleaning, and baked bread. She had found the routine work relaxing; she couldn't remember the last time she had such a quiet domestic day.

Now, she was learning that while she had enjoyed her domestic day, May had again been subjected to shock and questioning. After talking about it briefly, Fannie told May that she was convinced that Againsky was the man who had come into the basement and was also the man who killed the cook.

"He must have asked her about me, and she told him that I was downstairs with you. Since I think he meant to kill me, he wouldn't want a witness who could identify him," Fannie told May. "I tell you, that man is evil. You must be very careful. If he has any idea that you know me well, you will be killed. I know it."

May thought about this and had to agree that it was possible, but there is still a part of her that found the whole story fantastical, especially in this setting of a warm and friendly family.

"Deputy Marshal Leishke keeps asking about you," she told Fannie. "I've put him off, saying I want to hear the whole story before I talk to him about anything. If you can tell me everything I need to know tonight, then I can go to him tomorrow. I think Againsky could be arrested and in jail by this time tomorrow."

"Where did I leave the story?" asked Fannie.

"You had told me about the earthquake, but I don't know how you and Fannie met, or what you know of Againsky," replied May.

"All right," said Fannie. "A few days after the earthquake, the bartender, Joseph, and Ada and I walked back to the house where we had lived and where Bolek – he was my so-called husband -- and our friend Sasha were when the earthquake happened. The house was gone; in fact, the whole block was burned and gone. I found one of the neighbors in the camp about a week later. He said that Bolek and Sasha didn't make it out of the house. He was sure they were dead.

"I didn't know what to do, but I talked to Ada and Joseph and decided to continue being a working girl but this time I did it for myself. Joseph introduced me to a woman who had a house near the docks. She let women keep most of their own money; I rented a room from her and paid room and board. It was a safe place, and I started to realize that Bolek's death meant I was free from the Warsaw Club. I worked hard, not just as a working girl but also to learn English. I had decided I was going to stay in the United States. I learned reading and writing from another Polish girl at the house and began writing to my parents. I didn't tell them about Bolek, but continued to pretend I was married to a rich American. I still send them money – enough that they aren't really interested in asking questions."

"It worked out pretty well for several years. The money was good and I was able to buy pretty clothes and jewelry."

May had admired that jewelry – she noticed the small gold hoops in her ears and the two pearl rings on the hands she held.

"I also learned to speak better English – I sound like you now, don't I?" Fannie asked, laughing.

"You do – if I had an exotic accent. It is true that your English is excellent," replied May.

"Most of the money I made I have saved," continued Fannie. "I knew I couldn't do this work forever, so I'm saving to buy my own house and leave this work when I get older."

May released her hands and sat back, giving her a big smile. "You are so smart. I'm just trying to determine how to get back home, and you have an entire plan for your life. I'm so glad you escaped that awful man. I can't believe I'm saying this, but I'm also glad he's dead. I'm so sorry that your other friend didn't live. Did you know her well?"

"Yes, I knew her. All of us girls tried to be friendly – although not all of us were. Just like here at the Opera House, there were jealousies and envy and girls who didn't like other girls. But Sasha was a good girl. She was so young – I think only about 15 and had been with Bolek since she was 12. She had also gotten pregnant, and he made her give the baby to this woman back in Argentina who took the babies we had. We were told they would have a good life, but we didn't really believe that.

"We all heard that the woman had a baby graveyard behind her house." Fannie gave another shudder but summoned up a small smile.

"I escaped all that, and I've stayed escaped. Even when I met Jennie, I didn't get caught. My English was good, and I was very sure no one knew I was Polish." Fannie stopped and looked at May, who was looking puzzled.

"I'm sorry. I forgot you didn't know. Rosie's real name was Jennie. Jennie Poplosky. We all used new names in this work – you know that, right?"

May did know that, and realized she had never asked Rosie or Fannie what their real names were. She raised her brows at Fannie, silently asking her.

"I'm just going by Fannie Miller now. I'm sorry, but I really can't be caught again. And I'm afraid Againsky is going to figure it out but let me tell you the rest."

"I met Jennie at a local bar – we were both looking for customers. But I could tell pretty quickly that Jennie was different. And once I started talking to her, I realized she had also been a victim of the Warsaw Club. She had been brought to San Francisco by the man who called himself her husband, just like I had been. But he kept a close eye on her, and I couldn't figure out a way to get her away safely, Fannie said.

"Then, after two years, he said he was going to send her to Alaska. He didn't want to go himself, because by now he was running a house with six girls, including Jennie. He trusted her.

She had been with him the longest time, and he thought he had her completely. He thought she really loved him and would do anything he said."

Fannie sighed and looked at May. "I think he was partially right. She did love him, or at least thought she did, and she had proved it.

"There was a group of police in San Francisco who had heard of the Warsaw Club and decided to try to break it. They arrested Jennie, thinking she would tell them about it and they could then get the men who were bringing those girls to San Francisco. But even though she was in jail for six weeks, Jennie refused to tell them anything. It was in the newspapers. It made the police mad because they were sure she could tell them about it. And she could, but she didn't."

"She had only been in San Francisco for a few months when she was arrested, her English was poor and she was terrified. She was sure that if she said anything, Againsky would kill her. I think he would have."

May didn't say anything. If he had killed Jennie, or Rosie as she continued to think of her, it certainly went to prove that fear she had felt in the basement with Fannie was justified. The whole story just seemed unbelievable to May. She even found herself wondering if Fannie had created this to either draw attention to herself, or because she had some petty vendetta against Againsky. She looked at Fannie again. No, it must be true, she thought, however much she didn't want it to be.

"So, you went together to Anchorage?" she asked Fannie.

"Yes, I told her I would go with her. I was tired of being in the same place myself, and I wanted to help her." She looked at her hands again and added softly: "Like I couldn't help Sasha."

Fannie continued. "I kind of liked Anchorage, although it was pretty primitive. There were a lot of wall tents, as well as houses and some businesses. It was being built fast. Just a few years before, it had mostly just been a camp where railroad workers lived, but it was getting to be a big town. We quickly found the area where prostitutes lived and rented two little cabins, just like we have here.

"The other girls were friendly, and there was plenty of work, but we weren't ready for the weather, and the daylight. We got there in the spring, and before long, it was daylight almost all the time. Not like here – even if the sun doesn't set until midnight, it does set. There, it seemed like night never came. It made it very tiring – we were busy all day, and all night long. We made good money, but Jennie sent almost everything to Againsky, as he told her to when we left San Francisco. At least, she did at first. The longer we were gone from him, the more Jennie...blossomed, I think.

"She started to focus on learning the same things I had – how to speak English well and how to read and write. She even wrote to her family. She still pretended, like I did, that she had married a rich American and she was doing well. But she got news from home, and that seemed to strengthen her. She slowly began to keep more of the money she made for herself and send less to Againsky. She wrote to him that, as the fall and winter set in, it was much less busy. That wasn't true. Actually, as the weather got colder, we had more business because the men didn't have to work such long hours. We could really work as much, or as little, as we wanted."

"We saved a lot and decided to leave Anchorage. While the summer days had been long, the winter days were too short – it seemed to be dark and so cold, all the time.

"Jennie took off the wedding ring that Againsky had given her and told me the marriage was over. She told the other girls too, and some of them laughed at the idea that taking off a ring meant a marriage was over. When the marriage is just a ring, it makes sense to me that taking it off means it's over. Anyway...she was ready to really leave him. She didn't write to him about it or anything, just stopped sending money and we came here.

"We spent a year and a half in Anchorage, and we made a lot of money. I mean," Fannie said, opening her eyes wide. "A lot of money. Jennie had $3,000 when we arrived here last year. I had more because I didn't send anything to Bolek, but I also know enough to keep it in a bank. The day after we landed, I went to Mr. B.M. Behrends' bank and opened up a safety deposit box. I told Jennie to do the same, but she didn't trust banks, so she kept hers in the cabin. I'm sure it's gone now – no matter who killed her, they would know enough to look for her money."

May nodded in agreement; she certainly knew enough about the clients coming to the Opera House to believe most, at least, would be looking for money.

"Do you think it's possible that Againsky didn't kill her?" she asked Fannie.

"I don't think it's very likely. He certainly had the most reason to do so – she had left him and taken his money. That is not something that any of those men would take lightly. If word of a successful escape got back to the other women, it would encourage them to try the same."

Fannie silently agreed. She and Fannie sat in silence for a moment; May digested the story she had been told and Fannie seemed lost in memories.

"Well," said May as resolutely as she could. "I need to talk to that detective and we need to get you out of town. Have you given that any thought?"

"Yes," replied Fannie. "I've given it a lot of thought. Selena was going to send a relative to my cabin tonight to get my trunks. I will need to go myself to the bank to get my money, though. I'm not sure how I'm going to accomplish that. I feel safe here but know that Againsky will be looking for me. There are also enough men in Juneau and Douglas who would be happy to take his money to help him."

May knew that was the case; she saw that with the Usual Ones in Douglas, and suspected there were even more in Juneau. It meant that they really didn't know who was out there looking for Fannie. So, it would be impossible to avoid them – except perhaps for a limping blonde man, she thought with a small smile.

"Is it possible that I could tell the bank that I'm you and close your account?" she asked Fannie.

Fannie looked at her, and then shook her head. "That is a good idea, but I have been friendly with one of the cashiers. He would definitely know you aren't me, and the bank is small enough that he could possibly overhear you, even if you went to a female cashier."

"Hmmm. What if I create some sort of diversion while you go into the bank?" asked May, having no idea what that would entail.

"It's not a bad idea, but what do you have in mind?"

"Oh, I could faint on the sidewalk outside, or do something to bring a crowd."

"A crowd," mused Fannie. "I like that idea, but maybe we can accomplish it without you having to lie on the dirty sidewalk. I'll give it some thought." She paused. "When can we talk again? I miss talking with you, but I know it's difficult for you to get the time to come here. Do you feel confident that no one has associated you with me? That man this morning by my cabin?"

"I don't think so. He didn't see where I went after I left your cabin, and the weather was bad enough I don't think he got a good look at my face. I can come back tomorrow night if you like. If you need me before that, just send George."

George hadn't told anyone of his escapade earlier; he hadn't seen Joe so didn't know that the stranger who had been watching him earlier had followed Joe. His mother, of course, had noticed he had switched jackets, but had just told him to switch back at school the next day.

The two women agreed to meet the next day and Fannie headed back to the dock, hoping that Deputy Marshal Leishke would return to the Opera House tomorrow and save her the trouble of looking for him.

• • •

Leishke had had another frustrating day. He may have found where Againsky was staying – the Occidental Hotel and the Hotel Zynda had both registered single men after the steamship with Againsky aboard had arrived. With such a poor description, his only option would be to wait in the hotel lobby until the new guest returned, since neither was in his room and he didn't have time. He still hadn't found Fannie, or even any trace of her, and Selena Dowling seemed to be gone for the day. She still hadn't returned by 8 p.m., when he checked her hotel before taking a break for dinner at the City Cafe.

He sat at the table in the cafe, feeling as if he had gotten nowhere that day, much less had Againsky in jail, as requested by Marshal Calhoun. He hoped that Davies had been more successful than he had. He decided to map out his plans for the next day.

A trip to Douglas in the morning, he decided. He would talk again to Mrs. May Svenson, and then go to the Serbian church to see if the priest there could help with translation. Before heading for bed, he would return to the Occidental and the Zynda, in case their new residents had returned. Then, back to his office to type up his notes.

Chapter 20

May woke the next day feeling as if, finally, things would be getting back to normal, at least as much as possible.

Mrs. Montgomery had asked to see her as soon as she had gotten to work. The madam told her the new cook would begin the following day, and they agreed the new housemaid would be satisfactory. Mrs. Todd's family had asked for her body to be returned to her home in Illinois. It would be a long and expensive journey, but the family said they would bear the cost. May suspected that Mrs. Montgomery would also help with the expenses. The biggest problem could have been finding someone to accompany the body, because travel arrangements for an unaccompanied casket were impossible. Fortunately, the undertaker had a list of residents who were anxious to leave Douglas but didn't have the resources to do it. He had given the list to Mrs. Montgomery, and she had found a former prospector who was hoping to get back to his home in New Hampshire, and more than happy to have a large portion of the travel paid for in exchange for assisting with the transport.

After that meeting, May began her regular chores, focusing today on laundry; although Monday and Tuesday were laundry days, she was finding herself doing whenever she had time with the Opera House being so shorthanded. She had gathered a large hamper from the second floor and was trying to fit it and her down the back stairs, when she heard her name.

"Mrs. Svenson."

She looked at the base of the stairs, and there stood Deputy Marshal Leishke. She was caught off guard and found herself captivated by his intense gray eyes. She halted, and they both stared at each other. May realized she was holding her breath; she took a deep breath and resumed her journey downstairs.

Frank had been almost caught as off guard as May. He had heard footsteps on the stairwell, so looked up the stairs and there she was. He was beginning to become a little resentful at how easily he lost his composure around her. His first words to her reflected that.

"I've been looking for you. I can't wait any longer for any information you have. We must move forward with this investigation," Frank said.

May had reached the bottom of the stairs and he automatically took the hamper from her, following her as she walked to the basement door and down that set of stairs.

The small, high windows in the basement let in enough light to see where his feet were going without a light. May, still without speaking, led Frank to the washing sink, and began filling it with water. He waited until she had stopped pumping the water, and began to speak, but she interrupted him.

"I know," she said, surprising him as he was forming his next argument.

"I have the information for you, but I must talk while I work," she said. "We're still short-handed here, and I don't have time to sit down and be interviewed. Is that all right?"

"Yes," Leishke replied, gratefully. "I'm fine with that. What can I do to help?"

May had added soap to the water and begun gently washing under linens on the washboard, running them a few times over the rough surface and then putting them in a large basin of clear water for rinsing. Frank stood next to her, and began swishing the clothing in the rinse water, squeezing it dry and hanging it on the clothesline that had been run across the large basement.

May watched him, bemused. It was surprising and a little funny to see a Deputy Marshal hanging up pantaloons and chemises on the basement line. She didn't recall ever seeing a man doing laundry, and spent one moment enjoying the sight, before beginning the story of Rosie Brown.

As she told the detective what Fannie had told her, she left Fannie's name out of the story, telling the events as if Rosie had told her directly.

Frank knew there were key elements being left out; May couldn't help occasionally being confused or contradictory as she tried to revise the story. Frank heard the basic elements – the kidnapping and abduction of Rosie Brown, the attempts by law enforcement in San Francisco to use her as a witness, her decision in Anchorage to leave the Warsaw Club.

Frank knew that if the other deputy marshals heard this story, they would almost certainly have discounted it as dramatic nonsense. He knew something they did not. He knew the Warsaw Club existed.

Frank Leishke had been a Pinkerton detective for just 6 of his 12 adult years. Now age 30, his first job at 18 was as a police officer in Sacramento. He remembered hearing about the Warsaw Club from older police officers training him. The Club was then becoming notorious as more and more women were being brought to California from Argentina. Just as he suspected the deputy marshals wouldn't believe the stories around the Club in Juneau, it had taken some time for California law enforcement to acknowledge its existence. While bribes had silenced law enforcement in Argentina, disbelief had greeted any of the women who had first told their sad stories to California police.

When he heard May describe how Rosie Brown was jailed in San Francisco for her refusal to turn on her captors, he couldn't help a wordless exclamation.

"What are you thinking?" asked May, who was now scrubbing, more vigorously, the bed linens. She had been so wrapped up in telling what Fannie had told her that she hadn't really been watching Leishke's response.

"I'm thinking that I've heard about this group of men," said Frank. "And you're right, they are the worst of the worst. If they are moving into Alaska, all the deputy marshals need to know about it."

"You've heard of the Warsaw Club," exclaimed May. "I am surprised. I don't think that there are other women here who know anything about it. At least, I hope not." Of course, she didn't tell Leishke that Fannie knew – May was doing her best to protect her.

She continued with the story of the two women coming to Alaska, ending with the arrival of Againsky. For the first time, she told Leishke that she thought he was the man who had killed Mrs. Todd.

"I suspect you're right," said Frank. "But I'm not sure why – do you know of anything that Mrs. Todd might have seen or known to make her a target of the man?"

"I ... I," stammered May, trying to think how to respond. "Maybe."

"What do you mean, maybe?" asked Frank.

"I think I may have seen Againsky," said May. "I did the night she was killed."

A chill ran through Frank. "What!" he exclaimed. "Why didn't you say something before?"

"Well, as I told you before, I wanted to be sure I had the whole story before I talked to you. I saw a man leaving the building as I was outside the kitchen door – I was bringing in laundry, actually. He was tall and had dark, curly hair, a slight build, and a mustache. I also saw that he had a gun tucked in his back pocket."

"Did he see you?"

"I really don't think so. It was dark and I was standing to the side, not moving. He didn't glance my way at all. If he saw me, it would have been when he first came outside, and he didn't look my way or address me, so I really don't think he noticed me. Oh, and I forgot to tell you that he had a dark complexion – not like a Negro, but definitely darker than yours."

"Would you recognize him if you saw him again?"

"Probably. But I really hope that never happens," May said, candidly.

Frank and May had continued doing laundry as they spoke. Frank had changed out the rinse water twice, and they now had a basin full of clean but wet linens to hang outside. Frank realized he had hung up the chemises, pantaloons and petticoats of a dozen prostitutes – a task he would have guessed he would never do. May had the same realization but viewed it somewhat more humorously than did Frank. He knew he would never tell anyone about this; May knew that she would tell Fannie as soon as she could.

The two went outside, and without further discussion, hung the sheets, towels and pillowcases on the outside lines. The rain had stopped, and although the sky continued to be gray, May was in hope it would clear long enough to dry the linens.

Frank looked at May; he continued to fear for her safety but believed that he now had enough information to arrest Againsky and seek a solid conviction. He just needed to find him.

Frank had learned from Davies during their morning meeting that Againsky was most likely still in town. Davies said the suspect hadn't purchased a steamship ticket. Davies had also struck out on finding Fannie. Frank had given him the task of taking the letter to the priest at the Serbian church, ignoring the reproachful look from the younger marshal. It was a good lesson for Davies, thought Leishke – good detective work often consisted of tasks that seemed purposeless at the time.

Leishke was heading back to Juneau to the two hotels that had new residents. If he had to spend most of the day sitting in hotel lobbies, he was prepared to do so. Fortunately, he and Davies had escaped from the office before Marshal Calhoun had summoned either of them. He knew time was short, he was grateful to have escaped more exhortations for the need for haste.

Leishke's gratitude came to an end on the ferry to Juneau, where he ran into the Commissioner of Douglas, John Hensen. The commissioner was the official arm of the federal government in Douglas. It was his job to serve warrants and summonses, and to oversee any governmental duties in Douglas that fell to the federal government, and not the city government. Hensen, the commissioner, had an excellent reputation in Douglas and Juneau. In Leishke's experience, Hensen acted with restraint and judiciousness. When he initially saw him on board the ferry, Leishke was pleased and approached him to talk. Both men were in Leishke's habitual location on the ferry – the small stern deck.

"Leishke," greeted Hensen. "Just the man I wanted to see. Tell me what's going on with these murders. What do you make of them? How long until we've got someone in jail? Tensions are high in Douglas, and there's even talk of closing the Restricted District."

"Hello, sir," said the detective, noting they were the only two passengers outside in the rain, but still speaking in a low voice. "There are two of us assigned to the case, and we're both working hard to find our suspect. Marshal Calhoun is also very concerned about the situation, so he's giving us the men we need to work quickly." In making this latter statement, Leishke was hoping to convince Hensen to use his influence with Calhoun to support the investigation.

"Well, you must know what would happen if the Restricted District is closed," said Hensen. "The women there now – and I think there are about 40 of them – wouldn't leave. They would just relocate elsewhere in Juneau and Douglas. Keeping a close eye on them will be much harder for the marshals. We really can't let that happen."

"I completely agree with you on that point," said Leishke. "But, of course, I have no influence over what the town council does. My attention must be given to the investigation. And I do believe we are close to a resolution there." He had a sudden thought. "Do you have any contractors who could assist us?"

The commissioner often contracted with individuals to serve warrants and summonses as needed, and Leishke was hoping Hensen would be willing to pay for one of those men to help Leishke.

Hensen looked regretful. "I only have one man working for me right now, and he's kept plenty busy with the work from my office. But I'm sure Marshal Calhoun will supply you with additional deputies if you need more manpower."

Of course, Leishke had to reiterate that Calhoun was doing all he could but was disappointed that a possible source of help was blocked. The boat pulled up to the dock as the men concluded their conversation and they stepped off the boat and headed in opposite directions – Hensen up to the courthouse, presumably and Leishke to the waterfront hotels where he suspected he'd be spending the rest of the afternoon.

As Leishke walked toward the Occidental Hotel, he automatically checked behind him, glancing at reflections in the storefront windows. In one of them, he noticed a tall blonde man, who seemed to have a slight hitch in his step. "He isn't very good at following someone," Leishke thought. The blonde was staring fixedly at Leishke, as if afraid he would suddenly disappear from sight. Leishke had no intention of losing him; he wanted to ensure the man was following him, and possibly find out why.

As he continued walking, Leishke suddenly remembered where he had seen the man before. He had been in the dock during a court arraignment that Leishke had attended. He was one of a handful of prisoners waiting for a judicial hearing to make a plea of guilty or innocent. He didn't know what put the man there but thought the court bailiff would be able to tell him. The bailiff had an incredible memory for names and faces and was a resource that all the deputy marshals called upon regularly. Leishke added a trip to the bailiff on this list for the afternoon and entered the lobby of the Occidental.

The lobby held one couple sitting on a couch near a window and the front desk clerk, but otherwise was empty. Leishke checked with the clerk, who was fortunately the same one he had spoken with yesterday. The clerk said he hadn't seen the man in question yet that day, and his key was missing, so he believed he was still in the room.

Leishke sat in a chair with a direct line of sight to the stairs and lift doors. As he did so, he glanced toward the front door and saw the blonde man standing awkwardly outside by the door. "Definitely doesn't know what he was doing," thought Leishke, settling down for a wait.

Leishke didn't have long to wait. A short, dapper man exited the lift. He was carrying a satchel and in no respect matched May's description of the man she had seen, or that of the earlier witness, Sadie, but Leishke believed in thoroughness. He walked toward the man, halting his clear plans to leave the lobby. He removed the badge he held as a deputy marshal. Most of the marshals wore them in a visible location, such as a jacket or belt, but Leishke, in his investigations, wanted to be the one to decide when witnesses knew his identity.

"Excuse me, sir," he said. "I have a few questions for you."

"Oh, a deputy marshal?" replied the man. "I have an appointment in a few minutes," he began, then quickly backtracked after making eye contact with Leishke. "No matter. I have had as much time as you need. I'm sure my business associate will understand."

"Thank you," said the detective. "This shouldn't take long. Can you tell me what has brought you to Juneau?"

"I work as an accountant and have applied for a job with the B.M. Behrends Bank. I was on my way to that interview."

"And your name?"

"I am Roger Standwick. I am traveling here from Seattle, where I work for Washington Federal Bank."

Leishke knew enough. He would be stopping by B.M. Behrends bank later to confirm the story, but he believed the man. He thanked him, and Standwick left quickly.

"One down, one to go," thought Leishke, and noticed the blonde man still waiting outside the hotel's front door. "Or perhaps, one down, two to go."

As he left, he saw the man obligingly follow. Leishke walked two blocks along the waterfront, and then, suddenly, ran across the road and into an alley. Ducking behind a refuse can in the dark passageway, he waited for his pursuer to reach him. The man saw him at the same time Leishke reached out, grabbing the blonde man by the jacket, and throwing him against the opposite building. Although the blonde man was taller than Leishke, the detective was larger, not surprised by the encounter, and practiced in back street fighting.

"What are you doing?" was the somewhat lame exclamation from the stranger.

"What do you think?" responded Leishke. "You were following me. I want to know why. And I want to know your name." As he spoke, he tightened his hold on the jacket, so his fist was up against the man's collarbone, and just below the soft tissue of his neck.

The man continued to remain passive in Leishke's grasp. "I'm Lars Andersen. I wasn't following you. I just ... walked back here to take a piss."

"I don't believe you for even a second," said Leishke, grabbing the man's arm and wrenching it up his back. The man grunted, and Leishke could hear him expel air as he fell again against the wall.

"All right, all right. I was hired by this man who's new to town. He meets with me every morning and tells me what he wants me to do. Today, he wanted me to follow you. But I didn't find you until you got off the ferry. I had been watching it all morning."

"That's all you were supposed to do – just follow me?"

"Well, I was supposed to watch you unless you went to the Hotel Zynda. If you went there, I was supposed to go get him."

"Where is he?" demanded Leishke. "Where were you going to tell him if I went to the Zynda?"

"He's at the Imperial Saloon."

"What does he look like?"

"He's a dark guy – black curly hair and a mustache. Shorter than me – maybe five feet, 10 inches. He has a dark complexion, and always dresses well. He's pretty easy to spot."

Leishke thought quickly.

"Here's the deal," he said. "I want you to go ahead and meet with him and tell him I'm at the Zynda."

"I don't want to lie to this fellow," said Andersen. "He's a scary man – if he finds out I turned him in, he'll go after me."

"Don't worry about it," said Leishke, who certainly wasn't going to worry about it. "I'll take care of him. Just tell him what I said."

"Then what do I do?" asked Andersen.

"I really don't care," said Leishke. "Stay there and have a drink. Go someplace else. I don't care. But ... where can I find you if I need you later?"

"I'm staying at a boarding house near the AJ," he said, referring to the Alaska Juneau gold mine operation. "It's run by Mrs. Edison. It's on the lower end of Franklin."

"I'll find you if I need you," said Leishke, letting go of the man's arm and chest and stepping back. "Go on now, do what I said."

The man shook himself, straightened his jacket and turned to go down the alley, followed by Leishke.

The two crossed the street and headed up the hill toward the Imperial Saloon on Front Street. Once there, Andersen stepped in while Leishke crossed the street, bought a newspaper from a passing paperboy hawking it, and leaned against a building, an idle man reading the paper.

Within a few minutes, a man answering to both Andersen's and May's description walked hurriedly from the bar, headed downhill toward the Zynda, which was just a block away. As soon as he had seen him exit the bar, Leishke folded up the paper, put it in his pocket and stepped down a nearby alley, and from there to the narrow passage behind the buildings on this block. He ducked into the Zynda's back door, which led directly into its kitchen, and stepped quickly through the room, which held only a man washing dishes in this period between lunch and dinner.

Leishke went down a hallway and entered the lobby from the back, just as the man he suspected was Againsky came into the front door. Leishke stepped to the side of the door and stood quietly. Againsky was looking around the lobby, trying to spot Leishke. Fortunately, there were a half dozen occupants, which slowed his search. He didn't spot Leishke until he had stepped into the center of the lobby and didn't have time to duck back outside before Leishke was upon him.

He grabbed Againsky's arm, lifting it up his back, just as he had done with Andersen. Againsky's response was more aggressive, however. His other hand reached into his jacket as he struggled against the hold.

"You might want to think about your next move," said Leishke calmly in a low voice. "I am a deputy federal marshal, and there are three of us in this room. If you pull a weapon, you won't have time to use it."

Againsky looked around the room; of course, there weren't additional marshals, but the men's interaction certainly had the attention of everyone in the place. All the men in the room had stood; most recognized and knew Leishke, and he knew that at least a couple of them would come to his assistance if he needed it. Againsky must have recognized that also.

"No need for that," he said. His voice was deep, cultured with an accent that revealed his Eastern European roots. "I wasn't reaching for a weapon, just my papers." He pulled out a visa and passport to hand to Leishke. "I think there must be some misunderstanding. I haven't done anything that would need the attention of federal marshals."

"I disagree with you," said Leishke. "And in these situations, my understanding of matters takes precedence." He pulled out his handcuffs and handcuffed Againsky's hands behind his back. Nodding his thanks to the men who had stood ready to assist, he walked his prisoner out of the hotel. As he did so, he noticed there was no sign of Lars Andersen.

Againsky bit out a laugh as they walked up the street to the courthouse and jail. "There were no other marshals, were there? What a fool I am."

"No, there were no other marshals, but if you had pulled this out," said Leishke, reaching Againsky's jacket and retrieving a five-inch-long sheathed knife, "you would have been attacked by at least three men in that room. They knew me, and were ready to help, if needed. I don't think you understand how smaller towns work. You're too accustomed to big cities."

"Perhaps so," admitted Againsky, who was maintaining his calm despite the situation. "But carrying a knife isn't against the law, and you have no reason to be arresting me." He paused. "I am under arrest, am I not?"

"Yes," said Leishke. "You are under arrest for the murder of Rosie Brown, or should I say, 'Jennie Poplosky'?" He waited, but there was no answer from Againsky. "I also think you murdered the cook at the Opera House, Catherine Todd. But we aren't quite ready to charge you with that yet."

Againsky continued his silence, as Leishke led him to the courthouse, and took him down to the basement jail. He patted him down, finding another knife hidden in his sock gaiter, and a revolver in his back pocket, just as May had described.

He turned the still silent Againsky over to the jailers and went upstairs to begin the arrest paperwork. Hoping that neither the Marshal nor the Commissioner had noticed his arrival, he began typing.

Leishke had been working for less than an hour when Davies knocked on his door. "Come in," he called, welcoming a break.

"Deputy Marshal Leishke," said the young Welshman.

"I think we have worked together long enough to use each other's first names, don't you?" asked Leishke. "Call me Frank and you're..."

"Rhys," said Davies.

"Take a seat, Rhys. What have you been finding out?"

"Lots," the young man replied. "I took that letter to the Serbian cleric, and he translated it. It is very interesting. And...I stopped at the Opera House for... for ("a beer," thought Leishke). Anyway, I stopped there and talked to two more women there about that man who's been throttling them. You won't believe what I found out."

Leishke suspected it would have no trouble believing anything at this point in his career but gave his colleague an encouraging smile.

"Let's start with the letter," he said.

"Sure. The priest immediately recognized the language and was even able to read it. He told me what it said, but also said he would write down a translation and have it for us tomorrow. I left the letter with him so he could work on it."

"Sounds like excellent work. What did he tell you about it?"

"It's a letter to Jennie Poplosky from her parents. They tell her they are glad to hear she is doing so well in the United States and thanking her for the money. But then, they ask about their son-in-law, Mikel Againsky. They write that a friend from a nearby town had told them about a man named Againsky who had married a young girl in that town and taken her to live in America. They were wondering if the two Againsky men are related. There was also other family news, including that her brother was serving as a soldier in the Russian army."

"What do you think this means?" asked Davies. "Did the same man marry both girls? And does that mean that he married them to turn them into prostitutes?"

"I'll tell you more later. Tell me about your interviews with the other women at the Opera House."

"I talked to two other women – Delores and Ida. They told me more than the other women had been willing to say, I think because they hadn't had the man as a customer so weren't as frightened by him. They said they think he works at the Treadwell Mine, because he comes by the Opera House at shift changes. They said he is a dark-haired man with a small goatee. He is also a big man – they described him as about six feet tall, and burly, like a real prospector."

Leishke knew that referred to the type of work that prospectors did – vigorous hiking to find a claim, and then the tough work of sampling the claim, building a cabin, and building the apparatus needed to mine – the sluice boxes, pit, or tunnels, and even tram tracks if it was at a remote enough site. It was hard, tough work and dedicated prospectors were not men to challenge.

"What else did they tell you?"

"They said that the women who he paid were genuinely terrified by his behavior. Two of the three had blacked out as he throttled them, and all three had been too frightened to struggle. I wondered – is it possible this could be the same man the deputy marshal in Petersburg told us about?"

Leishke thought back to the meeting two or three weeks ago, when the deputy marshal from Petersburg had come up to bring a prisoner and told a few of the deputies about a man who had nearly killed a woman in Petersburg. She was a schoolteacher who had been found in the woods near his boarding house. She had been violated, beaten, and throttled. The poor woman had already left Petersburg when the Juneau deputy marshals were told the story. She hadn't left any description of her attacker, saying it was dark when she had been grabbed as she walked home, dragged to the woods, and assaulted.

Leishke realized he should have connected the cases immediately and blamed the distraction of meeting May Svenson. The idea that she could have compromised his investigation was galling and made him more committed to set his attraction aside as soon as possible.

"I think you may be correct," he said. "Let's take this description to the supervisors at the Treadwell Mine and see if they can identify him for us. Actually, I'm going to ask you to do that. I've just arrested Againsky, and I have to prepare to talk with him. I suspect I won't get much out of him, but who knows? I've got him downstairs in the jail and am going to let him stew there until tomorrow.

"Now, let me update you on what I found out about Rosie Brown and Againsky."

Without naming his source, Leishke told Davies everything that May had told him.

"I suspect my source for this information may have heard it from someone else, and there's an excellent chance that it was Fannie Miller," said Leishke. We need to redouble our efforts to find her. Did you have any luck at all on that front?"

"No. I've spent all day in Douglas, and don't think she's there," Davies replied.

In their visits to Douglas that day, both deputy marshals had checked for Fannie at her cabin with no success. The cabin looked as undisturbed today as it had been all week.

Davies continued. "Do you really believe this preposterous tale – men abducting young girls, forcing them into white slavery, and then the girls coming up to Alaska? It sounds too complicated and impossible to be true."

"I understand why you would think that" said Leishke. "When I first heard of it back in California, I had the same thought. But the more experienced police officers told me that, before these young girls had been taken to Argentina, the prostitution trade there had relied on Black girls. Offering the young white girls, many of them blonde, to the many men immigrating to South America, was an easy way to make money – a lot of it.

"And Alaska, just like California, and Buenos Aires, has attracted a lot of single men in recent years. In addition, many of those men have money. Here in Juneau, for example, even if you don't find a fortune in gold, you can still make a good life working in a mine, a store or even for the government. If you don't have a family to support – and many of us don't – you often have plenty of spending money."

Davies nodded his agreement but still looked dubious. Leishke didn't mind; it didn't matter at this point whether Davies believed the story or not.

Leishke said: "I need to finish up this report, and review my notes for interviewing Againsky, so if you could check with Selena Dowling at the Circle City Hotel, that would be helpful. Then, return here and type up your report. I want to read it before it goes to the marshal."

"Do you want to sit in with me when I interview Againsky tomorrow?" he asked Davies. "I'm going to go down early, to talk to him before he's had breakfast – probably around 6 a.m. Can you come?"

"I think so – another day of getting up early isn't going to hurt me, I guess," Davies observed somewhat reluctantly.

Leishke had again lost track of time, and days of the week, so he appreciated the younger man's willingness to give up some of his little amount of free time. He was also well aware, however, that sitting in such a vital interview could be an important lesson for the aspiring detective.

"I'll see you later then," Leishke said; Davies took the hint, grabbed his hat and jacket, and left for the next tasks that he'd been assigned. Leishke returned to his typing.

• • •

May had felt a great lifting of spirits after telling Fannie's story to Leishke. She was also encouraged by knowing she would soon have help with what now seemed like the endless cleaning and cooking demanded at the Opera House. She had genuinely appreciated Leishke's help with laundry, and now found herself wishing he had stayed to help with the afternoon's work as well.

After a good cleaning of the bar and putting the meat and vegetables in the oven for the evening's meal, which was pot roast, she poured herself a cup of tea and sat at the kitchen table to catch her breath. The task recalled Mrs. Todd, and the many times the woman's brisk, floury hands had placed a cup in front of her. May felt her eyes tearing up; losing Albert had been like a tornado of grief. Losing Mrs. Todd was more like one of the electrical storms that punctuated Minnesota's summers. It was hard to endure but didn't often cause permanent damage. As she had that thought, May wondered if her death would have the same effect on the ones she loved.

She thought it might – she no longer had that one person who loved her more than anyone else. While most of the time she was grateful their union hadn't been blessed with children; at this moment she grieved that loss. Her death would, she feared, be more an inconvenience for her family than a real loss. She found herself descending into self-pity, something she usually tried to avoid.

Shaking it off, May finished her cup of tea, stood up and resumed cooking dinner. The new housemaid came from pulling in laundry to help prepare the dining room, and May took a tray of bar snacks into the bar. There, she quickly glanced around, fearful of seeing either man she told Leishke about. Neither were there, but there was a burly man with a goatee who made her uncomfortable. Although he was sitting with one of the working girls, he seemed more interested in May. She avoided his gaze and returned to the kitchen as soon as possible.

May found the new housemaid in the kitchen and welcomed her assistance. The young woman's name was Olga Petersen. She wasn't a widow, but the teen daughter of a settler with a large family. It was a practical financial necessity that had allowed the family to permit their young daughter to work in a brothel. Olga was a hard worker and had completed school through the eighth grade. May hoped she would be able to find a husband who would value this girl's enterprise and obvious intelligence.

"Olga," said May. "I want to talk to you about being careful working in the front. For the time being, I'll be the one cleaning the bar and taking in snacks. There are plenty of customers here who think any woman in a brothel is doing more than just cleaning and cooking. If someone says something off color to you, I've learned the best approach is to pretend you didn't hear them. If they get too close or touch you ('although it was more likely to grab you,' she thought), then pull away if you can, and yell at them."

"Oh, Mrs. Svenson, I'm not sure I could yell at a strange man," said the obviously flustered Olga. "And what should I yell?"

"'Stop!' works pretty well," said May. "Just keep repeating it as loud as you can. And avoid being in an area where you could be trapped alone by anyone."

Olga was looking more and more terrified, and May decided she may have brought up too much information too quickly.

"Don't worry about that now," she reassured the girl. "I'll stay with you in any of the public areas."

The two women got down to the business of cleaning and cooking for a dozen women.

• • •

In spite of, or perhaps because of, the exhausting meeting with May, Fannie had slept well and upon waking, felt the same sense of hope that had touched May that morning. She rose, dressed, and went into the kitchen to help Jane.

"I've got good news for you," Jane said. "Our brother got the trunk from your cabin last night. He packed everything you thought you would want in it, but he's a boy. He probably left things behind. So, take a few minutes and go through it to see what is missing. He can go back tonight if he needs to."

Fannie had no intention of sending him back to the cabin; in fact, she had forgotten he had intended to go last night or she would have warned him about the blonde man that May had seen. Fortunately, it appeared he had gone and returned without incident, so Fannie guessed that her location was still unknown to Againsky.

She quickly looked through the trunk and Jane was correct; he had missed some items she would have included. A missing stocking and two silver teaspoons were not worth the danger he could encounter. She found her real treasures – the photos of family and her jewelry. Once she was able to get her money from the bank, she could leave, and planned to, as quickly as possible.

In the meantime, she would help repay Jane's hospitality by assisting her as much as possible.

• • •

The boarding house where Andersen said he lived was one of several that crowded the blocks near the gold mine operation. Among the hastily constructed buildings on South Franklin Street, it stood out due to its poorly maintained appearance – it was long overdue for painting, and the windows were dirty enough for its inhabitants to need no curtains; which was good, because there were none.

The harassed-looking landlady who answered the door said that the man that Leishke sought was a lodger, but his brief glimpse of the house made Leishke question whether she would even recognize Andersen. It was obviously a well-used place, and an excellent location for the workers at the Alaska-Juneau Gold Mine. It also appeared, however, to have a high turnover. The front parlor, where he had talked to the landlady, was worn looking, and not overly clean. Mrs. Edison herself was disheveled, wearing a well-worn and dirty apron that appeared to have missed more than one laundry day. Her response to his question was also telling.

"You say his name is Lars Andersen. I thought it was Lars Anton, but maybe that was the man who stayed here last week.

Tall and blonde? Yes, that sounds like the Lars I'm thinking of. He has one of the common beds, not his own room."

Leishke knew that meant that Andersen was renting a bed, not an entire room. Such an arrangement was common for the many transient men waiting for a mining job or seeking something more lucrative. The beds would be in a room with other beds, somewhat similar to barracks, depending on the boarding house. In some cases, the beds themselves were shared by men who needed to pinch pennies. Mrs. Edison answered Leishke's unspoken question. In a town like Juneau, where there were shift workers, the same bed might also provide a place for someone during a night shift to sleep in during the day, and a day worker be in it all night. They were occasionally referred to as "hot beds," since the bedding may still be warm from a previous occupant when the next person lies down.

"I think he sometimes shares a bed – it is just so expensive for these poor gentlemen to find affordable genteel lodging. I'm so fortunate to be able to provide it," said the landlady.

Leishke thanked her and left, hoping he was never in such a situation that the "genteel lodging" offered by Mrs. Edison was all he could afford.

As he walked back to the courthouse, he decided that after a meal at the City Cafe, he would head home. He wanted time to clear his head before meeting with Againsky in the morning.

Chapter 21

When Leishke and Davies entered the jail block the next day, they were greeted by a suspect who didn't seem at all cowed after his night in jail. Leishke took the keys from the jailers, pulled Againsky from his cell and took him upstairs to the first floor, where there was an interrogation room with a bolt on the floor for a prisoner's shackles. He ensured the shackles were tight, and then joined Davies at the table across from the prisoner. Againsky looked almost as well-groomed as he had the previous day; slightly disheveled hair and some wrinkles in his jacket and pants were the only evidence of a night behind bars.

"How can I help you gentlemen?" he asked the two detectives, with a smirk that both men ached to wipe off his face.

Leishke forced himself to lean back in the chair, stretching out his legs to the side and crossing his ankles. If Againsky wanted to pretend he was unbothered by his circumstance, Leishke would imitate him. He had found that to be an effective approach in previous interviews.

"Oh, we just have a few things we're hoping you can help us with," he replied. "The first is we're wondering what brought you to our fair city."

"As you may know, the steamship schedule was affected by the Princess Kathleen going aground," Againsky said, referring to the ship owned by the Princess Line, which operated all the ships that regularly plied the waters between Skagway and Seattle.

"That meant that, rather than quickly transfer to the next ship up north, I had to wait a week for the next available sailing. I've got a ticket for the next sailing – the Princess Sophia – tomorrow. Do you think I'll be able to board her?" Again, he gave the smirk that both detectives found infuriating.

"I'm not sure," replied Leishke, evenly. "What business do you have up north?"

"I was heading up to Anchorage to meet my wife. She moved there about a year ago and I had planned to join her long before now. But my business in San Francisco took much longer to resolve than I had planned."

Leishke considered this. The story was probably mostly true, which was indicative of how clever Againsky was. He knew that sticking as close to the truth as possible made it difficult to be tripped up.

"What has your wife been doing all this time on her own in Anchorage?" asked Leishke.

"She hasn't been alone; she was accompanied by a close friend, and the two women were sent up to oversee some new business interests I had just acquired there. They have been doing well, but the business I have there needs a man's involvement at this stage. There's only so much that women can do when it comes to business. I'm sure you understand."

"Yes. I'm sure she is looking forward to seeing you. Can you describe further the business interests you have, both in Alaska and San Francisco?"

"Of course," Againsky promptly agreed. "I have real estate assets in both communities. In San Francisco, I spent longer than I had expected finding a good property manager for my holdings. In Anchorage, my wife and her friend have been ensuring my purchases were properly recorded and overseen. I am going to be seeking developers once I arrive there."

Leishke decided that it was time to try to shake the man's composure.

"I'm surprised to hear that your wife is in Anchorage. We have information that leads us to believe that she, and her friend, relocated to Juneau. Have you heard anything about that in correspondence with your wife?"

For the first time, there was a crack in Againsky's composure, and Leishke saw a glimpse of seething anger, before the slight smile returned to his face.

"Oh, my wife – I'm sure you're familiar with the vagaries of the fairer sex. It is certainly possible that both women decided to explore a little of the beautiful scenery of Alaska before returning to California. Her friend has quite a wanderlust and may have convinced her to have a small adventure. Can you tell me under which name my wife is traveling? She sometimes travels under her family name, for safety reasons, I suppose," he said, somewhat unconvincingly, though Leishke. He also realized that Againsky had cleverly avoided identifying his wife under the name for which she was known in the underworld.

"What name do you think she was likely to use? It's possible that the information we have is about someone not related to you at all?"

The question was now turned back to Againsky. His smile looked a little strained.

"She sometimes went by her maiden name of Poplosky. And her friend's name is Fannie Miller."

Davies had been given strict instruction to remain silent without betraying emotion during the entire interview, but this was too much for him. His face had turned from Againsky to Leishke; Leishke attempted, without moving a muscle, to tell him to calm down. It worked. With a brief grimace of chagrin, Davies went back to studying Againsky.

Againsky had not missed the exchange, and now had a somewhat speculative look.

"It appears that these names are familiar to you," he said.

"Yes," said Leishke. "Both women have come to our attention recently under troubling circumstances." Againsky showed no reaction, other than raising one inquiring eyebrow.

"I'm sorry to tell you that I believe your wife has been murdered, and her friend is missing."

Leishke was impressed, despite himself, at Againsky's acting skills. Covering his mouth with one hand, he gasped in horror, and then let one tear slide down his cheek. It was a masterful exhibition.

"What ... what happened? I hadn't heard from them in some months, but I thought it was simply misplaced mail. Who killed her? Has the bastard been caught? What can I do to help?"

"We have not yet arrested the culprit, but we believe we are close to finding him," said Leishke. "I'm afraid we have even more distressing news. Your wife, and Fannie Miller, have been working in Douglas as prostitutes since arriving here last year."

"That is impossible!" cried Againsky, whose chosen career as a pimp was obviously a loss to theaters everywhere. "My beautiful Jennie would never do such a heinous thing! If it happened, which seems impossible to believe, it must be Fannie Miller's fault! I never liked that woman – a scheming harpy. I told Jennie she was not a true friend, but Jennie refused to believe me."

"I'm sure this is a shock," said Leishke, dryly. "You knew nothing of this? I understand you've been spending time in Douglas, and we have witnesses who have said you were seen near Jennie's cabin there."

"What witnesses? If I had found my Jennie in such a circumstance... ." He seemed to struggle for words, and Leishke waited. Would he claim he would reject her or "rescue" her?

"I would have gone immediately to authorities and had them arrest her, and that Fannie. Obviously, they were breaking the law."

Leishke waited, hoping silence would prompt more, less considered, words. It didn't work. Againsky just looked at him.

"I'm reluctant to admit this, but it's unlikely that anything would have happened to either woman. Juneau and Douglas officials turn the other eye when it comes to prostitution," Leishke said, and waited.

And waited.

Againsky broke first. "So, you're telling me that my Jennie was killed by some crazed miner after she had sold her body to him? What are you doing about it? And what are you doing to find Fannie? I'm sure she's the one who created this entire situation. Is she still here, or has she already left town?"

Leishke noticed the emphasis on finding Fannie. Was Againsky now expecting the marshal service to find the woman he wanted to kill next? That wasn't going to happen. He ignored the questions about her.

"We don't know yet who killed your wife, but I'm sure you understand why we felt the need to talk to you. Where were you last Wednesday night?"

"Last Wednesday night," mused Againsky, and Leishke couldn't escape the thought that he was being toyed with.

"When I first got off the steamship, another passenger directed me to a nearby boarding house. I stayed there a few nights, but the place was not overly clean, and the food was dreadful. I checked into the Hotel Zynda on Thursday, I think."

"What was the name of your landlady?" asked Leishke, with a sense of foreboding.

"I think it was Edison. I know she was short of beds, because I think it was Wednesday night that I had to share the bed with another man." He gave Leishke another of his smug smiles.

"I believe his first name was Lars. I don't remember his last name, but I'm sure Mrs. Edison will. You could ask her."

Leishke had noticed that Againsky was suddenly very sure of his landlady's name and knew he hadn't forgotten it for a moment. The entire story was a set up; he knew that both Mrs. Edison and Lars Andersen would corroborate Againsky's alibi. He had a sinking feeling in his stomach; the Warsaw Club was infamous for its success at bribery. In this case, Mrs. Edison wouldn't even need bribing; her boarding house was so poorly run that she would have no idea of who was in what bed last Wednesday.

"The bastard was going to get away with it," he thought, "and there's nothing I can do about it."

Or was there? After all, Jennie wasn't the only victim of this killer. There was also Mrs. Todd. Leishke was also convinced that, once Againsky found her, Fannie Miller would be another victim. At least, it appeared she had not yet been found by Againsky. It was still possible she had been killed, and Againsky was pretending otherwise, but Leishke's gut told him she was still missing. How could he use this information against Againsky?

As Leishke's mind raced through these thoughts, Againsky had remained silent, studying him, with that faint smile still on his face. Leishke made up his mind. He was going to play Againsky's game and see what happened. The most likely result could be another dead girl and Againsky leaving Juneau. But Leishke believed he might be able to turn Againsky's arrogance against him.

"Well, it does certainly sound as if you have an alibi. We will need to check on it, of course, and you'll need to remain here in the meantime. I'm sure you understand." Leishke offered his own insincere smile. "We'll work as quickly as possible, of course."

He gestured to Davies, and the two men unshackled their prisoner and took him back to the jail. They then went back upstairs to Leishke's office.

"My gracious," exclaimed Davies. "He's either very good at lying or a real son of a bitch."

"Very good at lying," said Leishke. "We don't have a lot of time. So, let's make the day's plans."

The two men spoke briefly and then parted ways; Davies to track down Lars, and Leishke to the Circle City Hotel.

Chapter 22

May had risen that morning, grateful for a short sleep in, and the day off. Even at a brothel, workers needed a respite, and while women could choose to see clients, the bar had short hours, and the women were expected to prepare their own food. Mrs. Montgomery gave her staff, except for the bartender, one day off a week. May had attended church the previous evening; as usual, she went to the Lutheran church in Douglas, which was well attended by the many Scandinavian miners and their families.

May only had one thing that she had to do that day, which was visit Fannie. She hoped that Againsky was in jail, but couldn't count on it, so knew she would need to remain cautious and vigilant making her way back to the Juneau Indian Village. She bathed and dressed. After a quick breakfast from the cold food that Mrs. Starling had laid out, she set out for the ferry dock.

She had seen the blue skies and sun when she awoke, but as she walked outside, May looked down the channel past the Treadwell mine and saw a cloudless sky stretching above the channel and the steep mountains that stood behind Juneau. Aboard the boat, she eschewed the cabin in favor of the deck, enjoying the warmth of the spring sun. The fresh green of the alder trees lightened the lower reaches of Mt. Juneau and Mt. Roberts, which loomed over the channel on the Juneau side. While most of the mountains were covered in evergreens, the alder trees took root where trees had been cut for the sawmill or development. They also tended to sprout in the many avalanche chutes that marred the mountains. The snow was now retreating to the mountaintops, although there was a deep pile of snow at the base of Mt. Roberts, marking a massive avalanche that had dropped onto the town of Thane in January. No one was hurt, which was a miracle, May thought. That particular place on the mountain was a well-known avalanche chute, and those who built Thane were smart enough to avoid building at its base. The road that followed the beach at the bottom of the mountain had been closed for several days after the avalanche. It wasn't until it was completely cleared that it was discovered no one had been on the road at the time.

She turned toward Juneau as the ferry docked; its arrival seemed to cause no interest from any of the few people near the dock on a Monday morning. The streets remained quiet as she walked toward the home where Fannie was staying, and she realized that it was still early. Now, as she walked into the community, she felt conspicuous – a white woman in the Indian Village. The few people who saw her didn't acknowledge her; most avoided her gaze and she was struck by the impression that they were more concerned about her noticing them than she was about being seen by them.

Even though her last visit had been at night, she had no trouble finding the house a second time; the map that George had given her was still a vivid memory. A soft knock on the kitchen door was quickly answered by Fannie. After a quick embrace, Fannie told her the children were at church, their father at work, and Jane was visiting a sister. She wouldn't return for at least an hour.

The two women caught up with each other, with May telling her of the meeting with Leishke. Fannie told her she had originally appreciated the sanctuary at Jane's house but was now feeling restless and increasingly worried for her safety, and the safety of the family protecting her.

"I don't trust him not to hurt anyone who stands in his way," she told May. "In Buenos Aires, if a girl escaped, once she was found, she was beaten and sometimes even worse. I'm worried that, given how people here feel, a Native family could be badly hurt and no one would care."

"Leishke would," declared May, who found herself a little taken aback at her own defense of someone she knew so slightly.

"I'm glad you think that, but wait ...," said Fannie. "Why do you think that way? Is there something you're not telling me about this man? Are you attracted to him?"

Unknowingly, May took a page from Leishke's interrogation techniques, and stayed silent. She didn't know what to say. She *was* attracted to the man, she realized. He was thoughtful and usually considerate. He was certainly handsome. She didn't know what to think about all of this. She had thought that Albert's death had also killed any feeling she may have for any other man. It was surprising and disconcerting to learn that wasn't the case.

"It doesn't matter," she said. "What's important is that I do think he's trustworthy. I don't think you would need to fear he would harm you or turn on you in any way. Could I persuade you to meet with him? I think he might be the best way to ensure that Againsky can't get to you."

Fannie paused. She was tempted to follow her friend's advice. She had learned long ago not to rely on a man, but it was in her nature to do so, and May made it sound easy. No, she really did know better.

"I can't," she said. "I'm hoping that I'll be long gone from Juneau by next week. So long as I can continue avoiding Againsky, I'll be alright."

She added, "I've been thinking about our discussion last time about getting my money out of the bank. Let's do that tomorrow morning as soon as the bank opens. There should be more people there, and the more people there, the better. I really don't want to try any distraction, though. I think that's too dangerous."

May disagreed with her and the two argued before finally agreeing on a plan. May promised to see Fannie the next morning and left for the ferry back to Douglas. She wasn't sure how she would get out of work the next day for the time it would take to go to Juneau and back, but with the new cook expected to begin work and Olga's strong work ethic, she thought Mrs. Montgomery would allow a short absence.

Leishke was pleased to find Selena Dowling in her hotel room at the Circle City. Maybe his luck in this case was finally turning. She was surprised to see him at her door, and not in a good way. She had opened the door only enough to see him and stood, holding it slightly open but not letting him in.

"I don't have time to talk to you," she told him before he had said anything. "And even if I did have time, I wouldn't."

"You really don't have a choice," said Leishke, bringing out his badge (the second time in two days, he thought – it might be a record). "We either talk here, or I take you out of here in handcuffs and we go up the hill."

"What is all this?" asked a man, who appeared behind Selena in the doorway. Leishke recognized him as the owner of the Juneau lumber company and realized his good luck may have turned. Max Whelan, who was a fit man about 50 years old, was fully dressed, but still slightly disheveled. It was clear that Leishke had interrupted a liaison. Unfortunately for Leishke, Whelan's wife had died the year before, so he apparently had no concern about his private life being made a little public.

"I'm not sure what a deputy marshal has to do with Miss Dowling," Whelan said. "But anything you have to say to her can be said in front of me."

"Oh, Max," said Selena, taking his arm and smiling at him. "I'm sure that Deputy Marshal Leishke just has some routine questions that I'm happy to answer. Why don't I just join him in the lobby for a few minutes and then send him on his way?"

"If you're sure, my dear," Whelan replied. "But," he turned to Leishke. "I don't want to hear any more intimidation on your part toward this young woman. No more talk of handcuffs."

Leishke nodded, took Selena's arm in a firm grip, and walked her down the stairs to the lobby. Other than the hotel clerk, they were the only two people there.

"What is this about?" asked Selena quietly, noticeably more compliant.

"It's about Fannie Miller," Leishke replied, also keeping his voice low. "She is missing and I'm concerned for her welfare. I believe you may have some notion of her whereabouts."

"What makes you think that?"

"I've learned you were friendly with her from someone in Douglas," Leishke said. "She's been missing almost a week, and I'm afraid she is in danger."

"From whom?" asked Selena.

"I can't tell you that, but I can say he is in custody now, but likely to be released tomorrow. I think the first thing he'll do is look for Fannie," said Leishke.

Selena paled. "I cannot tell you anything about where she is, but if I see her, I'll tell her you're looking for her."

Leishke felt his frustration rise. "Even if you won't tell me where she is, please tell her she is in danger. I'm going to try to keep him in jail, but it's unlikely I'll succeed. If you're a friend of hers, please tell her. Also, tell her that I can help. Any time you want to reach me, send me a message at the deputy marshals' office, or ask for me or Deputy Marshal Davies."

Selena nodded but didn't say anything. Leishke left and headed home. He didn't think he would be able to achieve anything more today.

Chapter 23

Mrs. Montgomery had been happy to give May a few hours off in the morning. With both newly hired workers at the Opera House, May thought she probably wouldn't even be missed.

Now, May walked toward the imposing B.M. Behrends Bank on Seward Street at 9 a.m. The large concrete building stood out among its wooden neighbors; May had heard that Mr. Behrends had wanted to ensure it wouldn't be a victim of the frequent fires that plagued the city. The rain had returned and May had again borrowed an umbrella from her landlady.

The workday was beginning downtown, and there was a short line of people waiting to enter the bank. One of them was Fannie, holding hands with a young child (another cousin of Selena's) and wearing a large hat tilted at such an angle to obscure most of her face.

May had walked up from the ferry terminal, and as she turned onto Seward from Main Street, she began walking slower, and weaving slightly. She was a few steps from the bank when its doors opened and the customers began streaming inside. Fannie was second in line, so May knew she would be leaving in just a few minutes if her transaction went smoothly. She put her hand on the edge of the bank building and leaned against it, biding her time.

Just as she saw Fannie stepping out the door, she gave a loud cry and slid (gracefully, she congratulated herself) to the ground. Instead of touching the ground, two strong hands grabbed her by the waist and pulled her against his chest. She realized the passerby had moved so quickly that many bystanders hadn't even witnessed her performance. She stood and turned to tell the man to unhand her.

She was shocked to see the face of the man whom she had seen the day before the Opera House bar – a large dark-haired man with a goatee and a chilling look in his cold eyes. The small smile on his face did not reassure her. In the second it took for her to recognize the man, he had successfully pulled her down the alley next to the bank.

"Let go..." she gasped, inhaling a breath to prepare for a scream. But one of his hands covered her mouth as the other moved from her waist to her shoulder, pressing his bent elbow against her throat.

She tried kicking, but her skirts were full enough to make her kicks ineffectual. He had pulled her to the dark end of the alley and she knew they were effectively invisible to passersby in the darkness of the narrow alley between two multi-storied buildings, and behind refuse containers.

May thought frantically and was surprised to realize that the physical dilemma she was in was not as foreign as it first seemed. After all, she had big brothers, and they loved rough housing, as her mother had called it. "What had I done to get away from them?" she thought, and then remembered.

She dropped limp all over, as if she was unconscious. That was the only thing that effectively ended her brothers' torment; fear that they had choked her too hard.

Initially, it worked with the man also. As she went limp, he loosened his hold on her neck and dropped the hand over her mouth, so he could check her breathing.

If May had waited a few more seconds, the ploy might have worked. In her anxiety to get away, she struggled too soon and both her mouth and neck were again quickly covered.

"You little bitch," the man snarled in her ear. "If I didn't need you to tell me where your friend is, you'd be dead right now."

May stared up at him, thinking that she couldn't possibly let this terrifying person know where Fannie was. For just a moment, she congratulated herself. Her plan to distract anyone watching the bank had worked – for Fannie at least. Now, she had to figure out how to rescue herself.

She pointed toward her mouth, trying to use gestures to reassure him that she wanted to talk, and wouldn't scream.

"If you make any effort to run or yell, you will be gutted like a fish," the man said, showing her a sharp knife that he had pulled out of his jacket breast pocket.

May nodded her head, assuring him as best she could that she would obey him.

He slowly removed the hand over her mouth, and asked, "Where is that other bitch – Fannie? I saw you at the Opera House, and I know you know who she is. I believe my friend is willing to pay me very well for finding her. So ... tell me."

"I would be happy to tell you, if I knew," said May, who had prepared with Fannie how to answer this question if she was forced to.

"I'm looking for her too," she told the man. "She owes me money. She pays me a fee to send her customers, and she owes me about $30. I would love to be able to find her. I need that money for my rent."

She stared at him, and he stared back, looking at a loss. May let loose a small sigh of relief; maybe this plan was going to work. She was sure that Fannie was now out of sight, and she wanted so badly to get out of this bad-smelling, dark hole of an alley.

"I don't think I believe you," he said.

"I don't really care if you believe me or not," May said. "Let me go, and I'll help you look for her."

"All right," he said reluctantly. "I guess." Then he paused. His hold around her neck had loosened, and now he dropped his arm altogether and put the knife back in his pocket. A hand remained tight around one of her wrists and she realized she still wasn't loose.

"I think you can help me find her, though," he told her. "We're in the same boat, after all. You need the money from her to pay your rent, and I need the money I get for finding her to buy a ticket out of this place. So, tell you where you think she might be."

"I think she's probably with her boyfriend," said May, slowly. "He's a miner in Treadwell. I think he works for the Ready Bullion Mine," she said, referring to one of the four mines that made up the Treadwell complex.

"The problem is, I don't know if he lives in Treadwell, or in Douglas. I've only seen him a couple of times and don't know his name."

"What do you know?"

"I think he's from Ireland, but I'm not sure. He's been trying to talk her into marrying him, but she isn't interested. She wants a more prosperous man; at least, that's what she told me." May realized that her fictional tale may have struck a nerve with this man, who looked angrier suddenly.

"Oh, so the bitch wants money, huh?" asked. "And what does she do to deserve that? Spread her legs for anyone who knocks on her door? I feel sorry for any poor bastard who's taken in by her."

May realized her imagination was not leading to the result she had hoped.

"Oh, but she deserves a happy life too," she said. "Fannie's life had been very difficult; she was abducted as a young girl and forced to become a prostitute."

"I don't believe that" was the reply. "Any woman who is willing to sell their bodies can make another choice – death. That is certainly more honorable than what this bitch chose."

May realized she was not going to be changing how her abductor viewed the women of the underworld, and she needed to focus on herself.

"Well, I've told you all I know," she said. "I can promise you, though, that I will tell you as soon as I get any idea where she may be. How can I reach you?"

He was obviously convinced of her sincerity. "My name is Constant Kilburn; I'm staying at Mrs. Furnace's boarding house in Douglas. Just send a message there." He dropped her wrist, and May thanked him, and moving as quickly as she could, returned to Seward Street.

There was no sign of Fannie, but she wanted to tell Frank Leishke what she had just learned. She didn't want Kilburn to see her walk directly up to the courthouse, so walked one block away from the bank before going up the hill to the courthouse.

At the courthouse, she was relieved to see Leishke as soon as she walked in the door. He was walking up the stairs from the building's bottom floor, where she had heard the jail was located, and his usually stern face appeared a little fiercer than usual. When he saw her, however, the smile she so admired appeared briefly. Then he hurried toward her.

"What are you doing here? Is everything all right? Has something happened?" he asked roughly.

She looked behind him and saw another deputy marshal – she remembered him as being Welsh but couldn't remember his name. He was looking at Leishke and had a grin on his face. It was attractive, but not as attractive as Frank Leishke's reluctant smile, thought May.

"I'm fine," she said. I just wanted to tell you about something I just learned. Is there some place we can talk?"

"Of course," said Frank, pointing toward the stairs leading up, while at the same time gingerly taking her arm to guide her. The Welsh deputy marshal began following them, still grinning. Leishke heard his steps and turned toward him.

"It's fine, Rhys," he said. "You go on and do what we discussed. Just come back later and update me."

The deputy marshal had stopped grinning when Leishke addressed him, but still looked cheerful as he nodded, and headed back toward the building's entrance. Frank and May continued upstairs to Leishke's office.

When they entered, May took a moment to look around before sitting in one of the two chairs facing the desk. She was surprised when Leishke sat next to her, rather than behind the desk. His hat and jacket were on a rack next to the door, so she saw him in his shirtsleeves for the first time in their acquaintance. His poorly cut and well-used jacket had disguised his powerful physique, she realized. He had big shoulders, well-muscled arms, and a trim torso. She found herself looking at him a little longer than was polite, but when she lifted her gaze to his, realized he was looking pretty closely at her also.

"Are you all right?" he asked again, less urgently.

She smiled and nodded. "I am a little shaken," she admitted. "I just had an encounter with someone who I think is working with Againsky."

"Oh," said Frank. "Who was he, and what happened?"

May went on to describe the encounter, leaving out the part that Fannie had played in the drama. Instead, May said she had been momentarily out of breath from walking up the hill so quickly, and was feeling faint when Kilburn grabbed her.

As she described her abduction, she noted that Frank had tensed up and was clutching a fist. He let her finish her entire story without interruption, however.

"Did he hurt you?" were his first words.

"No," said May. "Except for ..." she pointed at her wrist and slid up the cuff to reveal red finger marks she knew would be turning black in a few hours.

Frank took another deep breath, and she thought she heard a muttered curse.

"I'm sorry this happened to you," he said. "I will be picking up this man as soon as possible. Did he tell you his name? It sounds as if he didn't know I arrested Againsky yesterday."

"You arrested Againsky? That is good," said May. "Oh, and this man's name is Constant Kilburn; he said he was living at a boarding house owned by Mrs. Furnace in Douglas."

She was puzzled to see that Frank's face didn't display the relief she felt about Againsky's arrest.

"We're going to have to release Againsky later today," he admitted.

"What? How can that be happening? You know he killed Rosie and Mrs. Todd."

He nodded, and added, "Just because we know that doesn't mean we can prove it. And he has an alibi witness – a man named Lars Andersen."

"What?" May exclaimed. "But how could anyone believe anyone who said he was with Againsky? I think it's pretty clear that Againsky knows how to buy himself whatever help he wants."

"I understand, and I don't believe a word that comes out of that lying bastard's mouth," Leishke said grimly. "But I'm afraid our prosecutor and magistrate aren't going to agree. Even if we can prove he's in league with Againsky, and I'm not sure that's going to be easy, they are still not going to move to arrest Againsky without more evidence."

"I can promise you that I'm working on collecting that," Frank added. "But it's going to take time. And in the meantime, we're going to have to let Againsky go. And there is something you can do that would help, though."

"What is it?" said May. "I'll do whatever I can to get both those men locked up."

"I need your help tracking down Fannie Miller," Frank said. "You know her – I know you must. She came up to the Opera House regularly, and I've had a witness say you were seen together on more than one occasion. What can you tell me that would help me find her? I suspect her testimony could tell me the information that I'm missing."

May didn't know what to say. Her silence, and the stricken look on her face hit Frank like a punch to the chest. She did know Fannie, and he suspected that the story she had told him about Jennie's beginnings came from Fannie. He had to talk to Fannie. If she didn't come forward, he didn't see his way clear to making a convincing case.

"I know this must be difficult," he said, leaning forward and taking one of May's hands in his. Her hand felt cold and small under his grasp. He felt it tremble slightly and tightened his hold. He realized that the touch of her hand had so distracted him he had forgotten what he was going to say.

He cleared his throat and tried again. "It must be hard, but I promise you that I will do my utmost to keep you both safe. If you tell me where she is, I'll be careful in my approach. But I have to talk to her."

"I'm not sure what to do," admitted May. "She made me promise. I can't just break that promise. And she is so fearful – she has good reason to be frightened. But I trust you, and I will just have to convince her to do the same. It won't be easy, and I may never be able to tell you where she is."

She withdrew her hand from Frank's grasp and sat a little straighter. "I will not tell you where she is without her permission. She has had too many betrayals in her life. I can't add to that with any action of mine."

Torn between frustration at her decision and admiration at her loyalty to a friend, Frank knew he was not going to be able to force her to reveal Fannie's location. Whatever he told her now would have to be enough to convince her.

Frank said: "I truly believe that Fannie is the key to this entire business – the death of Rosie Brown and the death of Catherine Todd. In order to succeed in my efforts to bring their killer to justice, Fannie must become a witness. I will do whatever I can to protect her, and to ensure she is not treated poorly, but just as you can't betray your friend, I can't betray my calling to seek justice for the afflicted. If she wants revenge for the death of her friend, Jennie Poplosky, I am the one who can ensure it happens."

May looked at Frank's resolute face and knew he was right. The loss of both Rosie and Mrs. Todd couldn't be set aside. She also realized she had complete faith in his ability to make this right – to avenge the death of these innocent victims.

She nodded and stood, resolute. "I will try my best," she told Frank. "But I will ask that you don't have me followed or watched. I must act naturally when I see Fannie, and I can't if I know I'm being followed."

Frank agreed, but reluctantly. He had planned to have her followed not so she would lead him to Fannie, but so she would remain safe from Againsky and whatever confederates he bought.

"I am very worried about you," Leishke told her, looking at her in a way that made it difficult to move her gaze from his. "Will you do me a favor?" he asked, standing, and stepping over to his desk. He opened a drawer and withdrew a small knife in a sheath and buckled band. It was too small to fit around her waist; May wasn't sure how it was worn.

"It goes around your lower limb," said Frank, handing it to her. May noticed a slight flush in his face and thought incredulously that he was blushing.

"Oh, you mean," she pointed to her thigh.

"Yes," he replied. "Buckle it up high, and then pull out the stitches in the side seam of your walking dress, so you can reach in and grab it quickly. No one is going to expect you'll be carrying such a weapon and it may make the difference if someone grabs you again."

"Thank you," said May. She put the knife and its sheath and harness in her purse. It was a tight fit, but she was able to close the clasp. She stood, ready to leave. She felt much more ... solid, she decided, after talking with Frank. Impulsively, she walked up to him, put her arms around him and gave him a hug in gratitude.

Frank stood, arms at his sides, struck motionless by the warmth, smell and sheer womanliness of her. Just as he lifted his arms to return her embrace, she stepped back, a flush now on her face.

"I'll let you know what Fannie says," she told him, lifting her chin to look him in the eyes. "Thank you for...well, everything."

Chapter 24

May decided she would leave immediately for Jane's house. She hoped that Fannie hadn't already left, but she didn't think there was a steamship south for two more days.

She walked quickly to the Indian Village, slowing down as she approached people on the sidewalk. The sun had broken through the morning fog and drizzle and it promised to be another brilliantly beautiful day. The ravens circled overhead, and she heard the high-pitched chortle of an eagle as she approached the Village. The tide was out and there were several eagles at the mouth of Gold Creek as it flowed out onto the beach. As she watched, she saw the sharp fins of two killer whales diving in the channel. She knew from the previous year that it was also the time of year that killer whales often entered the channel in search of the spring run of candlefish north of Juneau. She felt her spirits rise along with the sun. It seemed impossible that anything bad could happen on such a lovely day.

In the Village, she slowed her pace, and walked past the alley way to Jane's kitchen door, trying to assess whether she had a follower. She didn't see anyone behind her or watching her, so made her way back to Jane's house.

Her knock was answered quickly; it was a school day and the children's absence made for a much quieter household. Jane greeted her and invited her in.

Jane led her to the bedroom where Fannie had been sleeping, and she found her friend completing the packing of her trunk. Fannie greeted her with a smile and hug.

"Oh, I'm so glad to see you. When you weren't at the bank this morning, I thought there must be something wrong," Fannie said.

"I was there, and there was something wrong," replied May, and then told the story of her morning's adventures with Kilburn.

Fannie paled and sat on the bed. "I am so sorry that you were put in such danger and through my actions. I hate to believe that another friend could have been lost to me." Her hands were so tightly clutched, the knuckles were turning white. May reached over and put her hand on her.

"I'm all right, though. And I walked up to the courthouse and told Deputy Marshal Leishke everything. He told me that he had arrested Againsky yesterday, but he is going to have to let him go, probably today."

"I told you that you couldn't trust the police or the marshals," said Fannie. "This just proves that. He must have bought them off, just like the Club does in Buenos Aires."

"He wasn't bought off," May responded before she could think.

That was the wrong answer, May told herself. She couldn't put up Fannie's back before she had even begun trying to convince her to talk to Leishke.

"I told him what Kilburn had done, and he promised to look for him. But he also asked me for something else," May said. "He wants to talk to you."

Fannie began shaking her head, and kept doing so as May continued talking, hoping to convince her. May's efforts were in vain, until she repeated what Frank had told her.

"He said that he has a calling to seek justice for the afflicted. He also referred to Rosie as an innocent victim. I really believe he will succeed in bringing Againsky to justice. Remember, he didn't doubt the story, and you know how fantastical it sounds," she said, hearing the pleading in her voice.

"He said she was an innocent victim?" Fannie asked. "No one calls any of us innocent. What do you think he meant?"

"I think he meant that she didn't deserve to be killed," replied May simply. "And she didn't."

"You say you trust him?" inquired Fannie. "If you trust him, maybe I can too. I will have to stay here for a couple more days anyway. There isn't a steamship out until then." She took a deep breath. "If you can set up a safe place for us to meet, I'll talk to him. But I can't make any promises after that."

"I can do that," said May, eagerly, while at the same time having no idea how she was going to do this.

May decided to leave Fannie before she could change her mind. May talked to Jane before leaving the house and agreed that one of the children would travel to Douglas that afternoon to find out from May where the meeting would take place. May left, consumed with thoughts about where this meeting was going to happen. She was almost at the ferry before she saw the man she thought of as Againsky. He was standing near the dock and appeared to be almost idly watching the boat traffic in the harbor. May halted, and her sudden movement caught his attention. He turned her way, watching her as she stood, frozen in fear.

Then, as she watched, his eyes went past her, and she remembered – he didn't know who she was. Kilburn might connect her with Fannie, but Againsky hadn't seen her the single time she had seen him as he left the Opera House. "No need to be frightened," she chastised herself.

She opened her purse and pretended to search in it, as if she had stopped because of something she needed. Then, closing it, she walked decisively toward the ferry, which had just docked and was letting off its passengers. Showing the skipper her return ticket, she stepped aboard.

As the boat pulled away from the dock, she saw Againsky still standing in Juneau, but he was again looking at her. She turned away from him and entered the cabin to take her place on the benches.

• • •

Leishke had watched as Againsky walked out the courthouse door and down the street. It was an infuriating scene. He hoped that May was out of the man's sight, and that she had successfully convinced Fannie to meet with him. In the meantime, there were things he should be doing. As he headed back to his office for his coat and hat, he saw the marshal's secretary walk toward him. That was not a good sign.

Half an hour later, Marshal Calhoun had again expressed the need for a quick resolution to the murders. Leishke had told him of both the arrest and release of Againsky, which hadn't helped matters. Leishke said he knew neither the prosecutor nor the judge would support filing charges unless Leishke could disprove the alibi.

"I'm going to try to do that today," he assured Calhoun.

"You need to not just try, but succeed," the Marshal said. "We need to get this wrapped up. And, while you're here, tell me what's going on with this Petersburg case. Do we have another killer in Douglas?"

Leishke told him that he was working on both cases and took the opportunity to praise Rhys Davies for his work. "He is going to be a fine detective," Leishke said. "I am impressed with how quickly he's learning."

Changing the subject seemed to work. Marshal Calhoun was placated at the thought of another trained detective on his staff. He told Leishke to leave and get back to work. Leishke was more than happy to obey him.

He headed to his office to finish typing his notes, which took another hour. He spent a minute reviewing his notebook before leaving. The items still needing resolution were the size of Againsky's boots, a talk with the coroner about Mrs. Todd's autopsy, and he needed to track down both this Kilburn fellow and Lars Andersen.

Leishke knew the jailers would have made measurements of the prisoner's feet because the territory had embraced the Bertillion method. Leishke had his doubts about its efficacy, but the method had helped identify specific prisoners in other cases in the country. Using a series of body measurements and a questionnaire about such things as skin tone, the method claimed to be able to conclusively describe a person in such a unique fashion that he or she couldn't be mistaken for anyone else.

Leishke wasn't sure it really helped find criminals, but it may lead to people not being falsely imprisoned. In this case, it would furnish him with Againsky's shoe size. He decided that today, he would focus on talking to Lars Andersen. He would visit the coroner later in the day.

With a plan in mind, he headed for the front door. Before he reached it, it swung open and the man he had last seen with Selena Dowling, Max Whelan, entered. Hatless and without a jacket, he was clearly distraught.

"Oh, you're here!" he exclaimed, grabbing Leishke by the arm. "Come, come quickly. Selena is asking for you, and I ... I'm not sure how much longer she will be able to talk."

Chapter 25

Leishke was alarmed to see tears in the man's eyes.

"What happened?" he asked, grasping Whelan's hand where it lay on his arm.

"I found her in her room at the hotel. She had been beaten – so badly that I don't know if she's going to survive. She's been taken to the hospital." As he spoke, his grip on Leishke's arm had tightened, and the detective found himself being dragged out of the courthouse and down the street to the hospital.

St. Ann's Hospital was just three blocks from the courthouse, and the men covered the distance quickly. When they entered the building, they found a cluster of sisters talking by the admitting desk. As soon as they entered, one sister walked toward them, wearing the habit and coif of a nun, covered by a nurse's apron.

"Oh, Mr. Whelan, I'll take you right back to your friend," the sister said, responding to the man's look of desperation.

"She's still alive," she said quietly as they walked down the hall. "That is surprising to us all. The extent of her injuries is severe, but she is putting up a valiant fight. Here she is," she said, opening a door to a single patient room.

The room featured a bed, small wardrobe, and a large window with a view down the hill to the Gastineau Channel. Another nun sat in one of the two chairs in the room. Sun streamed into the window, serving to highlight the gruesome sight of Selena Dowling. Her face had been so badly beaten as to make her unrecognizable; her hair was the only feature that Leishke would have known, and it was torn and matted with blood. Both eyes were blackened, her nose was broken and her mouth swollen and cut. She had also a bandaged shoulder, and bandaged arms. "Dreadful injuries," the sister whispered to the men. "A broken shoulder – there was a footprint on her dress. And burns -- it was as if someone had put his cigar out on her inner forearms. I've never seen such wickedness."

Selena's eyes appeared closed – it was hard to discern because they were so swollen. She lifted a hand as they entered, however, and used one finger to gesture them closer. Leishke took the sole chair in the room and pulled it close to the bed. Selena was lying slightly raised, probably to make her breathing easier. Lowering himself to the chair, Leishke put his hat on his lap and leaned toward her.

"I don't know who it was," she whispered, her breath raspy and the words slow. "He wanted Fannie. Everything he did to me was to get me to tell him where she was."

She paused, breathing hard. "I don't think I told him...but the pain was so great. I'm not sure."

Leishke had to ask. "What did he look like?"

The effort it took for Selena to answer seemed almost beyond her. She took another breath, wincing in pain and said, "Dark hair, dark complexion, curly hair, mustache." She breathed. "Do you know who it is?"

"I think I do," replied Leishke, thinking that the bastard must have gone directly from the courthouse to the Circle City Hotel. Leishke wasn't sure how Againsky had made a connection between Fannie and Selena, but it appeared that his jail stay had served to redouble his efforts to find Fannie and silence her. He looked at this bruised and battered person barely clinging to life, who had so recently been a vital, beautiful young woman.

He decided he had enough to go after Againsky. "You rest," he told Selena. He stepped into the hallway, where the sister had tactfully gone after he began talking with Selena. Mr. Whelan joined them.

"What can you tell me about her injuries, Sister?" he asked the blue-eyed nun, who appeared to be in middle age.

"As I said, this is a wicked thing," she replied. "The monster who abused her so much had kicked her repeatedly, which caused the worst injuries. We think she has a punctured lung, as well as the broken shoulder. He also hit her in the face, as you can see. Our biggest concerns right now are her lung and possible head injuries. So far, she is staying conscious, which is a very good sign. The doctor says, however, that she could lapse into unconsciousness at any time, and it would likely be a precursor to the end. She has a number of broken ribs, which is why we suspect a lung puncture, especially with the way she is breathing. You heard that rasp?" she asked both men. They nodded.

"If that doesn't resolve, the surgeon is likely to do a small surgery that would allow him to drain the lung. It isn't an uncommon surgery, but it is exceptionally delicate, so no doctor wants to perform it unless absolutely necessary." As she spoke, her face had brightened, and Leishke wondered how difficult it must be for this clever, experienced nurse to have to defer to every doctor, no matter how inexperienced or lacking in judgment. She had also caught a look on Whelan's face and decided that had been enough medical talk for the time.

"Despite these grievous injuries, we remain hopeful that she will recover. The next day or two will be critical." She turned to Leishke's companion.

"Mr. Whelan, we are grateful for your contribution to the hospital, and plan to keep Miss Dowling in a private room for the duration of her stay. As you can see, she is also receiving the sole attention of a dedicated nurse. We plan to continue such a level of care until the crisis is past, so you need not be concerned. She is getting every attention."

Leishke talked quietly with the sister for a few more minutes. Whelan had returned to the room, and now came back into the hall. The sawmill owner had somehow recovered his jacket and hat and looked more composed. After telling the sister that he would be back later that day, Whelan followed Leishke to the door and outside.

They walked in silence for a block before Leishke thought there was enough privacy to ask a few questions.

"How did you learn of this incident?" he asked.

"I certainly wouldn't call it an incident," Whelan responded. "It was an attack – it really can't be called anything else."

Whelan continued. "I had planned to visit Selena this morning, but my visit was delayed due an unexpected business matter. When I came to the hotel, I followed my usual practice of knocking on her door and waiting to be asked to enter. But this time, she didn't respond. Instead, I thought I heard a door closing, and then some faint moaning. That alarmed me. I have a room key, but generally don't use it. In this peculiar circumstance, I thought my use was warranted. So, I opened the door."

He took a deep breath. "It was a horrific scene – Selena was as you just saw her, but she was tied to the bed. Her dress had been torn almost completely from her body and she was covered in blood and burns. The burns were so foul – I could actually smell the burning flesh." He again took a deep breath. "I untied her and covered her, after feeling for a pulse. Then I told the hotel clerk to call the hospital ambulance. They were quick to arrive, but took a long time to move her, since they feared further injuries to the poor girl."

"Once at the hospital, she recovered consciousness, but wouldn't say anything about what happened to her," he continued. "She just asked for you."

"You can do something else to help me," said Leishke. "Can you come with me to the hotel? I want to see the room. The attacker may have left something."

At the hotel, the clerk asked after Miss Dowling, and Whelan told him that she was seriously injured. Leishke also took the opportunity to both find out more and plant some doubt.

"She is very seriously injured," he said sternly. "The doctor at St. Ann's doesn't believe she will recover. She is still unconscious, and we don't know if she'll ever come to her senses. If she doesn't, we may never know who did this."

"Is there anything you can tell us?" he continued. "Anyone in here today who was asking after her, or who you don't know?" As he asked his questions, he saw the clerk's hand pat his front pocket, as if checking to see if something was still there. Leishke suspected he knew what he was looking for – the bribe paid by Againsky.

He was made more suspicious by the clerk's reply. "I didn't see anyone this morning who I didn't know, and no one asked for Miss Dowling," he blurted out. "But there were a few minutes when I had to respond to another resident who had some questions, so the desk was not staffed. Anyone could have walked in – and anyone could have seen our registration book, which states who is in each room. So, I must have missed whoever assaulted her."

"That is unfortunate," said Leishke, who now grabbed Max Whelan's arm as he stepped toward the clerk. "We are going to go up and look around. If you think of anything else, please let us know."

"Certainly, sir," the clerk replied. "Do you need a key?"

The men shook their heads and walked upstairs to Selena's room.

"What was all that about?" asked Whelan. "Why did you say she hadn't regained consciousness, and we both know he was lying about not seeing anyone. Why did you let him get away with it?"

"Good questions," said Leishke, who was considering how much to tell the man, who appeared to be more than just another client of Selena's. He seemed genuinely concerned for her and deserved truthful answers.

"I didn't tell him she had gained consciousness, and you shouldn't either. I also asked the nurses at St. Ann's to keep that information private. So long as it is believed that she remains insensible, the man who attacked won't feel the need to finish the job."

He ignored Whelan's gasp, and continued, "I think it's clear that the clerk was somehow coerced into lying about seeing the attacker. It doesn't really matter because I know who did this. It just confirms my belief that one of the common tools used by this killer is bribery."

"Did you say killer?" asked Mr. Whelan. "Is this the same man who killed those women in Douglas?"

"I believe it is, but I'm trusting that you won't share that information with anyone – anyone," the deputy marshal said. "If that information becomes known, Miss Dowling's life will be in more danger, as well as the lives of other people."

The men had reached Selena's room and Whelan produced his key. Inside, the detritus of the torture that Selena Dowling had endured was evident. Bloody bedding, torn bits of rope still attached to the bed frame, and the lingering smell of blood and burning flesh presented a picture of the horrors that had occurred earlier that day.

"You said you heard a door close," said Leishke. "Did you see anyone else in the hall?"

"No, and I looked. I didn't see anyone in the hall until I answered the door to the ambulance crew."

Leishke walked over to the door that connected to the neighboring room. "Could it have been this door?" he asked.

"Yes," agreed Mr. Whelan. "But the other room's door is usually locked in hotels, isn't it?"

"But not this door," said Leishke, opening both doors and revealing the undisturbed hotel room beyond. "How do you think this happened?"

"I had paid for this adjoining room for a friend of Selena's last week, but she was only in the hotel for a night or two and left several days ago. So, I would have thought the hotel would have locked the door when she checked out."

"Hmmm. Did you know anything about this friend of Miss Dowling's? Was it another young woman? Did you ever see her?"

"No, I know it was another woman, but don't know anything else. I never saw her. I paid for the room as a favor to Miss Dowling, but never met her friend. But, again, don't you think the hotel would have ensured the room was locked?"

"It's possible that the clerk downstairs was paid for more than just keeping his mouth shut," said Leishke.

Leishke carefully searched the room, in hopes that the assailant's quick exit had meant he left something behind. As he looked, he marveled that Selena Dowling was still alive, if indeed she was. The amount of blood on the bedding, the torn clothing and, most of all, the lingering stench made it seem that someone must have died here. He was carefully going through the bedding when he found the knife sheath. The knife was missing, but the sheath not only remained, but had some distinctive tool work on its leather. He took it to the window to examine it more closely and saw what he thought might be the initial J worked into the scroll work, along with a six-cornered star. He slid the sheath into his pocket and returned to the search but didn't find anything else he could consider a clue.

While he had searched, Whelan had sat on a chair in the adjoining room, seeming overwhelmed by the scene of his paramour's torture. When Leishke was done, he went into the room where Whelan sat, and told him he was leaving.

"Did you find anything?" Whelan asked, looking, and sounding exhausted.

"Maybe," said Leishke. "I'm done here and I was going to head back to my office. Do you want to remain here or...?"

"I guess I'll go back up to the hospital," replied Whelan. "I ... I'm not really sure. I've been just sitting here thinking. When I took up with Selena, I surprised myself. I didn't think I would ever find myself thinking that way toward anyone other than my wife. And I thought it would be a ... transaction. Just that – a transaction. I didn't expect to develop feelings for her. But I've been here thinking about her, and I know that I do have feelings for her. What do I do now?"

Leishke didn't think he had ever before been asked for advice about matters of the heart. He considered his response carefully. This was a well-known and respected local businessman who was confessing his love for a woman of the underworld, and one who was Alaska Native. He found himself hoping for just a second that she would die – it would be hurtful initially but could also save this man a lot of hurt. Then, he reconsidered. His feelings toward May had awakened a new awareness of the power of passion, and of feeling an unremitting desire for someone. He knew if something had happened to her like it had happened to Selena that he would be broken by it.

"I know little of such matters," he said. "But Juneau is still a pretty remote community with lots of unconventional people and relationships. If this young woman is that important to you, then I would recommend seeking a permanent and public alliance with her. There will be talk, but you have a strong position here and it will eventually die down. If you want to pursue this, I think you should."

Whelan looked initially surprised, and then grateful. He stood and held out his hand. "Thank you. If she will have me, I hope you will stand with me."

Leishke didn't understand at first what he was asking, and then realized he was being invited to be part of a wedding party. He bit back his first response, which would have questioned whether the to-be bride would live to be married. Instead, he shook Whelan's hand. "I would be honored."

***

May got back to the Opera House at midday, just as breakfast was being cleared away. Quickly tying on her apron, she assisted Olga and the new cook, Mrs. Sherwood, as they cleaned. As they were finishing up, Mrs. Montgomery entered and asked to speak with May.

The meeting was in Mrs. Montgomery's office. She sat, as usual, behind her lovely desk – a fine piece of furniture that was definitely not made in Alaska. The lacquered wood surface perched on top of four slender curved legs. Her chair was of a matching design, and may not be comfortable, but was certainly attractive.

Mrs. Montgomery was her usual pragmatic self, although her light makeup didn't fully hide the circles under her eyes. It reminded May that Mrs. Todd had been a longtime employee of the brothel's madam.

"How are you?" May asked, and then wondered if the question was a bit presumptuous.

"I am fine. Thank you for asking. I'm sorry to interrupt your working day, but I learned something recently that I hope you can tell me more about," said Mrs. Montgomery.

"Oh?" asked May.

"Yes. One of the girls was telling me about a conversation she had with Fannie Miller while she and Rosie lived here. They were here for a few months before getting their own cabins. I can't recall if you were here then, but I think so."

"Yes, in fact we all three arrived here within a week of each other."

"I was hoping that was the case," said the madam. "Were you close enough with them to learn anything of their past?"

"Some of it," said May, cautious about giving away too much. She couldn't understand Mrs. Montgomery's interest in this. She had always made it clear to May that personal privacy was essential for anyone working at the Opera House – it is rare for any of the working girls to reveal much of their pasts, except possibly to each other.

"Can you tell me what you learned?" asked Mrs. Montgomery, then, possibly realizing her question had been too abrupt, she added, "I don't trust the federal marshals to try to find Rosie's family and wanted to be sure they were informed of her unfortunate death."

May wondered why Mrs. Montgomery hadn't asked her these questions last week, shortly after Rosie's death, but thought that Mrs. Todd's murder may have, understandably, been too distracting. She thought about her reply. She wanted to give enough information but not too much. "I did learn something about both girls," she said. "They were both Polish, although Rosie was from Russia and Fannie was from Germany. And they were both Jewish, but I think you know that."

Mrs. Montgomery nodded, motioning for May to continue.

"I'm not sure I know much more," said May. "Except I think that Rosie's real name was Jennie Poplosky, I think that's right."

"Thank you. Did you hear where the two met?"

"Yes," said May. "They met in San Francisco and then traveled to Anchorage together." Mrs. Montgomery had a pen and pad of paper and was taking some notes as May spoke. She glanced up. "Do you know how they met?"

"I think they were working at the same establishment," May replied.

"And do you know how both arrived at their occupation? Was that in San Francisco also?"

May hesitated. She couldn't tell the truth, but maybe she could tell part of it.

"I think they said they had come to San Francisco from someplace in South America?"

Mrs. Montgomery's attention was now fully engaged. "South America? Was it Buenos Aires?"

May was startled by Mrs. Montgomery's response. She seemed much more interested in this answer than any other. The women's families weren't in South America. So why was the madam so interested?

"I'm not sure," she decided to reply. "Maybe."

May thought she might have revealed too much and told Mrs. Montgomery that was all she knew. Mrs. Montgomery sent her back to work.

Chapter 26

When Harry, Jane's older son, arrived at the kitchen door that evening, May was ready. She hadn't been able to send a note to Leishke, but believed he would meet anywhere she chose if he could talk with Fannie.

"Tell her to meet us at the Juneau Lutheran Church at 5 p.m.," she told the boy. "I've also got a note for you to give to Deputy Marshal Frank Leishke at the courthouse. If he isn't there, slide it under his office door. It's on the second floor."

She gave the boy a day-old cinnamon roll and sent him on his way, hoping he hadn't been followed.

May had chosen the Lutheran Church because it was near the courthouse, and only a block from the B.M. Behrends Bank. She guessed that if Fannie could go to and from the bank without being detected, she could do the same at the church. It wouldn't be dark at 5 p.m., but the church had a family gathering that evening at 6 p.m., so she knew the church would be unlocked at 5 p.m., and while there may be a few people there, they should be able to find a quiet place to talk.

Leishke had spent a futile afternoon, evening and much of the night yesterday looking for Kilburn, Againsky or Andersen. They weren't at the boarding houses in Juneau or Douglas, and Mrs. Furnace, at the Douglas boarding house, had no record of a Mr. Kilburn boarding with her, so he had lied to May, which wasn't a surprise. He also couldn't locate them in any saloons or hotels. No one with those names had purchased steamship tickets. He described them to the Douglas ferry skippers, in hopes that they would be seen on a ferry. He enlisted Davies' help, who was also unable to find any evidence of any of the three. Unfortunately, there were enough small boarding houses to make a real search difficult. There were also plenty of small charter boats that could easily whisk the men away from Juneau and Douglas altogether.

Leishke had also talked to the mining supervisors in Treadwell and learned that there had been a miner employed there named Kilburn, but he was fired after only a week when he got into an argument with his boss and knocked the man out.

"It was no loss to any of us to fire the man – it was last week, sometime," said the supervisor at the 700 Mine. "I don't think he is missed by anyone."

This morning, Leishke had typed up his notes and given his report to Marshal Calhoun. He told the Marshal that he wanted to begin a public search for the two men. Providing their descriptions to the newspaper and offering a reward for their arrest were effective tools that had been used in the past, most notably with Edward Krause, the killer who had abducted two Juneau men, which had led indirectly to Leishke coming up to Alaska.

Marshal Calhoun, however, was unconvinced that such lengths were necessary. His interest continued to appear to be appeasing local politicians. Putting out a public plea for the three men would make the marshal service look like it couldn't handle the job, he said. He reminded Leishke that the reward for Krause's arrest was paid for by the fraternal organizations to which two of his victims belonged, not by the territorial government.

Leishke had argued as best he could, saying he believed a reward and public appeal could wind up the case in a few days. Without it, he told Calhoun, he was afraid the men would escape the region altogether. Looking at Calhoun's face after making that statement, he realized that Calhoun hoped for exactly that outcome. The Marshal wanted Againsky, Kilburn, and Petersen to just be gone, and not arrested. An arrest would lead to a trial, and the topic of the women of the underworld in Douglas would continue to be on the front pages of territorial newspapers for months to come.

He left the meeting feeling discouraged – not just with this case but with his future as a deputy marshal. As a Pinkerton detective, he realized there was often an agenda for his investigation that was dictated by the agency's client, but the machinations of local politics didn't reach his level in the organization. It was now clear to him that as a deputy marshal, he would also work at the whim of the head marshal, as well as the local city council, mayor, police or all four.

Leishke returned to his office to review his notes. He had checked with the jailer, and discovered with no sense of surprise whatsoever that Againsky wore a size 10 boot, matching the size of the print he had found in Douglas. Now, he recalled that the print had also shown a missing tread on the boot; amidst the past few days' events, he had forgotten to check Againsky's boot tread. A missed opportunity – he cursed softly.

He had talked to the coroner about the autopsy of Mrs. Todd's body. There were no surprises there. She had been strangled by a window sash cord. Two of her fingernails were broken; Leishke wondered if she had injured her assailant in the struggle, but there was no other evidence of her fighting back. He guessed she had been surprised by an attack from behind.

Leishke's musings were interrupted by a knock at his door, and he opened it to Deputy Marshal Rhys Davies.

"Frank?" the young man inquired. "I was hoping to catch you today. I've found out some more about the Petersburg suspect."

"Sit down," said Leishke, stifling his impatience. He had hoped to begin today's search for Againsky and his confederates. "What have you discovered?"

"I'm not sure, but I think he may actually know Againsky."

"What?" exclaimed Leishke, feeling himself jolting upright. "Who told you that? Tell me everything."

"I had gone back to the Opera House to talk to the women there again about the man who had threatened them," said Davies. "One of the girls told me that he had seen him talking on a ferry run from Douglas to Juneau with a man who sounds like he answers Againsky's description. They were standing outside, so she didn't hear what they said, but she thought they knew each other. And she said she saw them leave the ferry together."

"That is very ... interesting," said Leishke, wondering if Againsky had a third confederate. It seemed a little unlikely, given his short time in Juneau and his need for confidentiality. Then, he had another thought. What if Kilburn was the Petersburg suspect? He hadn't asked for a physical description from May because she had told him a name and an address. Leishke had assumed he would have no trouble finding him. What if May had described a big man with dark hair and a goatee? He needed to ask her as soon as possible.

"Let's break up our tasks for the rest of the day," he told Davies. "I need to check on Selena Dowling's condition, and I think we should both focus on finding these sons of bitches."

Rhys looked a little surprised at the profanity, but the severity of Leishke's face made it clear he would not appreciate being questioned on the topic. "I can take the boarding houses and places in Douglas, if you like," he said.

"Sounds good. I'm going up to St. Ann's Hospital and then will go back to the saloons and as many boarding houses as I can find. Let's also both check at the harbors for any charter boats who may have carried the men from here. Just ask if there were men of their description seeking charters. After all, a tall blonde fellow, a burly man with a goatee and the third man with a mustache and curly dark hair are pretty unusual, right?"

"I guess?" said Rhys, then realized that Leishke had actually tried to joke. "Oh, you mean there are a lot of men who look like these suspects? You are right – everyone has a mustache, many have goatees, and there are a lot of Scandinavian miners and fishermen. I think what might be less typical is seeing all three together."

"Right," Frank agreed. "I think finding a witness who has seen two or three of these men together is going to be easier to locate than anyone seeing just one of them. Let's focus our attention today on that. Maybe we'll have better luck."

The men separated at the door; Rhys to walk down toward the ferry dock, and Leishke toward St. Ann's Hospital.

At the hospital, he was pleased and more than a little surprised to hear that Selena Dowling was still alive. Her condition had deteriorated, however, and as yesterday's nurse had predicted, she was now scheduled for chest surgery. He reiterated the need to keep her condition confidential and left to begin his inquiries.

• • •

May dressed carefully for the evening's meeting at the Lutheran Church. She had picked out the seam stitches of her walking dress on the right side, below the waist a few inches. She put on the dress and saw that the heavy material pulled the skirt straight, closing the seam when her hand wasn't in it. Her hand touched her upper thigh; she realized she would need to buckle the knife outside her bloomers so she could reach it.

She slipped on her chemise, corset, and bloomers, then the knife belt. She had to wear it at an uncomfortable tightness to ensure it didn't slide down. She decided to tie a strip of fabric around the belt and then around her waist to keep it in place. She walked a few steps, trying to become accustomed to the uncomfortable feel of the knife and its harness. Slipping her hand through the opening in her dress, she found the knife in the perfect location to be grasped. As long as she was careful when she sat so the seam didn't gap open, it seemed like an excellent form of protection. She silently thanked Frank Leishke.

After telling Mrs. Starling that she was again going to be out late, she made her way to the ferry and over to Juneau. She walked up Main Street to the Lutheran Church, which was across the street from the courthouse. It was early – about 4:30 p.m., but the next ferry would have made her late for the meeting. It was still broad daylight; the sun wouldn't set until about 8 p.m. The light, and the number of people on the streets on this fine spring evening made her feel safe. She was beginning to think her earlier tailoring was unnecessary.

As she crossed the street toward the church, however, a man grasped her arm, as if assisting her to cross. She instinctively pulled away, but his grasp just tightened. Looking around, she saw Kilburn, again smiling that chilling smile she had seen the day before.

"Why, Mrs. Svenson, I think you may have lied to me yesterday. I heard from several of my acquaintances that the marshals have been looking for me since I last saw you. Is it possible you told someone about our encounter?" As he spoke, he was guiding her toward another alley, this one between the church, which was a large log building, and its neighbor, another log building that May thought was a store.

Once again, she found herself in a narrow, dark alley behind some refuse bins, which hid both of them from the street. Again, her mouth was covered and his arm around her neck. She knew her trick of pretending to faint was not going to work. Her right hand moved cautiously toward the open seam in her skirt.

"I really don't appreciate being lied to, especially by a self-righteous bitch," said Kilburn. As his arm tightened against her throat, May feared she may genuinely faint from lack of air. Kilburn thrust his pelvis against her stomach, and she could feel his arousal, which served to add to her sense of lightheadedness.

She forced herself to breathe as deeply as could, as her hand found the knife handle.

"I think you deserve to be taught a lesson," Kilburn said. "It's the kind of lesson that every married woman should have already learned, so I expect you to cooperate."

As he spoke, she could feel his yanking at his pants fly. She now had a firm grasp on the knife, which she eased from its sheath. As he began lifting her skirts, she pulled out the knife, bit the hand covering her mouth, and stabbed.

The knife entered at the top of his thigh, near his hip. He gasped, dropping her skirts and the arm against her neck. She didn't hesitate but pulled the knife from his leg – finding it surprisingly difficult to yank out from his muscle and turned toward the street to run.

Kilburn tried to grab her, but she twisted her arm away and escaped; she heard a grunt and thud behind her. As she reached the end of the alley, she looked behind her and saw that he had fallen to the ground. The blood from the wound was now evident on his pant leg, and he appeared to be fumbling to close his fly.

She turned back to the street and looked into the gray eyes of Frank Leishke.

Chapter 27

Leishke had gotten back to his office at about 4:30 p.m. and found May's note under his door. He had had a frustrating afternoon – unable to locate Againsky or either of his confederates, the only good news was that Selena Dowling had survived the surgery, although her survival was still an open question.

Rhys Davies had returned to the office at the same time he did, and the two men were going to the Lutheran Church for the meeting with Fannie when he heard a cry and footsteps from the adjoining alley. He waved Davies into the church, while he went down to investigate the noises and there was May.

She saw him, gave a small smile and then, as he came closer, leaned her head against his chest and put her arms around him. Learning from his late response to her last embrace, Leishke encircled her with his arms, and felt her collapse completely against him.

"That man – the one who grabbed me yesterday. He just did it again. He's in that alley – Kilburn? I stabbed him. Thank you for the knife. You told me to take out the skirt seam, and that worked. I think...he was going to violate me."

As she spoke, Leishke yelled for Davies, who had just poked his head out the door of the church to see where Leishke was. Lifting May in his arms, he told Davies to check on the man in the alley but warned him that he was probably armed. Davies pulled out his gun and approached the alley, while Leishke carried May into the church.

A large bench sat in the narthex, between the outer doors of the church and the inner doors of the sanctuary. Frank sat on it, placing May in his lap, in a close embrace. She had stopped babbling during the walk but began again after a minute or so.

Tears streaming down her face, she said, "It was the same man. I know it was. He told me that I had lied to him, and that I had to be taught a lesson. He put his arm against my throat again, and then began ... began...."

Frank patted her back clumsily and tried to think of soothing words. They did not come naturally; if a colleague had acted like that, he would have told him to snap out of it. Frank didn't think that was a suitable response in this situation. He said instead, "It appears that you took care of yourself. I'm very proud of you. You did an excellent job." Even as he spoke, he could hear his stilted tone.

The awkwardness of his response seemed to pull May out of herself, however. With a watery chortle, she lifted her face from Frank's shoulder, and he instantly missed the contact.

"I did an excellent job?" she asked. "Thank you?"

He looked down at her face, tear stained, but smiling, and found himself leaning toward her. She met his mouth with her own, and the initial contact was as awkward as his speech. Their teeth clashed, and May let out a brief "ow," but they both persevered, turning their chins for a better fit.

May had experienced such kisses from only one man in her life before this moment. Frank's experience was certainly greater, but the embrace seemed to have surprised both of them in equal measure. After an immeasurable time, Frank lifted his head and stared at her.

He was at a loss.

Rhys Davies broke the spell they were both under. He had thrust open the doors, grasping a handcuffed Kilburn, whose hip was still bleeding sluggishly. It was apparent he was standing only due to Davies's strength.

"So, do I take him to the hospital or the jail, Frank?" Davies asked, obviously unaware of the encounter he was interrupting.

Leishke stared at him for a moment or two, still lost in the recent kiss. May poked him in the side, obviously not quite as affected.

"The jail," he said. "Take him to jail. We'll have the doctor see him there. If he has to go to the hospital, one of the deputies will need to go with him."

"I need to go to the hospital," Kilburn almost yelled. "I think I'm bleeding to death. That bitch there," he gestured toward May, "just attacked me. I've never seen her in my life. I am the victim here. She is the one who should go to jail."

As Kilburn said "bitch," Frank had carefully set May next to him on the bench and stood, walking over to the prisoner. Without saying a word, he hit Kilburn in the jaw, sending him down to the floor and out cold.

"He deserved that, but it certainly makes hauling him across the street harder," said Davies. Looking at Frank as if seeking his assistance, he apparently realized that wasn't going to happen.

"I'll leave him here and step across the street for some help," he said.

As he left, the Lutheran pastor stepped from behind the sanctuary's closed door into the scene. He was joined shortly by his assistant, and a couple of parishioners, and the narthex became a crowd of people exclaiming and asking questions that Frank was hard pressed to answer. He kept his eye on May, who seemed more amused than shaken by the situation.

May was enjoying seeing Leishke appearing somewhat rattled when she realized the time. It was now past 5 p.m., and Fannie should have arrived. She stood and walked over to Frank. Reaching up on her tiptoes, she pulled his arm and he obligingly leaned down.

"Fannie should have been here by now," she whispered in his ear.

He checked his pocket watch. "Yes," he agreed quietly. "But the hullabaloo right now could very well have discouraged her from entering the building."

"Maybe," May agreed. "But I'm worried for her, especially after what just happened to me. What should we do?"

Their conversation had not gone unnoticed, especially since Frank had been trying to respond to the many questions about the hand-cuffed unconscious man on the floor.

"I'm afraid that I must ask you to explain yourself. Now," said the pastor, a newcomer to Juneau who apparently did not recognize the deputy marshal.

"It's a matter for the federal marshals," Frank told him. "I'm a deputy marshal and this man is under arrest. He will be removed from the premises shortly." He looked at Kilburn, whose leg was now being tended to by a parishioner. He was pressing a cloth to the wound on his leg. Frank recognized the good Samaritan as one of the territorial governor's assistants. Obviously, a man of good sense, he was the only bystander, including the pastor, who was actually doing something useful.

Davies again burst through the doors, this time with another deputy marshal and a stretcher. Telling Frank only that he had sent for a doctor, Davies and the other deputy loaded Kilburn, who was now conscious and cursing, onto the stretcher and bore him to the courthouse.

Frank and May thanked the pastor and the congregants and departed, leaving behind several frustrated people still teeming with questions.

May realized that she was holding Frank's arm as they walked past the courthouse. It was the same way she had held her late husband's arm the day they arrived in Douglas. For a moment, she wondered if she was being disloyal to Albert. Her grip slackened for a moment, and Frank looked down at her. She smiled at him and grasped his hard bicep even firmer as she told herself that she knew Albert wouldn't have expected her to grieve his loss for the remainder of what she hoped would be a long life. Albert was a man who had embraced all aspects of his life and would have wanted the same for her.

"Where are we going?" May asked.

"To my house," Frank replied, and May realized that she had hoped that was the answer.

Frank's cabin was only two blocks from the church, and as they walked into the small house, May realized she felt completely comfortable with whatever happened next. A large part of her was hoping that the next part would be something that no self-respecting widow should welcome.

But, as Frank slowly unbuttoned her jacket, pushed her carefully into a chair, and then kneeled in front of her to remove her walking boots, she simply smiled. She leaned forward, unbuttoning his jacket, vest and then shirt, as if she had done this hundreds of times before. The kiss they exchanged as he knelt there seemed just as inevitable and natural, as did the ensuing joining on the very large bed in the small bedroom.

It was more than an hour before May realized that her mind had completely lost track of its concern over Fannie.

"Oh, my goodness," she sat up, dislodging Frank, who had drifted asleep next to her, one arm across her and a leg pinning her down.

He grunted, and reluctantly opened his eyes. "What's wrong?" he said, somewhat perfunctorily. Everything appeared very right to him, for a change.

"Fannie," said May. "What about Fannie?"

At her question, Frank realized he had one of his own, and felt it was definitely more pertinent.

"Are you a widow, May?" he asked, lifting himself up against the headboard, and suddenly feeling very awake.

"Of course," she replied. "Do you think I would have kissed you and done this?" she gestured between them, "if my husband were alive? What kind of woman do you think I am?"

"That is excellent news," replied Frank, leaning over to kiss her bare shoulder. "And I think you're the best kind of woman. Now, what was your question again?"

May was momentarily nonplussed at the idea that Albert's death was "excellent news," but then remembered her concern for Fannie.

"Fannie!" she exclaimed. "Where is she? Has something happened to her? Is Againsky still loose? How could I have forgotten?"

"May," said Frank calmly, rubbing May's back. "I think she's probably fine. But we should go to where she is and find out. Are you ready to tell me where she's been hiding?"

Fannie shut her eyes. She would never have gotten into bed with a man she didn't trust, but the issue wasn't just who she trusted. She also had to be Fannie's voice in this decision. Fannie had agreed to the meeting, though, so maybe she would be all right with her taking Frank to Jane's home.

"I'm not sure," she said. "Let me think for a minute."

Frank waited, while also feeling a little sad for himself. It was clear that they would not be remaining in bed for much longer. As he thought that, May pushed back the bedding, and stepped over to the chair where her clothes lay. The fading daylight entered the window and he would see her clearly as she dressed. He gave a heavy sigh and stood up to dress himself.

Chapter 28

Fannie had arrived at the Lutheran Church just as a man came out from a nearby alley, appearing to be almost carrying another man who was bleeding from a wound on his upper leg. After pausing for a moment to look at the spectacle, she continued walking. She again held the hand of a child – this time it was George, who was not very fond of holding hands with anyone but was also obedient to his mother's commands.

"I thought we were going over there," George pointed to the church.

"We were, but I'm worried that now might not be a good time. You and I are going to walk around the block and see what we can see," she replied.

The news of Selena's attack, which Fannie had heard about from Jane earlier that day, had made what she knew was going to be a worrying outing even more concerning. She knew her nerves were on edge, and welcomed the comfort of George's hand, despite knowing his clear resistance to the contact.

The two turned at the corner to walk past the church, now putting themselves in front of the courthouse. They kept walking, turning at the next corner to walk behind the church. A few minutes later, they were again nearing the church, and saw two men coming out of the courthouse with a stretcher and entering the church.

"Oh, my God," gasped Fannie. "Is May hurt?" She and George kept walking, glancing toward the church. The stretcher came out again, but with the injured man on it. Fannie saw no sign of May and decided she had seen enough. She got a firmer grasp on George's hand and headed back down the hill to the Village.

"Where are we going?" asked George.

"We're going back to your house. I've seen enough. Now is not a good time to be meeting with anyone at the church."

As they walked toward the Douglas ferry dock, before turning right to go toward the Village, George tugged on her hand. She learned toward him.

"I see him," he whispered. "But don't look."

Fannie obeyed him and tugged her large hat a little closer toward her face.

"Who?" she whispered back.

"The man who followed me when I went over to Douglas to give your friend a message."

"What!" Fannie hissed. "You didn't say anything about being followed."

"I had almost forgotten about it," said George. "I was very clever, and he ended up following my cousin Joe instead and my uncle told him off."

"This sounds like an excellent story. Tell me the whole thing later," said Fannie. "Can you still see him? What does he look like?"

"He's dark with a big mustache. He's looking this way, but I don't think he is really seeing us. I think he's watching the ferries."

Fannie shuddered. She just knew it was Againsky. She was grateful for her hat, for George and for the street that separated her from the man. "I think we just need to keep walking, and to pretend nothing is wrong," she said quietly. "I'm going to let go of your hand and you're going to pick up the stick in front of us and start poking at things. That will let you keep an eye on him as we keep walking."

"What a good idea," said George, happy to let go of Fannie's hand, especially since he had felt it begin to tremble through her glove. He grabbed the stick and began hitting the new grass, skunk cabbage and wild celery spouting next to the wooden sidewalk. As he did, he kept an eye on the bad man. George's actions had caught his attention, but it was fleeting. George was suddenly glad that he hadn't worn his favorite jacket today; the one with the eagle embroidered on it. When Joe finally returned it, it was dirty and a pocket needed mending, so his mom had taken it from him for cleaning and repair. Today, he was wearing a hand-me-down jacket of his brother's that was still a little large.

The man's eyes now turned to follow the ferry, which was just pulling into the dock. George saw a tall blonde man step off the boat and join the bad man. The two walked toward the steamship dock.

"I think we're safe," he told Fannie. "He and a friend are walking toward the steamship dock."

Fannie stopped and turned, seeing a man she recognized as Againsky, even from the back, next to a tall, blonde man. She thought it was the man who had chased her and Selena on her first trip to the Village. He turned his face toward Againsky, and she recognized the overly elaborate mustache. He was the same man. She was doubly grateful for the man in the Village who had knocked their pursuer down.

Once back at her temporary lodging, Fannie told Jane what had happened. She also asked George to tell of his adventure with Againsky. She couldn't help but smile at the trick that George and Joe had played on "the bad man," as George called him. The incident heightened her concern about Jane's family and what could happen to them from Fannie's choices. Dinner plates had been kept in the oven for George and her, but she declined food. Leaving George happily eating at the table, Fannie told Jane that she was going to lie down for a few minutes and retreated to the bedroom she shared with Sally. She was lying there when she heard a knock on the kitchen door. Jane answered, and she heard two new voices – her friend, May, and a man's voice.

Her first instinct was to run, but May sounded calm, and very much like her usual self. Fannie crept to the bedroom door and opened it just a crack so she could see into the kitchen. Jane was there, along with May and the detective, Leishke. George and the other children were gone. She opened the door and entered the kitchen.

"Oh, Fannie," exclaimed May, rushing to give her a hug. "I was so worried when I didn't see you at the church. What happened? Why weren't you there?"

"Before I answer that," replied Fannie. "Why did you bring that man here? I thought we had agreed to keep Jane's home and family out of this. It's bad enough that Againsky almost saw me today. If he finds out I'm here ... bad things could happen to everyone."

Leishke had been startled to hear the reference to Againsky, and opened his mouth to interrogate Fannie about it, but looked again at Fannie and May. The two young women were obviously good friends; he suspected that May would have much more success getting information from Fannie than he would.

"You saw Againsky?" asked May, unknowingly confirming Frank's belief in her. "Where ... and when?"

"I'll tell you that later. Tell me about that man near the church – the one whose leg was bleeding," said Fannie.

May described her abduction, and her defense. She was showing Fannie the opening in her dress seam, and how she could reach the knife if it were there (she had left it at Frank's house), when Leishke interrupted her.

"I'm sorry to interrupt, Miss Miller, but can you tell me where you saw Againsky? I've been looking for him and his confederates for some time now. Any information you have about his whereabouts would be helpful," said Leishke.

"Today, it was at the Juneau side of the ferry dock – and I think I saw him joined by one of his 'confederates,'" Fannie replied. "A tall blonde man came off the ferry from Douglas and they walked together toward the steamship dock."

"This is very helpful," said Leishke, silently cursing the Douglas ferry boat skippers for paying such little attention to the information the marshals gave them. He then continued:

"Would you be willing, Miss Miller, to tell me what brought you and your friend, Miss Poplosky, to Juneau?"

Fannie looked at him. Jane had excused herself a few minutes ago, saying she was going to go visit her sister, where the children were also. Her husband had begun his 12-hour shift in the afternoon, so wouldn't be expected home until late tonight. She didn't want Jane and the children to think they couldn't return home, so she decided to tell Leishke all she knew as quickly as possible and then let Jane know she could return.

"I'll tell you," she told Leishke. "You must promise me, though, that you will keep my host and hostess out of your investigation. They know nothing of this but have simply been helping a stranger out due to kindness." She didn't tell him of the relationship between Selena and Jane; the least said there, she thought, the better for Selena.

The three sat at the kitchen table – the center of this close and warm family – and she told Leishke the same story she had told May. Under his skilled questioning, she provided a more thorough description of Againsky, and also told him of being chased by a tall blonde man who she had seen just today with Againsky. She ended with her plans to leave on the next steamship. When she said that, Leishke shook his head.

"I can't let you leave town until we bring Againsky to trial," he said. "But I will be arresting him soon – hopefully, today – and you won't need to worry anymore about him hurting you."

"I don't think so," said Fannie. "You might have him in jail, but you've already seen that it is easy for him to buy people to help him." She pointed toward May, who had sat silently during the interview, occasionally patting Fannie's hand, and once getting up to make them all some tea.

"Frank will keep you safe," said May. "You can stay with me until the trial is over." As she said it, she realized that she wasn't sure her landlady would agree with this proposal. If she had to find another room, she could do so. She also thought that Mrs. Montgomery would help. After all, she had been so concerned about informing Rosie's family of her death.

"But that could mean weeks without work," said Fannie. Then, anticipating May's next comments, she added, "and you can't pay for my keep. Besides, I don't want to share a room with anyone. I've been on my own too long. I just want to be able to leave and continue with my life."

"We both understand," said Leishke, and he looked at May in a way that made Fannie think she may have missed something.

She realized that his chair was just a bit too close to May's, and May seemed to be hiding a blush at his look. She told herself she would be asking May about that later.

Now, she had to find a way to convince the deputy marshal to let her go.

"I can't stay; I never promised I would do that. I didn't even want to have this meeting with you but May convinced me of the need. I am not going to testify against this man – you mean speak in an open courtroom with him sitting there looking at me? No, I absolutely cannot do that." She spoke so firmly that Leishke knew he had little chance of changing her mind.

He stood. His next act was not going to be a popular one, but he saw no other course.

"I'm arresting you, Fannie Miller, and charging you with perjury. You lied to the coroner's jury about your knowledge of a suspect in the murder of Rosie Brown," he said, pulling out his handcuffs.

The women had been struck initially with silence, but Frank looked at them both and knew this wasn't going to last.

Their ensuing exclamations and complaints were oddly similar.

"How dare you?" from May, was followed by "You dare to do this!" from Fannie. "Putting her in jail can't make her talk," said May, while Fannie said at the same time, "staying in a jail cell is just going to ensure my silence."

He ignored them as best he could but knew looking at May that this arrest was not going to help their budding relationship. He couldn't see an alternative – Fannie would be safe, and he hoped would become more compliant in the harsh conditions of the jail.

Leishke had rarely arrested a woman, and knew the jail was not prepared for a female occupant. He would need to ensure there was a female jailer, which he knew would not be easily done. Once Againsky was arrested, though, Leishke was convinced that Marshal Calhoun would be more supportive of all aspects of this arrest.

The three left the house, after May went the short distance to Jane's aunt's house to let the family know they were departing. Leishke planned to send for Fannie's trunk the following day; he thought the contents might give him more information to convince Fannie to remain, on her own, until the trial.

Chapter 29

As they walked from the Indian Village and up Main Street to the courthouse, Leishke realized they were all looking for Againsky by the ferry dock. There was no sign of him, however. Leishke wondered if he and Andersen were planning to leave town, or if they had gone to the steamship dock to look for Fannie. He suspected the latter.

When they entered the courthouse, it was almost 10 p.m., and the jail was shut down for the night, meaning the common secure area outside the small block of jail cells was vacant, and the large wheel that connected to all the cell doors was turned, closing, and locking all the cell doors. There were only two cells occupied; Leishke noticed that Kilburn was not in a cell. He must have been moved to the hospital. Leishke would be checking on him before retiring for the night. May gave her friend a fierce hug and he turned Fannie over to the jailer, asking for some accommodation for the female prisoner and quickly noting the intake information in the jail log.

As he and May left the building, he looked down at her. Her face was not happy; her lips were tightly shut and she looked up at him with a harsh glare. He bid farewell to his earlier hope that he could convince her to spend the night with him.

"I'm sorry," he said before she could utter the recriminations that he saw practically trembling on her lips. "I really didn't have a choice; she wasn't talking to me, and I didn't have the time I needed to bring her around. With Againsky and Andersen still not apprehended, she isn't safe." (And neither are you, he thought, keeping the words to himself). "But I hate leaving her at this horrible place," cried May. "Who knows what kind of riff raff she'll be exposed to? And there's no privacy, and no other women there. Surely there's a better solution."

"If there were, I would love to hear it," Frank said. "I know this isn't ideal, and I'll be talking to Marshal Calhoun tomorrow about getting a female warden." He didn't address the riff raff comment; he suspected that Fannie was accustomed to riff raff.

The two had stood outside the courthouse during the exchange. May now turned to go down Main Street to the ferry dock. "I must get to my boarding house. It's late and I have a full day tomorrow."

"I'll escort you home," said Frank.

"That isn't necessary," May said. "I have made my own way home dozens of times. I don't need your assistance."

"Perhaps not, but you'll have it," said Frank. "If I have my way, you'll be making very few walks in the future on your own." He grabbed her hand and tugged it up, against his bicep in the crook of his bent arm. She resisted initially, but then gave in.

The couple completed the walk, the ferry journey across the channel and the walk in Douglas to May's boarding house in silence.

May unlocked the boarding house door, and they stood in front of the darkened building. Frank bent and kissed May's cheek.

"I understand your anger, and appreciate your loyalty to your friend," he said quietly. "That loyalty is one of the many things that drew me to you. I will do everything I can to take care of her, but you must know it's because of how I feel about you."

"My feelings toward you are significant," he said. "Please remember that. I'll see you tomorrow." He pressed one more kiss on her cheek and squeezed her hand. He turned to go.

"Thank you," May whispered, and opened the door to enter the building.

• • •

Fannie was bewildered – how had she ended up here, in jail, when it seemed like a few minutes ago she had been so relieved to have finally told Rosie's story to the deputy marshal? She wondered about May. Had she been wrong to trust her friend? Did May know that Leishke would have gone to the lengths that he had obviously gone?

"No," she decided. May would not betray her like this. May had believed Leishke, and Fannie suspected May's feelings toward him may have influenced him in favor of his decision making.

So, now she was in a cell in the basement of the federal courthouse. There were two men also in the jail. Her entrance had excited their curiosity, but after it became clear their shouted questions and rude comments were receiving no response from Fannie, and just calls to "shut up" from the jailers, they had quieted down. Fannie knew at least one of them was asleep because of his loud snoring.

She had been placed in the cell furthest from them, so was against the outside wall on one side of her cell. The cell included a toilet, bunk, and sink. At Leishke's insistence, the jailer had put a small screen in front of the toilet to offer her some privacy.

Fannie washed briefly, used the toilet, and lay on the bunk. She expected to be unable to find sleep, but the stress of the past few hours caught up with her and she drifted off.

• • •

Leishke had made a brief visit to the hospital to check on both Miss Dowling and Kilburn. He talked to the night nurse in charge and found that Kilburn had needed stitches and it had been late enough when that minor surgery was done that the doctor asked to keep him for the night. Deputy Marshal Davies was in his room, guarding him, she said.

Selena Dowling was continuing to have a difficult recovery; the thoracic surgery had gone well but had revealed an infection from the lung puncture. She had a high fever and it was unclear if she would survive the night. One man had come by earlier that day asking for her – a tall, blonde-haired fellow, the night nurse said. He had been told she was very ill and had not been fully conscious since being brought to the hospital. Although the daily newspaper usually wrote an account of who was in the hospital, and why, nurses had continued to keep her presence there quiet.

Leishke had talked to Davies, telling him about arresting Fannie Miller, and that she had seen Againsky and Andersen together at the docks. He also told him he would be in early the next day to report the day's doings to Marshal Calhoun. Leishke promised to send Rhys a deputy marshal to relieve him in the morning.

When he walked into his cabin, it was close to midnight, and Frank was exhausted. He smiled, looking at the disheveled bed, and remembering what took place there earlier in the day. He was going to do his darndest to ensure that May would be back soon.

Chapter 29

Leishke arose early the next day and after a quick breakfast at the City Cafe, went into the courthouse with his usual tepid cup of coffee, planning to devote the next hour to typing up his notes. He was almost done when he was summoned to Marshal Calhoun's office.

As usual, Leishke pulled the slightly larger chair up to the marshal's desk. The weather had reverted to its usual gray skies, dropping rain so light as to seem like the faintest mist. Leishke knew he could get just as wet in that rain as in any other; it would just take a little longer.

"What can I do for you, sir?" he asked the marshal.

"I'm surprised I had to summon you, Leishke," Calhoun said. "I would have thought that arresting the murderer we've been searching for would be reason enough to seek me out this morning."

"Arrest the murderer?" asked Leishke.

"Yes. Davies was just in here telling me about the arrest last night. The doctor released the man this morning, and he's down in a jail cell where he belongs. The best part of this arrest is that it is really two birds with one stone – both the Douglas killer and the Petersburg killer in the same person. This really couldn't be better news. I've already summoned Douglas Commissioner Hensen to tell him. He should be here shortly, and I want you to be part of the conversation. After all, it was your work that led to this case being solved."

"You think it's been solved," commented Leishke. And then he caught on – the Marshal just wanted to close up the entire case. It had been all he had been looking for this past week. And Kilburn certainly made a good pawn.

"He is certainly involved in this case," Leishke told the marshal. "But he is not the killer – I am convinced that is Againsky. And I arrested a woman yesterday -- a friend of the prostitute killed in Douglas -- who will be a damning witness against Againsky."

"So, you're saying that you've broken the man's alibi?" asked Calhoun.

"No, I haven't, but ..."

"But nothing – if he has an alibi, he didn't do it. And I don't want a woman in my jail, even a woman of the underworld. I'll have the added expense of a female jailer, which is completely unnecessary. Why should we provide free room and board to some working girl?" Calhoun demanded. "The case is now officially closed. I'm happy to excuse you from my meeting with the Douglas commissioner. If Hensen has additional questions, I'll answer them myself."

Leishke was at a loss for words, and Calhoun took his silence as assent. He walked to his office door and told his secretary to come in to take dictation on some letters he wanted typed.

Leishke left and made his way back to his office. He had left the door unlocked and found Rhys inside, sitting while he waited.

"I can see from your face that you just met with Marshal Calhoun," Rhys said. "I tried to catch you before you talked to him. I think he has everything completely wrong, but I'm not sure what we can do about it."

"I'm not either," admitted Frank. "But I plan to find something. If we leave Againsky on the street, and I'm forced to release Fannie, she will almost certainly be his next victim."

Rhys agreed, and added, "I do believe that Kilburn may be the Petersburg attacker, and he is almost certainly the man who has been tormenting the working girls in Douglas, but that's not a good enough reason to put him away for the murders in Douglas."

"And the Douglas murders don't match the patterns of the Petersburg attack or what the women had been telling you," Frank noted. "Jennie Poplosky, or Rosie Brown, was killed by a hammer and knife. Mrs. Todd was strangled, but not in some fit of passion. It was simply a cold-blooded murder to shut up a possible witness."

Frank suddenly wondered – what had Mrs. Todd witnessed? He needed to ask Fannie, and maybe even May. Was Againsky at the Opera House the evening that the cook was killed? How could he have forgotten to focus more on the motive of this death?

Rhys brought him back to the present. "What can we do?"

Leishke smiled. "I have an idea," he said. "Why don't you just stay here for now? I'm going to try to waylay the Douglas commissioner, and I might need your help."

Davies ushered Commissioner Hensen into Frank's office about an hour later. The two men had been waiting for him – Frank had felt himself getting more anxious and frustrated as each minute ticked by. He was having to spend time on a political matter instead of doing what he needed to do – find Againsky.

Hensen took the chair that Frank offered and sat with a sigh.

"Why do I have the suspicion that you may not agree with Marshal Calhoun's decision to close this case?" he asked, assessing the deputy marshals. Frank was behind his desk, since there were only three chairs in the room, and Davies sat next to Hensen. Frank stood, picked up his chair and brought it around, so the three were in a close huddle. Both Davies and Leishke were in their shirt sleeves and looked intent.

"You are correct," said Leishke. "Neither of us agree with the Marshal's decision. We believe the man in jail – Kilburn – is a killer but is not the Douglas killer. More importantly, we believe that the real killer is still in Juneau because he's waiting to kill again."

"You have my attention," said Hensen. "Explain."

Leishke, with Davies's backup, told the story of Jennie and Fannie. Leishke described Mrs. Todd's death and the difference between her killing and Kilburn's usual attacks on women.

"This all seems somewhat farfetched," Hensen responded. "But I certainly wouldn't want to see more murders and you have proven yourself in the past. I'm willing to advocate for you with the Marshal. What are your next steps in solving this investigation, and – I can't emphasize this enough – you will have very little time. I doubt I'll be able to buy you more than a day or two."

"I don't know the connection between Kilburn and Againsky, but there is one," said Leishke. "My first task after this is to interview him and find out what I can. If you can convince the Marshal to give us two more days, I do believe we'll have this solved and the real murderer in custody."

Hensen stood. "I can do that. After all, it's my community that has been affected by this murder. I'm the one who calls the coroner's juries and will be in charge of the court hearings. If I don't move forward, neither can the Marshal." He smiled. "But I certainly know better than to tell Marshal Calhoun that. Especially since he already knows it." He left the office.

"That went much more easily than I expected," Frank told Rhys. "I'm going to go downstairs and get Kilburn for an interview. It would be good to have you with me, but I'm going to need you to keep looking for Againsky or Andersen. And I've had an idea about that. We know they've been seen at the docks, and I'm wondering if it's because they've given up boarding houses for boats."

"What do you mean?" asked Davies. "I don't think there's such a thing as a boarding boat."

"No," said Frank. "But there are boats that are vacant for extended periods. Perhaps Againsky is using one of those as a temporary place to live. Why don't you go talk to the harbormaster? Ask him if anyone has seen newcomers in the harbors and remember to ask him about seeing those two men together."

"Certainly," said Rhys. "I'll head down there right now. If I find them, do you want me to arrest them? I'm not sure I could handle both of them."

"No," agreed Frank. "Just get a word to me and I'll come assist. And in the meantime, watch them and, if you can get away with it, try to stay unnoticeable." He looked at Rhys, thinking that this stalwart young man's appearance screamed "federal marshal." "Well," he said. "I guess all you can do is try."

Leishke thought about checking in with Marshal Calhoun to see if the Douglas Commissioner had been successful in his efforts, then decided against it. Better to ignore the caged lion, rather than to poke it with a stick. He was going to continue as if he had been granted the reprieve. He noted that interviewing Kilburn was completely in keeping with Calhoun's decision to pin the murders on him.

Both Fannie and Kilburn were awake and had eaten breakfast. Fannie was sitting on her bed, hands on her lap, staring at the floor. Kilburn was lying on his bed, complaining of pain, and asking for medicine.

Leishke was pleased to see that the jailers were ignoring Kilburn and that Fannie was still safe in her cell. He was afraid that Calhoun may have already released her. He asked the jailers to assist him in getting Kilburn from his cell and up the stairs to the interview room. As the two jailers unlocked the door and prepared to lift Kilburn, Leishke went to Fannie's cell.

"How did you sleep?" he asked.

"All right," she replied. "But I'm still not inclined to remain in Juneau so I can attend a trial."

"I understand," said Leishke, who had been giving the matter of Fannie's presence in the Village some thought. "I'm wondering if you know what happened to Selena Dowling."

"Who?" asked Fannie, but her quick glance at his face had already given away her knowledge of the name.

"She's fighting for her life at St. Ann's after being beaten nearly to death by Againsky," replied Leishke. Fannie let out a small gasp, but he had no time to respond. He saw the jailers were on their way up the stairs with Kilburn between them. "You think about that," he told Fannie. "I'll be back to talk with you later."

He followed the jailers, knowing he had planted a seed with Fannie. He now wanted to give it room to grow.

In the interview room, he provided a chair for Kilburn to set his foot on, so the prisoner could extend his wounded leg. For someone who had not hesitated to throttle women, Kilburn was being awfully whiny about a few stitches in his thigh.

"How do you know Mr. Againsky?" asked Leishke. He had decided a direct approach might serve him best, and he had little time for his usual cautious approach. He also decided to set aside the Petersburg case and the complaints from the working girls. Those would be questions for another day.

"He's an acquaintance," said Kilburn. "We met on the steamship from Petersburg. He was coming up from Seattle, but I embarked in Petersburg. We ended up playing a game or two of cards. Why?"

"I am interested in talking to him about two murders in Douglas."

"Oh," said Kilburn. "I think I heard about those – they occurred a day or two after our steamship arrived?"

"Yes," said Leishke.

"Well, I don't see why Againsky would have anything to do with those. After all, he was only here because the steamship heading up north was delayed. He was en route to Anchorage."

"I also heard that," said Leishke. "But what we now know is that the woman he had expected to meet in Anchorage had moved to Juneau. And shortly after he found out she was here, she was dead," he added. "Againsky is not someone to spend time with; he will almost certainly get you in trouble. And in this instance, he already has."

"What do you mean?" asked Kilburn, as he winced and grabbed his leg, lowering his foot to the floor. "And hey, I've been asking for something for the pain all morning. That bi ..." he looked at Leishke's face, "woman who stabbed me really did some damage. The doctor had to give me seven stitches and said I may have permanent damage to my muscle. He said I might end up with a limp."

Leishke stopped himself from his first response, which was not a sympathetic one. Instead, he replied. "I'm not in charge of pain medication, but I'll say something to the jailers about it. But what I think you should know is that Againsky has pinned those Douglas murders on you. And our federal Marshal believes him. You are going to be indicted on two counts of first-degree murder."

Kilburn's shout of laughter surprised Leishke.

"What – that bastard is saying I killed those women? What the hell! I wouldn't know them if I saw them. Why would I do that? You can't really believe him; after all, he's a common pimp. Now, he had a motive to kill that first woman – the slut. She had stopped sending him money. I don't know about the second one, but I can tell you, I had nothing to do with it. With either of them. Where is the bastard? Why isn't he in a cell downstairs?"

At that question, Leishke thought, they finally agreed on something. He was pleased by Kilburn's response to his somewhat fabricated statement. It was only fabricated because Againsky wasn't present to cast the blame. Leishke was sure that Againsky would have been more than happy to throw Kilburn to the wolves.

"Mostly, he's not downstairs with you because we haven't seen him since getting his letter casting the blame on you," said Leishke, blithely adding to his fabrications. "We are also looking for another confederate of his, a Lars Andersen. Do you know where the two have been hiding?"

"Yes," said Kilburn. "They're sleeping aboard a boat in Douglas; it's docked down near Treadwell. It's named the *Lanie B.*; a bartender told us the owner of the boat was not due back until the beginning of next month. He was being paid to keep it pumped out and dry and offered to rent it to us for a couple of weeks. You can find the bastard – both bastards – there. I'm happy to tell you what you need. I refuse to be fingered for a crime I didn't commit."

"So," said Leishke. "Keep talking. What do you know about Againsky?"

"He was heading to Anchorage to collect this slut he had in his stable. He had sent her north from San Francisco a couple of years ago and all was fine until this past fall, when she stopped sending money or letters. He decided he was going to have to act and was heading north to bring her back into the fold."

"Did he say how he intended to do that?" asked Leishke.

"Nothing specific," was the reply. "But he had bragged about teaching some of his other whores lessons if they didn't do what he asked. So, this was nothing new to him. When I heard a Douglas whore had died, I thought that Againsky may have just gotten a little too 'enthusiastic' with his lessons. I understood, though –

you probably do too. You know you have to be firm with these sluts, or they don't respect you."

Leishke certainly didn't understand but didn't plan to get into an argument with this dreg of a human. Instead, he said, "What did he ask you to do? Why did you abduct Mrs. Svenson last night?"

Kilburn looked caught off guard for a moment. "He didn't really ask me to do anything," he said. Then, catching Leishke's glare, he added, "I mean it. He didn't ask me to, but I knew he was trying to find that other bitch, Fannie Miller, and Mrs. Svenson had told me when ... we met earlier, that Fannie owed her money. I thought she would be able to tell me where to find Fannie. Againsky had told me that if I gave him any information he could use, he would pay me. And he had the money; I think that whore he killed in Douglas must have had a lot of cash, because after her murder, Againsky had a big roll of bills."

"What did Againsky tell you about a woman named Selena Dowling?" asked Leishke.

"Not much," said Kilburn. "He just said that Dowling was a friend of Fannie's and he thought would tell him how to find her. But after he visited her, he said she was a waste of time."

Leishke was struck with the image of Selena as he saw her last night – unconscious, battered and bruised, fighting for her life. Againsky called his torture of her a 'waste of time.' He turned back to his interrogation.

"One last question," said Leishke. "Did Againsky know that Mrs. Svenson was connected to Fannie, or knew anything about her? Is Mrs. Svenson likely to be a target of Againsky's?"

Kilburn smiled, and Leishke realized that his fist to Kilburn's face last night had revealed Leishke's interest in May.

"I don't know," said Kilburn slowly. "Maybe, and maybe not. I can't remember if I told him about Mrs. Svenson being at the bank or not. If I did, though, I'm sure that Againsky would have been very interested. He is really desperate to get to Fannie Miller. I think he would do practically anything to find that bitch."

Leishke heard Kilburn laughing as he stalked from the interview room to direct the jailers to lock Kilburn back up. He, meanwhile, had the remaining jailer unlock Fannie's cell so he could escort her upstairs. They passed Kilburn on the stairs. He winked at Fannie and made a lewd comment but didn't appear to recognize her or call her by name. Leishke wondered if the jail was the safest place for Fannie now that there was a known confederate of Againsky's in the same place.

He walked her into the interview room and pulled out a chair for her. She sat, and he did the same. For the first minute or so, they looked at each other. Leishke had discovered that, in some circumstances, it was best for the suspect to begin an interrogation. Silence had a way of prompting that turnabout, and it worked in this case.

"What happened to Selena?" asked Fannie. "She is the reason I was hiding in the Village. In fact, her cousin is Jane, the woman who was hosting me."

Leishke chastised himself – Jane and Selena certainly bore a resemblance. He should have seen the relationship immediately, but his liaison with May had obviously distracted him.

"She was tied up, tortured and beaten in her room at the Circle City Hotel," he said, deciding he didn't have time to mince words. Looking at Fannie's suddenly white face, he regretted that decision.

"She is still alive," he said in a softer tone. "She is gravely ill but has kept fighting. I've been checking on her regularly at St. Ann's Hospital. And so far as Againsky knows, she hasn't gained consciousness since she was found."

"Has she – gained consciousness?" asked Fannie.

"Yes, when she was first found, she described her attacker as someone fitting Againsky's description," said Leishke.

He thought how best to tell Fannie what else Selena had told him and decided to just be forthright.

"She said he was trying to get her to tell him where you were."

"Oh, no," said Fannie, now beginning to cry. "I put her in that situation – it was my fault!"

"It was not," said Frank emphatically. "It was Againsky's fault. I have seen too many victims blame themselves. It is not your fault, and it was not Selena's fault – the blame is all Againsky's."

He decided to take advantage of the moment. "The only way we can make him pay for this is if you testify against him during a trial. Otherwise, I'm afraid he'll go free."

Fannie had dropped her head into her crossed arms on the table, still sobbing. Frank pulled out his handkerchief and handed it to her; the lace-trimmed scrap she had pulled from a pocket wasn't going to do much.

She took the handkerchief, raised her head, wiped her eyes, and blew her nose.

"I'll do it," she said, tearfully but firmly. "I will do whatever I can to see that – that bastard – behind bars."

"Thank you," said Frank. "I have every hope that I'll arrest Againsky today. Once he's in jail, I can release you. In the meantime, I'm going to ask the jailers to give you, paper, and pen so you can write a statement. Are you willing to do that?"

"Of course," was the quick reply.

"Good. Please write down as many details about Rosie's past and what has happened since you met her – include dates and as many names of Club members as you recall. I can send a copy of this statement to officers I worked with in California. It could be used to shut down the Club, at least in the United States, and in Alaska."

"I'll do that," said Fannie. "Is there anything else you need from me? If not," she added with a watery smile, "You need to go find that bastard and get him in jail."

"Doing it," said Frank, standing and crossing to Fannie's side of the table so he could pull out her chair.

"Oh, and one more thing," said Frank. "Why do you think Mrs. Todd was killed by Againsky? Was he there that night?"

Chapter 30

Rhys Davies was pleased with himself; he had earned the trust of the law enforcement officer he most admired – Frank Leishke. If Frank didn't trust him, he wouldn't have sent him, by himself, to find Againsky and Andersen. Davies thought he might be close to finding them. The Juneau harbormaster hadn't known of anyone living on board a boat in the Juneau harbor – except for those who always lived aboard. It was discouraging news, especially since Douglas didn't have a boat harbor. Davies decided to go to Douglas anyway and ask around. In Douglas, the Natives pulled their canoes ashore, and homesteaders did the same. Both ensured their watercraft was above the high tide marks, so they wouldn't float off. If their boats were too large to pull ashore, owners would anchor the craft in the channel, or tie them to a grounded buoy. They then used dinghies to go to and from the anchored boats. In addition to these individually moored boats, there were a very few boats that Davies had noticed always seemed to be tied up to one of the docks. The company town of Treadwell had a number of docks for use by steamships and ferries. They had regular and frequent use, with steamships routinely dropping off passengers, supplies and equipment, and picking up people and sometimes gold. Douglas also had several docks to account for the same traffic. All those docks featured one or two boats who were tied up on a regular basis. Davies decided to track down the harbormaster in Douglas to question him about those boats.

The harbormaster's office was on the short end of the longest pier stretching out from Douglas. Located on Front Street, it was just two doors down from the Opera House. Davies tried the door to the office, but it was locked. He looked up and down the street, thinking he might spot someone walking toward the building. Instead, he caught the eye of one of the men hanging outside the Opera House. The man gestured for him to come there. Yesterday's drizzle had become a bit more serious today and had combined with a nasty wind swooping down from the steep mountains across the channel. The ferry trip had been bumpy; even the rain hadn't prevented several passengers from seeking the open air. Now, Davies clutched his hat as he crossed to the brothel.

"You looking for the harbormaster?" said the man who had waived him over. He was a typical Treadwell miner – roughly clothed, mustache and hair a little too long. He pulled back into the shelter of the porch. Davies followed him, glad to escape from the blowing wind. He asked, "Do you know where I can find him?"

"Sure – he's probably at the harbor," the man said – a remark that made the handful of men on the porch burst out laughing.

Davies was irritated, but tried to imagine how Frank Leishke would react. He would probably not pull out his badge, he told himself. His fingers let go of it, still in his pocket.

"Well, he's not in his office. So where in the harbor do you think he'll be?"

"I think you've got the wrong harbor," said his erstwhile helper, with a broad grin. He pointed up the street.

Davies looked where he pointed and saw the name on the saloon in the middle of the next block. "The Harbor" was painted on the sign that hung over the door of a small building.

"Thanks," he said, and headed for the saloon.

Inside, the Harbor was a ratty old dive. A handful of men sat at the bar, peanut shells littered the floor, and the two spittoons on the floor dripped tobacco split. Davies didn't consider himself fastidious, but he found himself almost tiptoeing across the mess.

"What can I get you?" asked the aged bartender; Davies suspected he was the owner. He wondered if he had seen the light of day anytime in the past decade. His pasty face said otherwise.

"I'm looking for the harbormaster."

"That's me," said a man who appeared to be in his 50s. He was well dressed and looked relatively sober for someone in a bar before 1 p.m. "What can I do you for?"

"I was hoping to talk to you privately," said Davies.

"Well, you're out of luck with that," said the harbormaster. "Hey boys," he told the other men at the bar. "This young fellow wants to talk to me privately. So just shut your ears."

"Done," he told Davies. "Go ahead."

"Maybe we could sit over there," Davies gestured toward a table near the door.

"Sure," said the harbormaster. He grabbed his glass of beer and they went to sit at the table. As they sat down, a large drop of water hit the center of the table.

"Hey, Lucky," the harbormaster called to the bartender. "You're out of luck!"

"That joke never gets old," he told Davies. Davies looked at the bartender and thought that it probably did.

"The roof you just got fixed has sprung a leak," he yelled at the bartender.

"Criminy – I'll bring you a bucket," the bartender replied. In a short time, he proceeded to drop a mop bucket on top of the table.

The harbormaster held out a hand, around one side of the bucket. "I'm Robert MacDonald, Douglas harbormaster," he said.

"Rhys Davies, deputy federal marshal," Rhys replied, shaking the offered hand.

"A marshal. Wow – what have I done?" asked MacDonald. "Hey, fellas," he bellowed toward the bar. "He's a federal marshal. Hope you're all going to come bail me out when I'm hauled away."

The "fellas" looked their way and all of them shook their heads, then turned back to their drinks.

"They are such comedians," MacDonald said, chuckling. "So, what can I do for you?"

"I'm looking for a couple of men who may be staying on a boat here in Douglas," the deputy marshal said.

"What do they look like?"

"One is slight, dark complexion, mustached and has dark curly hair. The other is tall, blonde, and also with a mustache. They will have been staying here for about the past week or so."

"Hmmm. You know that we don't have a small boat harbor here, right?"

"Yes," replied Davies. "But I've seen some of the same boats tied up on the city docks, and in Treadwell. I'm wondering if any of those boats have anyone living aboard."

"They shouldn't," said MacDonald. "They're really transitory tie ups, but sometimes someone will arrange for a longer mooring. Let me think. ... The *Beverly J.*, the *Lanie B.*, the *Henrietta*. They're all owned by fishermen who are out of town for a couple of months and arranged for temporary tie ups."

Before Davies could object, MacDonald again yelled toward the bar.

"Hey, any of you boys know of anyone living aboard the *Beverly J.*, the *Lanie B.*, or the *Henrietta*?"

The men, who had looked up at this shouting, looked back down at their drinks, not bothering to answer.

MacDonald drained his drink and stood up. "I guess I can go check in my records at the office," he said, staggering slightly as he headed toward the door.

The two men left the Harbor and headed across the street to the office. As they passed the Opera House, Davies glanced toward the front door, and saw a shorter man with curly black hair and a dark complexion, walking out, next to a tall blonde man with an elaborate mustache.

He stopped, frozen, as he stared at the two men for whom he'd been searching. MacDonald had kept walking, making Davies stand out in the middle of Front Street. Againsky looked at the deputy marshal, and then grabbed Andersen by the arm and began walking, then running, toward Treadwell.

Davies began running after them. MacDonald, oblivious, continued toward his office, turning to usher a nonexistent Davies in before him. He looked down the street in time to see Davies turn the corner at a flat run. "Oh, well," said MacDonald, shut the door he had just opened, and headed back to the bar.

"Stop, in the name of the law!" Davies yelled at the two fleeing men. He felt for his gun in his pocket and thought about what to do next. Leishke had told him to watch them, and he was certainly doing that. He wasn't sure how he could catch them, and then arrest them both. He looked around for assistance and saw none. Shift change wouldn't happen for more than an hour, and most of Douglas's occupants were inside on this rainy and windy day. He was out of sight of the men loitering at the Opera House.

The two men kept running, and Davies kept going after them. He was slowly catching up, he thought, as they turned toward the large sawmill on the water side of the street. He turned to follow them, and realized they were no longer in sight.

The mill had a number of buildings and large equipment on its block-long site. In addition to the warehouse that stored the cut lumber, there was the mill building itself, as well as the water-driven apparatus that drove the giant sawmill. There were carts and wagons interspersed among the buildings and equipment, offering a number of places for Davies' quarry to hide.

He stopped, looking for any evidence of the two men. The sawdust covering the ground held a number of footprints, and he noticed the boot toes that indicated running men. The prints also looked relatively fresh. They led around the warehouse, and Davies stepped cautiously around the corner.

Not cautiously enough. He felt an arm grab him around the neck and turned his head to look into Lars Andersen's face. Andersen was looking past him, and Davies turned his head back to see what he was looking at. Againsky was in front of them, holding a wicked-looking knife. Without a word, he plunged it into the deputy marshal's chest. He dropped to the ground, and Andersen and Againsky turned to walk calmly back to the street.

Davies collapsed on his back, couldn't get up, and could feel his sight getting blurry, but he knew he had to seek help. Slowly, he dragged his leg up, and then dug his boot heel into the ground to propel him forward. He didn't know where he was going, but knew that somehow, he must keep moving. Another knee up, and then another heel pressed against the ground. He was moving, but he felt the blood leaking from around the knife. He wondered idly if it was hard to breathe because of the pain, or because his lungs were filling with blood. He heard a man shout, "Hey, what happened?" as he lost consciousness.

Chapter 31

After seeing Fannie back to her cell, Leishke headed out of the courthouse and back down to the ferry to Douglas. He felt a visceral need to see May, and ensure she was safe. After hearing from Fannie that Againsky had almost certainly killed Mrs. Todd because he had questioned her about Fannie, Leishke was convinced he needed to move quickly.

Leishke had thought he might see Rhys either in Juneau or near the ferry dock in Douglas. He wondered fleetingly how his search was going. He hoped that the young marshal was being suitably cautious around Againsky.

Leaving the ferry, he walked quickly to the Opera House, intending to enter through the kitchen. As he neared the building, he saw two men carrying a third on a stretcher. They were walking a block away on Second Street, and he thought probably heading toward the Weyerhauser Hospital, a small private hospital about two blocks away. It wasn't as well staffed as St. Ann's Hospital in Douglas, but closer.

He paused, wondering if he should find out more. His attention was still focused on May. Inside the brothel's kitchen, he saw two women he hadn't met before. They turned to stare at him. The older woman who he thought might be Mrs. Todd's replacement, addressed him.

"Customers are to enter the other door," she said firmly.

"I'm not a customer," said Leishke. "I'm Deputy Marshal Frank Leishke, and I'm here to talk to Mrs. Svenson. Where can I find her?"

"Oh," the woman replied. "She's meeting with Mrs. Montgomery upstairs. Olga," she addressed the other young woman. "Take the marshal to Mrs. Montgomery's office."

"Of course," the woman – Leishke thought she looked more than a teenage girl – answered. She led Leishke upstairs to the madam's office.

May had slept surprisingly well and thought it might be due to her activities with Frank the day before. She had laughed to herself about Frank saying his feelings were "significant." What a romantic man, she thought with a smile. She guessed her feelings could also be called "significant," but the real word might be "infatuated."

She dressed, had breakfast, and came to work. While she remained upset about Fannie being in jail, May admitted to herself that it lessened her anxiety about her friend's safety, at least with regard to Againsky. She was counting on Frank to keep Fannie safe in the jail.

At work, she continued working with the new cook, Mrs. Sherwood. She was a good cook, but needed help from May regarding quantities, and the timing of meals, as well as food favorites for the working girls. She was not the baker that Mrs. Todd had been but May knew she was going to miss more than Mrs. Todd's bread and pies. Mrs. Todd's comforting pats, never-ending cups of tea and gentle gossip had become an important part of May's life. She anticipated becoming close to Mrs. Sherwood but knew it would not be the same.

It came as a relief when Mrs. Montgomery sent Olga to summon her to the office. It was hard spending so much time in the kitchen, which resonated with memories of Mrs. Todd. May was thinking it would be nice for there to be some kind of service in Douglas for Mrs. Todd, since her body was being sent south. There couldn't be a funeral, but maybe there could be some kind of gathering, she thought. She greeted her boss and sat in the chair across from the desk.

Mrs. Montgomery's eyes had the same dark circles that May had noticed earlier in the week, and she seemed a little paler than usual. She was cheerful in her greeting of May, and they talked for a few minutes about how well Mrs. Sherwood and Olga were settling into their new jobs. May then brought up the idea of a memorial service or gathering for Mrs. Todd, and Mrs. Montgomery was pleased with the notion. They were discussing where and when the event would happen when Olga brought Leishke to the office.

"I'm sorry to interrupt, ladies," he told them, his presence seeming to overwhelm the very feminine room. "There are a few things I need to talk about with Mrs. Svenson, and I also have a question or two for you, Mrs. Montgomery."

"Of course, detective. You are welcome to sit down," said the madam.

"Thank you," Leishke said, carefully sitting on one of the room's delicate chairs. "I have been reviewing my notes from the death of Mrs. Todd and wanted to ask you both about that evening."

"Yes?" inquired Mrs. Montgomery.

"I believe we know the identity of the person who killed Mrs. Todd, but we need to find out more about the motive," said Frank.

"Well, of course I'm delighted to hear that. I hope he has been arrested," replied Mrs. Montgomery.

"Not just yet, but I anticipate arresting him today," replied Frank. "I believe that Mrs. Todd was killed because she witnessed something. We know that this killer has been looking for Fannie Miller. Do you know of any connection between Mrs. Todd and Miss Miller?"

"Yes," said Mrs. Montgomery. "Before she and Rosie began working on their own in the district, they worked here and became friendly with all the other girls, as well as the staff." She addressed May, "You were close with Rosie and Fannie, weren't you?" she asked.

"Yes," said May.

"So, is it possible that this man came here looking for Fannie?" asked Frank.

"Yes," replied both women, simultaneously.

"Would Mrs. Todd have known where she was?"

"If she did know where she was living, she wouldn't have just told some stranger," May replied. "She was very careful about protecting all the working girls."

"I agree," said Mrs. Montgomery. "She wouldn't have said anything. But May," she said, looking at her maid. "Was Fannie here that evening? You stayed late with the laundry because I saw you leaving after dark. Did you see Fannie?"

May took a deep breath and tried to decide how much to say. Could anything she say now hurt Fannie? No, Fannie was safe in jail. Mrs. Todd was dead. There was no harm to telling the truth.

"Yes," she admitted. "Fannie and I were in the basement while I worked on the laundry. She and I were down there talking when a man opened the door and came down. Fannie was terrified, and I threw a plate across the basement to distract him. We ran upstairs and tried to block the door. Fannie got away, and I went outside to take the dry clothes and linens off the clothesline. It was after dark, but I saw the man leave through the kitchen – he had gotten through the basement door."

She turned to look at Frank. "Do you think he killed Mrs. Todd so she couldn't tie him to Fannie? Do you think he would have killed us also?"

"Yes, I do," said Frank, reluctantly. He hated to see how frightened she had become. "If he had succeeded in catching up with Fannie that night, Mrs. Todd could have identified him as having asked for Fannie. I think he killed her and hid the body as best he could before going down to the basement."

"Oh, my goodness," said Mrs. Montgomery. "It appears that you and Fannie had a very close call. Thank heaven you were able to escape from him."

"I certainly hope you have him locked up as soon as possible," she told Leishke. "Is there anything else I can help you with?"

Frank knew he had been dismissed, and his questions, at least for Mrs. Montgomery, were answered. He was also reassured seeing May looking as lovely as ever, although she still appeared shaken about the information he had provided. Before he could say anything to her, May stood and told Mrs. Montgomery that she would show the detective to the door.

They walked down the hall to the top of the stairs. Frank looked around and seeing no one, tugged May into his arms for a quick kiss. She reciprocated, and the quick kiss became not so quick. Then, she pushed him away.

"How is Fannie?" she asked.

"I saw her this morning, and she has pledged her cooperation with a trial," he told her. "I now need to locate a place where she can live in relative safety until this case goes to court. I hope to have Againsky arrested, but I don't trust him not to bribe someone to attack her, even in jail."

"That's easy," said May. "She can stay here."

She continued, "She is accustomed to the Opera House, and the girls are pretty good at looking out for each other. Mrs. Montgomery also has a buzzer from each girl's room to the bar downstairs. If something is happening in one of the rooms, the girl just presses the buzzer, and the bartender shows up with a shotgun."

"What about the girls who were being throttled by Kilburn?" asked Frank.

"They would have been protected if they had pressed the buzzer," argued May. "They just didn't do it because they didn't want to discourage a client. Fannie would know better than that." She added, "I just wish there were buzzers in the kitchen and the basement."

"Maybe you should suggest that" said Frank. "You may be right. This could be a good solution. Fannie could continue making an income, but in a safer place. And it would certainly be easier to keep her safe here than in that little cabin down the street."

"Can you bring her here today?" asked May.

"Not so fast," he said. "Davies and I are tracking down Againsky and his friend. I have some information about where I can find them, and I'm heading there now. I'll stop by before I take the ferry to Juneau if I have time."

"Thank you – and be careful," said May, giving Frank a quick hug before sending him down the stairs and out the door.

Chapter 32

Out on the porch, Leishke saw the typical crowd of men, but they were unusually agitated. The detective stopped, pulling out the newspaper he had bought that morning in Juneau, unfolded it, and leaned against a wall. He didn't have to wait long to find out what had stirred them up.

"That man who just walked into the bar?" one man said to another. "He's the one who told us. Some marshal was shot today by the sawmill. He helped carry the body to the Weyerhauser hospital. He said there is no way that marshal is going to see another morning. We're suspecting it is the same fellow who was talking to the harbormaster this morning."

Leishke, surprised to see his hands trembling, shoved the newspaper back in his pocket and headed to the hospital. It was a small building, owned by Dr. Weyerhauser. Leishke was a little surprised the wounded person hadn't been taken to St. Ann's, but perhaps this small hospital was closer? He would find out.

When he arrived, he was unsurprised, but still shaken, to be told the patient was Rhys Davies. He had been found stabbed in the chest – the knife still in him – and lying in the sawdust in the mill yard. The nurse told him the men who found and carried him to the hospital had known enough to leave the knife in the wound.

"If they had pulled it out, he would not have survived the trip here," the male nurse said, sounding a little too ghoulish for Leishke's taste.

"But he is still alive?" Frank asked. "Is he conscious? I need to talk to him if at all possible."

The nurse summoned Dr. Weyerhauser, whose bloody apron showed evidence of having just attended to Rhys.

"He may be able to talk. I don't expect he'll live through the night, so you can go see," said the doctor. Leishke hadn't met the physician before and was not impressed. The man was unkempt – he needed a haircut and beard trim, and his hands hadn't been washed since seeing to Rhy's wound. The doctor followed Leishke back to Rhys's room, which Frank thought could have been cleaner. Rhys's shirt had been unbuttoned and pulled apart, but his chest was unwashed, and Frank could see the volume of blood he had lost either when stabbed or when the doctor pulled out the knife. The wound had been stitched. There were no attendants in the room.

Frank pulled a chair to the bedside and grasped his colleague's hand. Rhys's eyes flickered open to look at Frank's face, and then fell closed again but he spoke:

"Frank. I'm sorry. I thought ... I thought I was being careful. But that bastard ... Againsky ... nailed me. That other man ... he was with him. They took off ... went toward Treadwell." His voice had been getting progressively weaker and now faded away altogether.

"I'll get them, friend, don't you worry," said Frank. "And I'm going to get you better care also." There was no response, and he hoped that Rhys was asleep and not unconscious.

The doctor was not to be seen when Frank returned to the front desk. Frank told the nurse there that he wanted the deputy marshal moved to St. Ann's Hospital as quickly as possible. The nurse objected, but Frank was insistent.

"I'll assume the expenses of moving him," he said. "I'm going there now to arrange it."

He left the hospital and walked the half mile to St. Ann's, the large hospital that loomed above the Douglas Indian Village, managed by St. Ann's nuns and sharing its campus with a Catholic school and the priest's rectory. His visit there was reassuring after being at the Weyerhauser Hospital – the sister he spoke to was clean and concise, and the hospital's front room was remarkably clean. The sister arranged for a pair of orderlies to take a horse-drawn ambulance to pick up Rhys.

He described the man's injuries to the nurse in charge, and while she was too experienced to look alarmed, her instructions to the orderlies included that the patient be kept as still as possible during the transport. Leishke had worked with the nurse before, and she took a few minutes to listen to his concerns about the private hospital.

"I understand," the nun said carefully. "We have heard about some ... concerns regarding Dr. Weyerhauser. I understand that the territorial government is reviewing his medical license. Please don't share that information; I'm telling you because of your standing in law enforcement. I pray for discernment and wisdom on the part of the government agents, and for the health and safety of his patients. And of course, I pray for the soul of Dr. Weyerhauser."

If there was such a thing as a half-hearted prayer, I think it might be that sister's prayer for Weyerhauser, thought Leishke as he left the hospital to go seek out the *Lanie B.*

He found the boat quickly – a surprising event in a case which seemed replete with missteps and delays. It was tied up to the steamship dock in Treadwell – tucked close to one end to be out of the way of the much larger steamships.

He stood behind a dock building so he could observe the gas fishing boat without being seen. As he watched, Lars Andersen stepped outside the wheelhouse, and tossed a bowl of refuse overboard. Leishke deduced that the stairs to below decks were located in the wheelhouse, because the boat's galley, or kitchen, would be below. Lars went back into the wheelhouse, which was surrounded by windows to allow a skipper unimpeded views. Lars stepped out of sight, confirming to Leishke that he had gone below.

One sitting duck was found – Leishke hoped the second duck was also on board. Glancing around, he saw no one paying attention to the dock, which currently held no steamships. He retrieved his gun from his pocket and began walking quickly, but as quietly as possible, down the ramp to the floating dock. Fortunately, the tide was high, so the ramp was not at a steep angle and it was easier to approach without noise.

He walked the length of the dock, and stepped slowly on board, so as to minimize the boat's response to his weight. Then, he deliberately stomped over to the wheelhouse. The move had its intended effect, and Lars popped up from the rooms below. He was greeted at the wheelhouse door by Leishke and his gun.

"You're under arrest," said Leishke calmly. "Where is Againsky?"

"Not here," said Andersen. "And what are you arresting me for? I haven't done anything."

Leishke had not seen any movement from Andersen that indicated Againsky was aboard – no raised voice or looking toward below decks. Disappointing, but perhaps not surprising.

"You are being arrested for the attempted murder of a federal deputy marshal," he said. "Put your hands up so I can see them and walk slowly toward me."

Andersen did so, apparently silenced by the attempted murder charge. As he neared Leishke, the detective told him to drop to his knees. Leishke then came up behind Andersen and handcuffed him to the boat's railing. He then conducted a quick search for weapons, confiscating one knife from the man's boot. He was not carrying a gun.

"Stay here," Leishe said, somewhat unnecessarily. "I'll be back."

Leishke entered the wheelhouse. The steps below were positioned next to the boat's wheel. He stood for a few seconds but heard nothing. After first lying on his stomach to look below, he turned outward from the stairs and somewhat awkwardly descended, one hand on the stairs rail and one holding his gun as he looked behind him during the descent. Below decks, the boat held four bunk beds, a small boat's galley, a head with a hand-pumped toilet and a small dinette that could be converted into another berth. In the bow, a hatch opened to a small hold that held lines, buoys, and other needed equipment, but no Againsky.

He ascended to the deck, and opened the main fish hatch, but found it empty. He retrieved Andersen, handcuffing his hands behind his back. Grasping an arm, he led him to the Douglas ferry dock for transport to the Juneau jail.

As he walked Andersen into the jail, he noted the alarm on Fannie's face when she saw his prisoner. Leishke knew he would need to move her soon. It was almost impossible to keep the prisoners completely separated from each other, given the jail's design. Frank was not going to put Fannie in jail for her protection and then leave her to the mercy of Againsky and his confederates.

He went upstairs to meet with Marshal Calhoun.

Calhoun was not happy; his earlier conversation with Hensen meant he was forced to allow Leishke to continue his investigation. Now, he was learning from Leishke that one of his deputy marshals may die from being attacked as a result of that investigation.

"I told you to just let this go. We have the killer in custody, and your job is done. Your need to be proven right may now end in Davies's death. Are you proud of what you've done?" he raged.

"Yes," said Leishke. "I am proud of what I've done. I've brought in two men who were implicated in a white slavery ring that has been imprisoning young girls for years. And I expect to bring in their mastermind today. Of course, Deputy Marshal Davies's sacrifice is not a small thing, but it just points to the danger that everyone is in until Againsky is behind bars. And you, sir, should be proud also."

He continued: "You have put the resources of your office in the battle behind this international conspiracy, and in so doing, have saved countless innocent girls and their families. I think you will be a hero to the entire marshal service."

Leishke thought he may have been laying it on a little too thick, but looking at Calhoun's face, decided that no flattery was too much flattery for the Marshal.

Mollified, Calhoun agreed to release Fannie to Leishke, and to send a deputy marshal to guard Davies at St. Ann's Hospital in Douglas. He also agreed to assign another deputy to Leishke, this time McIntyre, the same deputy marshal who had guarded Rosie Brown's house.

Thanking the marshal, Leishke looked for, and found, McIntrye, an American whose grandfather had emigrated from Scotland. He was young enough to appear to still be in his teens, although Leishke thought that unlikely. Another new recruit to train, he thought.

He gathered his thoughts and decided that he would be the one to go after Againsky this time; he did not want to be finding McIntyre in either the hospital or the morgue. He told the young man that he wanted him to help escort Fannie to the Opera House, and then quickly went down to the jail to get Fannie released.

He brought her up to his office so they could talk quietly. McIntyre had been told by Leishke to listen, but not talk, and the detective was pleased to see him obey orders.

Fannie was happy to be free, but understandably concerned that Againsky had not been found. He told her about Davies, in part to ensure she understood why she was going to be staying at the Opera House, and the need for her to remain in the building, and to remain wary.

"I do understand," she said. "I feel comfortable there and I know Mrs. Montgomery takes good care of her girls. But how much longer do you think I'll need to stay in Alaska? As each day goes by, Againsky could be hiring more men to do his bidding, or there could even be more of his confederates coming up from San Francisco."

Leishke thought the latter was unlikely but agreed that Againsky would probably have no trouble finding replacements for Andersen and Kilburn among the idle men waiting for work in Juneau or Douglas. He assured Fannie that he believed he was within a few hours of arresting the killer. He and McIntrye briefly discussed how to handle any potential attack on Fannie and left the courthouse for the dock.

Fortunately, Fannie still had the large hat that she had used earlier to hide her features. McIntyre walked with her, her hand resting in the crook of his elbow. Leishke walked a few paces behind, as if separate from the pair, scanning for threats and prepared to draw the gun he clasped in his pocket.

The trip to Douglas, however, was uneventful. Leishke left the couple at the kitchen door to the Opera House and walked quickly down to the dock where the *Lanie B.* was moored. The boat appeared deserted and Leishke repeated his earlier search, finding no one on board, with no evidence that Againsky had yet returned. He went into the steamship offices, located on shore at the head of the dock, and introduced himself.

"I'm watching for a dangerous criminal who I plan to arrest," he told the two clerks in the office. "I was hoping to take advantage of your windows and watch from here."

They agreed with alacrity, and Leishke stationed himself at the window. One of the clerks brought him a chair and coffee, and he decided that this surveillance was going to be a relatively easy one.

Chapter 33

Hours later, as the twilight turned to full night, Leishke realized he had misjudged the ease of his afternoon. He had seen no sign of Againsky and was chafing at the hours he had spent to no effect. He had received no updates on Davies, Selena Dowling, or Fannie. The clerks checked with their boss and had told him he could stay as long as he wanted. They even left Leishke with a key when they departed the office at the end of their workday.

It was now dark enough to make surveillance difficult, and Leishke was increasingly convinced that Againsky was not going to be returning here. He must have seen Leishke with Andersen, or even seen Leishke on board the *Lanie B*. He had gone to ground elsewhere. Leishke sighed; his search was going to have to begin anew.

For right now, Leishke made his way to St. Ann's Hospital to check on Rhys. The deputy marshal was holding on, the night nurse said. He had regained consciousness after moving to the new hospital, and had been checked on, cleaned up and his wound checked. He was now sleeping. Frank decided against waking him, especially since he had no news to tell him.

Leishke walked down the street toward downtown Douglas, turned onto Front Street, and entered the Douglas Opera House through the kitchen. After having a quick look into the bar for Againksy, he made his way upstairs. He was looking for May, but when he didn't see her. He knocked lightly on Mrs. Montgomery's door.

"Come in," the madam said.

Lieshke opened the door. "Mrs. Montgomery," he said. "I was hoping to check on Fannie Miller. Has she settled in?"

"Yes. Fortunately, I had an empty room that she could occupy," the brothel owner replied. "I've suggested that, for the next few days, she stay away from our public rooms, such as the bar and front parlor. She has agreed."

Leishke knew that the front parlor referred to by the madam was a room off the bar where men who wanted more than a drink could choose a working girl. He agreed with Mrs. Montgomery that Fannie was safer staying upstairs in the building. He knew that May would ensure she received meals and had some company. He was trying to think of a way to ask about May when Mrs. Montgomery said:

"I was hoping you could give me an update on your efforts. Of course, I am most concerned about the investigation into Mrs. Todd's death – she was an excellent woman and a loyal employee. However, I'm also concerned about the killing of Rosie Brown. I don't know if you're aware that she and Fannie lived here when they first came to Douglas. I was fond of her. I am also, of course, worried about the safety of all the working girls under my care, as well as those in the Restricted District."

"I understand," said Leishke. "My investigation so far leads me to conclude that Fannie Miller is the most likely potential victim at this time."

He thought for a moment and decided to tell Mrs. Montgomery what he knew of Constant Kilburn.

"I know that some of your ... residents ... had expressed concern about a client who had been ... rough ... with them," Leishke said.

Mrs. Montgomery nodded, folding her hands on the desk blotter in front of her and silently encouraging him to continue.

"Yesterday, the man I suspect of this behavior was arrested after abducting Mrs. Svenson in downtown Juneau."

"What!" exclaimed the madam. "I don't know anything about this. May doesn't seem hurt. In fact, she appears her usual cheerful self. What happened?"

Leishke described the previous evening's events, making it sound as if Kilburn had arbitrarily chosen to grab May, and not mentioning Againsky's involvement. Mrs. Montgomery was appropriately alarmed and expressed her relief at hearing of Kilburn's arrest.

"I believe," said Leishke, "that Kilburn may be connected to the attack on a schoolteacher in Petersburg. Frankly, I think your residents were much more at risk from him than they are from Againsky."

"I understand why you would think that," said Mrs. Montgomery. "I suspect time will tell."

Leishke left the office after thanking the madam for her time. He was slightly puzzled by Mrs. Montgomery's closing remark, but he stopped thinking about it when he spied May leaving a room at the end of the hall. She saw Frank at the time he spotted her and greeted him with a smile. The couple met in the hall and embraced briefly, after ensuring they would not be seen.

As they walked down the back stairs to the kitchen, May told Frank that she had spent the past hour visiting with Fannie, who seemed happy to be back at the Opera House, "or at least out of jail," said May with a laugh.

She led Frank into the hall outside the kitchen and collected her jacket and hat. Frank offered to walk her home, and she happily agreed. As they left the Opera House, however, Frank admitted he hadn't eaten all day.

"We cannot have that," protested May. "There's a little restaurant down the street that I think may still be open."

The restaurant was still open. It was a hole-in-the-corner place with about six tables, and two staff – the owner/cook and a dishwasher. Customers knew to place their orders in the kitchen; when it was ready, their table number was called out. The middle-aged man who ran the place was from Eastern Europe, recalled Leishke, who had been here before. It was crowded, even at the late hour, which was a testament to the cooking.

As they entered, several people turned toward the door. Those who recognized Leishke greeted him and appeared especially interested in seeing him with a woman. One man near the door grabbed him by the arm.

"Howdy, Frank," he said, and Leishke recognized him as the Douglas Commissioner's office manager. "I've heard you've been busy," he said, and added with a smile: "And who is this little lady?"

Frank was irritated – he didn't like the grab or the question about May but he also wasn't going to offend the commissioner's right-hand man. He could see other eyes on the interaction.

"Hello, Mr. Sullivan," he said, gently pulling the man's hand from his arm. "I've been busy. This is Mrs. Svenson. She is ... helping me with a case."

The couple sat at the only open table in the room; the number 5 was in a placeholder in the middle. It was the last table available because it was located near the kitchen in a corner, and the kitchen noise was noticeable. The day's special was meatloaf, and even seeing the word on the chalkboard by the door made Frank's stomach growl. May heard it and laughed.

"You need someone to look after you," she said.

"Are you applying for the job?" asked Frank. "Because if so, you're hired."

May blushed slightly and laughed. "I didn't say I was applying, but I might consider it if the job is open."

Frank surprised himself with his quick response. "It is," he said, wondering when he had abandoned a lifetime commitment to avoid female entanglements.

He and May agreed they both wanted meatloaf, and he went to the kitchen to place their order. He made his way back to their table, again exchanging greetings with several patrons.

He sat down and faced May.

"I know we haven't known each other very long, but I can also say that I have never felt this way about anyone," he said, reaching over to quickly grab, and release, her hand. They were both aware of the watching eyes and kept their voices low.

"Thank you, Frank," said May. "I know you don't say this lightly. My feelings toward you have taken me by surprise also. I did not think I could feel about anyone the way I felt about my Albert."

Frank hated the sound of "my Albert," but tried to imagine how she would talk about him if Frank were killed. He hoped she would say "my Frank" in the same way. It would be even better if he didn't have to die for her to say it.

"I have spent my entire adult life without entering into a relationship with a woman," Frank said, slowly and quietly. "I had just about come to believe that I would live my life alone."

"That is so sad," said May. "I come from a big family, and I know the love that family can bring into a life. My marriage to Albert also taught me that I liked being a married woman. In one way, I'm sorry that we didn't have children, but with Albert gone, it has made my life much easier. I would hate to have children who had no father."

"I would hate that for you," said Frank. He thought and then added, "I think Albert would probably have not wanted to leave children behind."

"I'm not sure how I feel about children," he continued. "My family was small – I was an only child and my parents were older. They have both passed away. We didn't have any other extended family, except my mother's family back in Norway. I've been on my own for a while now.

"I had decided that my choice of profession made it much better to avoid entanglements. I have moved pretty frequently, and when I'm working on a case, I have a hard time thinking of anything else, like eating," he said, gesturing around them.

"So, this is a big decision for you," said May. "Perhaps you should be sure that you've given this all the thought you need. I think we would both be better off if you give this the needed attention before we go any further."

Her words made sense in Frank's brain, but his heart overcame his reasoning.

"I don't want to wait," he said vehemently, and realized he had spoken loudly when May shushed him, with a little laugh.

He told himself that he was glad someone thought this was funny. He certainly didn't.

"I mean it," he said. "I sometimes feel as if I've been waiting my entire life for this ... for you. I don't want to wait any longer. As soon as this case is over, I want to be married."

"Number 5," bellowed the cook. Frank rose from his chair to pick up their food.

Chapter 34

The next morning, Fannie lay in her bed, trying to decide what to do next. She had slept poorly, haunted by memories of her time here with Jennie, and wondering what was happening with the search for Againsky.

Last night, it was good to see May and talk with her. Fannie thought about how she felt around May. She was a young woman of her same age, but May's life had been so different. Even though she had become a widow, her life was still full of goodness, and purity. Fannie thought about the evil that the Warsaw Club had brought into her life, and wondered if she could ever be in the sort of world that May inhabited.

Jennie's death had released her in one way, Fannie realized with some surprise. Although Fannie had escaped from the Club in San Francisco, she had felt its tendrils still clinging to her through her friendship with Jennie. With Jennie gone, Fannie could finally fully escape. But the realization didn't lessen her grief for Jennie. She, and all the other girls trapped by this organization, should have had the same world that May had – a world of love and goodness. Now, because of some selfish men who believed their needs are more important than anyone else's, Jennie, Fannie, Ada and all those other poor girls – they were lost to their families and the world. Innocence, goodness, purity and even love were taken from them.

Fannie found her hands gripping the bed's blanket. She felt filled with anger, and a sense of injustice. Those men were still out there, "marrying" innocent young girls, deceiving families, and ruining lives. Staying in Juneau to testify against Againsky suddenly seemed like the only thing she could do to battle the Warsaw Club. She no longer felt any hesitation about doing it; she only wished she could do more.

She got up, washed, dressed, and felt filled with a new resolve. She was going to ask May to bring Deputy Marshal Leishke to meet with her so she could answer any more questions he might have. She walked down the backstairs to the kitchen for breakfast and entered the room just as someone knocked on the door. The cook was in the kitchen, but up to her elbows in dough. She smiled at Fannie and nodded at the door. Fannie answered it.

She was startled to see Harry, Jane's oldest son. He looked upset; his shirt was untucked and his hair not brushed. She was surprised that Jane had let him out of her sight without his being tidier. She didn't have an opportunity to ask him any questions before he blurted out:

"You have to come with me."

"What?" she asked. "What is happening? Come inside and talk to me. I'll fetch you a bite to eat."

"I don't want anything to eat," he retorted. "I just need you to come with me."

"Harry," she said. "You must tell me what is going on. I'm not just going to go wherever you say; it's dangerous for me to leave here."

"It's more dangerous for my family if you stay," he said. "That man who is looking for you has George. He says he'll do something to him if you don't come now."

"Oh, my goodness," said Fannie. "George? Againsky has George? Your poor mother must be frantic. When did this happen?"

"This morning when we were walking to school. A man stepped out of an alley near the school, grabbed up George, covered his mouth and ran. I chased him, but couldn't catch him," said Harry, who was beginning to cry.

Fannie reached over and hugged him. "It's going to be alright," she said. "We'll get him back."

• • •

George saw the bad man just before Againsky grabbed him up. He struggled, kicking and punching, but the man was strong. He put his hand over George's mouth and had a cloth in his hands. It smelled funny; George realized there must be something that was making him sleepy. His struggles became weaker, and he closed his eyes.

George didn't know how long it was before he woke up. He felt lumps poking into his back, arms, and legs – everywhere. It took a few minutes before he opened his eyes; his stomach was in an upheaval and his eyelids were heavy. The place he was in was dimly lit by the daylight that entered the two dirty portlights. The lumps, he saw, were heavy ropes; he was lying in the bow of a boat's hold on top of a pile of ropes. None tied him, however, but they weren't needed. The boat's hatch above him was closed and he wasn't tall enough to reach it.

After spending a few more minutes waiting for his stomach to settle down, and trying to find a more comfortable position, he stretched and stumbled to his feet. He tried to reach the hatch, even though he knew it was out of reach, and discovered that, yes, it was out of reach.

George wasn't sure why the bad man had taken him but thought it must have something to do with the woman who had been staying at his house. He wondered if any of the rest of the family had been abducted, like he had. He hoped not. George was convinced that he could get out of this situation but wasn't as confident about his mom and dad. They seemed to have trouble understanding sometimes the circumstances in which he got himself – something he always found surprising.

Right now, he looked around for the next step. The boat was gently rocking, but there was no engine noise, or motion indicating the boat was moving forward. So, it was either tied up at a dock, or anchored. George hoped it was tied up, because once he got out of the hold, it would be easier to leave a dock than an anchored boat. Like most Alaskans, George couldn't swim. Fishermen always said it didn't make sense to learn how to swim; the water was too cold to allow anyone to survive long enough to get to shore.

The hold smelled like all boats did – gas fumes, bilge water, fish, and the tang of the wet ropes. He realized that his stomach was still a little upset and these smells weren't helping. But the ropes gave him an idea. The ropes were the thick, heavy lines used for mooring. They were also wet, most likely from bilge water – the water at the bottom of any wooden boat. He could see the standing water under the ropes he stood on, and the sight of the dirty, oily water jolted his stomach one more time.

He thought that he could pile the ropes up, making a makeshift tower he could climb to reach the hatch. He began tugging at them to carry out the plan.

• • •

May come into the kitchen as Fannie was putting on her jacket.

"Where are you going?" she asked, alarmed. "I thought we agreed..."

"We did," said Fannie, tight lipped. "But Harry, Jane's son, just told me that Againsky has little George, and is holding him until I go there."

"That's ... awful," said May. "But please wait. Frank said last night he would come by this morning and I want to ask him about this. I'm sure you're just going to walk into a trap and end up just like Jennie."

Fannie swallowed, knowing that May was correct, but also knowing she could not put Jane's family in any more danger. "How soon will he get here?" she asked. "Harry, Jane's other son, is waiting for me."

"I'll go talk to him," said May. "And then let's talk to Mrs. Montgomery. She may be able to give some good advice also."

May went outside, where Harry was waiting, and coaxed him in. It took some doing, but the offer of breakfast and a chance to meet the famed Deputy Marshal Leishke, persuaded him. She looked for Leishke coming from the ferry dock, but he wasn't coming yet. May wasn't sure how long she could persuade Fannie to stay but knew it wouldn't be too long. She prayed that Frank would be there soon.

Frank had woken that morning with the belief that the case was going to resolve itself today. He thought he could almost hear all the pieces clicking together. Andersen in jail, Kilburn in jail, Fannie safe at the Opera House, and Frank now knew where to look for Againsky. He had hidden away on one boat, and Leishke was convinced he would be found on another.

He washed, dressed, and walked over to his office to type up his notes. He had asked McIntyre to check on Selena Dowling's status last night, and McIntyre had left a typewritten status report. She was finally on the upswing; her fever had abated and her breathing was less labored. It appeared that she would live. Leishke hoped that Davies's condition was also improving. He knew, however, that it was often several days after an injury before the risk of infection had passed. Rhys was a strong, young man and Frank let himself be hopeful that he would survive the attack.

This news also meant another witness against Againsky. Even if Leishke couldn't prove the man guilty of Jennie Poplosky's murder, or Mrs. Todd's, he would still be convicted of kidnapping and attempted murder. Leishke believed he could make the murder charges stick also, but he had been a detective long enough to know that prosecutors and juries were often looking for eyewitnesses. There were plenty in this case, he thought.

After a brief meeting with an unusually acquiescent Marshal Calhoun, he made his way down to the ferry dock and crossed over to Douglas. The weather continued to be rainy, but yesterday's wind was gone and the rain had lessened. He stood on the deck and looked at the mountains. Southeast Alaska was an evergreen forest – Sitka spruce and cedar trees dominated with occasional alders coming up in areas that had been logged or experienced snow avalanches. North of Juneau, where the glacial icefields rolled down the mountains through Mendenhall Valley, the alders were the first trees to come up after a glacier retreated and were favored by the black bears in the spring, who climbed up the trees to reach the tender spring shoots.

This morning, the evergreen forest reflected the almost ferocious spring – a bright green predominated on the steep mountain slopes that overlooked Gastineau Channel. Leishke knew that the bright green spring spruce tips were prized for tea, and also used in jams and jellies.

The ferry pulled into the Douglas dock, and Leishke stepped off, thanking the boat's skipper, and heading up the ramp, its steepness dictated by the low tide. He approached the Opera House, and spied May peering out of the kitchen window. The sight of her face, even as he wondered what worried her, lightened his mood even further. Everything appeared to be on the upswing.

May opened the kitchen door as he approached. She ushered him in and he quickly removed his jacket and hat and hung them up. A young Native lad sat in the kitchen with a cup of tea and partially eaten sandwich before him. He stared at Leishke, who looked back at him and smiled. May tugged his hand and pulled him upstairs before he could greet the boy.

"Who was that?" he asked as they reached the top of the stairs. She pulled him to a stop and gave him a quick hug before answering.

"His name is Harry; he's Jane's son – the woman who took in Fannie, remember?"

"Of course, I remember," replied Frank. "Why is he here?"

"That's why we need to talk. He says that Againsky took his little brother, George, and is holding him until Fannie turns herself over to him – Againsky, that is. Harry is very worried, but he and Fannie agreed to wait until you got here before they decide what to do," said May. "You must act quickly, however. I don't think either of them are going to give you much time before just leaving to meet Againsky."

"Where is he going to meet her?"

"Here in Douglas at her cabin," said May.

"That's a clever location," Frank admitted. "We haven't been checking there for the past few days, and it's the last place we would have looked. Have you told anyone else about this?"

"Yes," said May. "I wanted to ask Mrs. Montgomery for her advice, so we told her what had happened. She agreed with me that we needed to talk to you first." She smiled, and added, "I'm so glad you came so soon."

"So am I," said Frank, with a smile of his own for May. "Now, let's make a plan."

Chapter 35

George was exhausted and discouraged. After what had seemed to him to be hours of moving heavy, smelly, and wet rope, he had finally built a small mountain in the boat's hold. He had climbed to the top, slipping over and over, and then returning to climb again. When he got to the top, he found the hatch couldn't budge. It must be latched on the outside; no wonder the bad man hadn't worried about leaving George alone. There was no way he could escape.

He slid down the pile of ropes, and found himself standing in the dirty bilge water, which was now uncovered by the ropes. He realized that he had left himself without a dry place to sit; he would need to take apart his hard-won tower of ropes in order to sit down without sitting in water.

As he stood, staring at the water, he also became aware that the water was deeper, and seemed to be getting deeper even as he watched. Could the boat be sinking? In his mind, he saw the abandoned boats that sometimes sank in the harbor, still tied to the dock. Their hull could be completely underwater, but the mooring ropes kept the boats from disappearing altogether. If their owners couldn't be found and the boats were small enough to not be a hazard, the harbormaster would just cut the moorings and allow them to sink.

This boat was not large; George played at the Juneau harbor often, and suspected it was one of the smaller fishing boats that could be operated by a solo fisherman. He was in the ship's bow, with the hatch above him the only access point to the hold. The heavy ropes could make this point the heaviest in the boat, especially if there wasn't a gas engine. If this was one of the older sail vessels, it would likely sink at the bow.

He knew now he didn't have time to find another way out. He was going to have to make enough noise to attract attention. George had avoided doing that before now because he didn't know where he was and was afraid that any noise he made would only attract the attention of the bad man.

He grabbed an old, rusty gaff hook from underneath the water at his feet. The large metal hook at one end of the thick, squat pole was used to grab fish by their gills and it had a substantial handle. Clambering back up his tower, he began pounding on the hatch above him with the handle end, and yelling. As he did so, he realized that it had probably been his earlier efforts that had prompted the water rising in the hatch. He felt the boat shift beneath him and saw the water below him was now noticeably rising; the portlights were beginning to leak water as the portholes went under water. His cries became more frantic, and he doubled his efforts at hitting the hatch with the handle.

He didn't know how long he had been yelling and pounding but knew he didn't have much time left. The boat was slipping further underwater, and it was becoming clear that the moorings were unlikely to prevent the boat from swamping. The water was now up to his waist, despite his standing on the pile of mooring rope.

For the first time, George felt a sense of despair; perhaps this was the end. He wouldn't see his family again, he wouldn't finish school, or ever learn to commercial fish as his uncle had promised. He felt tears slide down his cheeks.

Just then, the hatch above him was yanked open.

"George!" exclaimed his cousin, Joe. "I've been looking and looking for you. We both need to get off this boat before she goes down."

Joe dropped the hatch door on the deck and grabbed both of George's wrists. George could see that the boat was tied up at the Juneau harbor. He could also see they were both in a precarious position; Joe had his feet wedged against the short railing running along the bow, and it was the only reason he wasn't in Gastineau

Channel. George climbed to the top of his rope tower, using Joe's grip for purchase, and stepped onto the boat deck. Without pausing, Joe swung George around to the edge of the boat and pushed him onto the dock. He then jumped after him.

The weight of the boat had yanked down one side of the floating dock, and the boys nearly slipped into the water toward the sinking boat, but George grabbed the side of the dock with the gaff hook, to which he had clung during his escape, and grabbed Joe with his other hand. Joe pulled his way up the inclining dock by grabbing George by the pants leg, working up to George's arm and then his shoulder. The two boys then crawled their way, hand over hand with occasional grabs of the ever-useful gaff hook, to a more level place on the dock. They stood up and smiled at each other.

George was covered in filthy bilge water, and his bloody hands told the tale of his attempts to rescue himself. Joe's hands weren't as beaten up, but he was almost equally filthy.

Joe told George he had been looking for him for hours. He said he had seen the bad man grab his cousin, and had followed, trying to keep out of sight. When they got to the harbor, Joe was chased off by the harbormaster before he saw where George had been taken. Joe had come back to the harbor and had been walking around, looking for any evidence of George or his abductor ever since. Joe was about to give up when he heard the pounding on the hatch.

From their safe vantage point, the boys looked at the sinking boat that had been George's prison. He was correct; it was a smaller boat, and it was sinking. With the boys' weight now off it, the boat had evened out somewhat, but was still mostly underwater. Once the mooring lines were cut, it would quickly sink. George felt grateful that the boat had been tied to the dock; it would have sunk much sooner if it had been at anchor.

"Did you see the man who took me while you've been down here at the harbor?" he asked Joe.

"No," said Joe. "He could be anywhere."

"Well," said George, "he's not here now, so let's get out of here. I want to go home and get something to eat." He added, "I hope

Mom is willing to feed me because I'm pretty sure she won't be happy about the state of my clothes."

• • •

At the Douglas Opera House, Leishke, May and Fannie had discussed how best to capture Againsky. Leishke thought the man could already be waiting at Fannie's cabin, so it would be impossible for him to accompany her. He flatly told May she was staying at the Opera House. May didn't argue, but also didn't agree. She just nodded.

Leishke said he would approach the cabin first, trying to ensure that Againsky didn't see him. Fannie would come to the door and knock; Frank would be as close as he could get and would arrest Againsky before he could harm Fannie.

It was risky, and Leishke knew he should involve more marshals, but Harry was becoming increasingly frantic, which made Fannie more anxious. He was also concerned that Againsky may have already abandoned the plan and harmed the boy. They couldn't wait.

Leishke decided to approach Fannie's cabin from the water; with May's help, he found a man among the "Usuals," as she called them, on the Opera House porch, who had a dingy he could borrow. While Fannie would walk to the cabin, he would row there. He left quickly, knowing he needed to reach the cabin before Fannie did. He told her to give him 10 minutes, and then leave.

The borrowed dinghy was pulled up to the beach below the Opera House, so he was able to be aboard and moving within five minutes. As he rowed along the beach, he was grateful that it was an incoming tide. He rowed under the three docks and among the pilings holding them up. The tide meant he would be close to First Street when he left the boat, and it also meant he could easily pull the dinghy to higher ground, above the tide line and safe from floating off.

As he approached the cabin, he could see two female figures walking down First Street toward his location. As he now realized and had feared, May had decided to accompany Fannie. Leishke pulled ashore, slipped the oars from their locks, and laid them in the boat, grabbed the tie-up line and stepped into the water, ankle deep. He walked up the rocks to the street, pulling the boat to high ground and leaving it. The two women were near him now but were pointedly ignoring him. He had instructed Fannie to do that so if Againsky were watching, he wouldn't be clued into Frank's arrival.

The cabin's back window faced the water, but was curtained, and Frank was convinced that Againsky would be looking toward the road and not the channel. At least, he hoped so. He walked behind the cabin and around to the side. He stood at the corner, facing the road. May and Fannie walked up to the cabin and began turning toward its front door.

Leishke was confident that he hadn't been seen; there was no window facing the next-door cabin, which had been Rosie Brown's, so unless Againsky had seen him come up from the beach, he wouldn't be visible.

As he stood there, watching Fannie and May, they looked toward him, and for a split second, he saw the shock on their faces. Then, as he heard the shuffle of boots behind him, everything went dark.

It had not been difficult for May to convince Fannie to let her come. Fannie was petrified; despite her resolution to help law enforcement, she couldn't banish the years of fear that her experience with the Club had instilled. May had assured her that she, May, would not go anywhere near Againsky, but would give Fannie moral support for the walk from the Opera House to the cabin.

Both women were terrified when they saw Leishke drop from the hammer blow dealt by Againsky, who had walked up behind the detective. They hadn't seen where he had come from; Fannie knew her cabin had no back door, so where had he been waiting?

Againsky looked remarkably calm for someone who had just attacked a federal marshal. In one hand, he held the hammer and in the other, a wickedly sharp knife. He smiled at them, stepping over Leishke's immobile body.

"Ah, girls," he said. "I see you received my message, Fannie. And I see you've been kind enough to bring me a replacement for my lost Rosie."

While May's first instinct had been to run toward Frank's prone, Fannie had a death grip on her arm, and was slowly backing away.

"I am glad to see you," said Fannie, her voice shaking slightly. "I've been wanting to tell you about what happened with Rosie."

"Yes," said Againsky. "Do tell me what happened with Rosie." He kept smiling, and kept advancing, but now, he dropped the hammer, and took the knife in his right hand. He was still a few steps away, but Fannie felt as if the knife was already slicing into her. She stepped back again, still holding onto May's arm.

"Well, we were in Anchorage, and Rosie decided she could do better business down here in Douglas, with the gold mine so busy," she said, speaking quickly now. "I came with her because business wasn't going so well in Anchorage. In fact, I don't think she had been able to send you any money for some time before we left.

"When we got here, I told her to write to you right away and tell her she had moved, but she ... she wanted to be sure it was worth her while before letting you know."

"And yet, when I met with her here, she had $3,000 in her trunk, as well as this handy knife," said Againsky. "So perhaps things had been going better than you knew."

"Oh, it was definitely busier here than it had been up north," said Fannie. "She wanted to surprise you with a big payout. I think she was planning to send you the money this week."

"Hmmm. That is not what she said," said Againsky. "And by the way, does this pretty little thing with you know the story of how Rosie and I met?"

"Oh," said Fannie, looking at May. "No, no, she doesn't know anything. She was just heading in the same direction and offered to walk with me."

"You know," said Againsky. "I do not believe a word you have said. I think that you and Rosie decided to cheat me, and that you're the one who set the marshals on me. Without you around, I don't think they will have a witness to anything. And now, I'm afraid that you've doomed your friend here to the same fate."

He was now close enough that another step would put him within stabbing distance. He took that step, his arm stretched out to slash across Fannie's neck.

A shot rang out.

Againsky dropped, face down. His body would have struck them if they hadn't instinctively stepped back. May watched, frozen, as the small hole in the back of his head sprouted red. She realized that she couldn't stop staring – his head had been turned slightly from a rock beneath him, so the blood went to the left, dripping into a pool on the ground.

She wrenched her gaze away to the front door of Fannie's cabin and saw Mrs. Montgomery, lowering a large revolver. She was smiling. It wasn't a happy sight.

Chapter 36

May ran forward to kneel next to Frank. He was pale, and unmoving, but she felt a pulse in his neck. He was still breathing. The wound on the back of his head was bleeding heavily. She reached under her skirt and yanked at the lace ruffle that she tacked to the bottom of her petticoat. The ruffle was meant to come off easily to allow it to be laundered after picking up street debris. She folded it into a thick pad and pressed it to his head.

She looked up and caught Fannie's eye. "Could you please go to St. Ann's hospital and send an ambulance?" she asked. "I think they can probably notify the Commissioner about him," and she motioned toward Againsky's body.

Fannie had moved to Mrs. Montgomery and they were talking in low voices. She looked up at May's request and nodded, then began running back down Front Street toward St. Ann's Hospital. The Weyerhauser Hospital was much closer, only about four blocks away, but Frank had shared his concerns about the care there, and May knew he would want to be treated at St. Ann's.

Mrs. Montgomery had walked over to Fannie, and now said, "Is there anything I can do?"

"No," said May, "I'm just trying to stop the bleeding until someone comes who knows how to care for him. He hasn't moved since he was knocked out. I don't know...I don't know if he'll gain consciousness." May had seen head injuries before that sometimes took days to kill the injured person. She prayed that would not happen to Frank.

"Can I get you anything? Would you like me to take over for a few minutes?" asked the madam.

"No. I don't think I could bear to be away from him," said May, shaken by the circumstances into frankness.

"I suppose not," said Mrs. Montgomery.

"Where were you?" asked May. "How did you get here?"

"You told me where you planned to meet Againsky," Mrs. Montgomery reminded her. "I had my own reasons to want him dead, so I came down here right after we spoke. I've been waiting in Fannie's cabin for him to arrive but he never did."

May thought about this. He must have been here before they got here. Where could he have been? And then she realized. "He was in Rosie's cabin," she cried. "He must have been watching for us and planned to surprise us."

"Which he did," said Mrs. Montgomery.

"Which he did," agreed May. "When he saw us outside, he must have gotten out of her cabin, maybe through a back window? And come over here, where he saw Frank. I guess Frank is just lucky that he chose a hammer, and not a knife." She looked down at Leishke. "I guess you were lucky," she said in an undertone and brushed his hair from his forehead.

"But why did you come down here, Mrs. Montgomery?" asked May, looking back at the woman standing near her. "I know you are upset about Mrs. Todd, and Rosie, but this was an enormous risk."

"I had my reasons," said Mrs. Montgomery. "I'm going to wait for Fannie, and then I'll tell both you girls. You deserve to know, especially Fannie. Now," she said briskly. "I'm going to go into Fannie's cabin and see if I can find some clean towels or linens that you can use against that bleeding."

May thanked her. She pulled the bloody wad of fabric from Frank's head. It did appear that the bleeding was slowing. She pressed it back, and prayed the ambulance would arrive quickly and that Frank would survive.

• • •

At George's home in the Juneau Indian Village, his concern about his mother being angry over his appearance quickly disappeared in the clamor and excitement of his arrival. He found the entire family gathered in the kitchen when he arrived. In addition to this immediate family, Joe's parents, his other aunt, and uncle, and his five cousins were present. The room was so crowded there was barely room to stand, but the uncles had brought extra chairs, so those who wanted to sit could.

His mother, who George had never seen cry, had tear tracks running down her cheeks and a red nose; his father looked grim and angry when he and Joe walked in.

George couldn't ever recall one of his escapades ending with such joy – they were more likely to end with a paddling and a stern talking to. He wondered if this was the beginning of a new attitude toward his arriving home looking dirty and with torn clothes but feared otherwise.

He was hugged by everyone, while at the same time being bombarded with questions. He and Joe both answered as best they could, with George ensuring that the whole family understood the important role that Joe played in saving his life.

"Oh, that evil, evil man," cried his mother. "We must all take a moment to pray for your safe return, and for God to watch over Fannie."

Everyone stood, held hands, and prayed, led by his Uncle Michael, a church deacon. George found himself suddenly struggling with tears – it felt as if he was standing in a great heap of love, in place of the heap of rope he had spent so much time struggling with today.

• • •

The ambulance had arrived as May and Mrs. Montgomery were placing the fourth towel on Frank's head wound; it had almost stopped bleeding, and May tried to tell herself that she had not imagined the faint squeeze she thought he had given her hand.

The ambulance driver and orderly jumped off the wagon and quickly lifted Leishke onto a stretcher and then into the bed of the wagon. At their request, the orderly helped both women into the wagon, to sit on a bench next to the stretcher. A canopy covered the bed of the wagon, but the wind had picked up, and May busied herself trying to protect Frank's head with her own hat.

When they arrived at the hospital, May walked into the building holding Frank's unresponsive hand. Mrs. Montgomery was next to her. The hospital staff appeared to recognize the owner of the best-known brothel in Douglas but did not act untoward. The nurse in charge greeted her by name, and May wondered what connection Mrs. Montgomery might have with the hospital.

The question was quickly answered when she heard the nurse quietly thanking the madam for her generous monthly contributions. The sister directed that Leishke be taken to a private room, appearing to seek approval for the move from Mrs. Montgomery, who nodded her approbation.

In the room, the orderlies transferred Leishke to a bed, and a doctor came in to examine him. The doctor briefly asked May to describe the injury, before telling her that she had done the right thing by applying pressure to the wound. He excused both women from the room, saying the orderlies would be undressing and cleaning the patient.

They walked out to the hospital's waiting room; they had not walked through it when they entered with the stretcher as that came in through a side entrance. May was pleased to see that Fannie was in the room and went to thank her for getting help.

Mrs. Montgomery joined the two young women; they were, fortunately, the only people in the waiting area at this time. May suspected it was busier earlier in the day, but it was approaching the dinner hour, and visiting hours for patients had probably ended.

"Mrs. Montgomery," said Fannie, "you said you would tell us why you put yourself at such risk today to kill Mr. Againsky. Can you tell us now?"

"It's a long story, but I'm afraid that Fannie, at least, will find it a familiar one," said the madam. She reached to take Fannie's hand. "My dear child, were you abducted from your home by a man who promised marriage, but instead took you to Buenos Aires?"

"Yes," said Fannie, sounding surprised. "That happened to both Jennie and me. Do you know other women here who had the same dreadful thing happen to them?"

"Yes," said Mrs. Montgomery. "It happened to me also. I was only 12 years old when my parents were approached in Germany by a man who said he was from America and wanted to marry me. They were so happy to give me such a grand opportunity.

"They had no idea they were condemning me to a life of misery. The man who took me – a devil on this earth if there ever was one – got me with child as quickly as he could. I bore the baby but had to give it up to a woman in Buenos Aires. The word was that once she had her hands on your child, the infant was never seen again."

Mrs. Montgomery appeared to choke back tears, and May and Fannie now found themselves reaching to hold her hands.

"Oh, you sweet things," she said. "That was the beginning of many years of heartache and anger. But the year I turned 20, a young man who was a regular client of mine came to tell me that he had just inherited a fortune and wanted to buy my freedom. I didn't think it would possibly work, but my 'advanced age' and the amount of money he was offered persuaded my so-called husband to let me go."

"My protector brought me to California and set me up in business. He didn't want to, but he had been engaged since he was very young, so marriage wasn't a possibility. After he married, I left for Seattle; I didn't tell him I was going and for the first time, I was free to do what I wanted to do.

"I worked hard, and by the time I was 35, I had earned enough to make my way to Alaska and open the Opera House. I thought I was safe from the Warsaw Club here, but have found that is not the case, as you poor girls know. By the time I moved here, my German accent was gone, and I chose the name Montgomery because it was the name of a friend I had made in Seattle. I have always been very careful about who I let work there, and I've tried to treat them well. I would never want any of my girls to feel the desperation I had felt in Argentina."

She turned to Fannie. "When May told me that you, Rosie, and Jennie, had worked in Argentina, I just knew that same organization that had captured me all those years ago was still in operation. I had to do something, and I just did it.

"That man had to die. I'm glad that I was the one who killed him."

"You saved our lives," said May. "I'm sure the marshals and the Douglas Commissioner will understand it was done in self-defense."

"I'm honestly not worried about what happens to me," said Mrs. Montgomery. "I've sent to hell one more devil, and that is enough for me."

Epilogue

Three months later

It was July, and the days were long; May knew she wouldn't be seeing the sun set tonight because it would have necessitated that she remain awake until midnight, and her days were too full to miss out on sleep.

It was a beautiful summer day; the Fourth of July celebration had occurred the previous week, and the sunny, warm weather had continued since. Fourth of July in Douglas marked the biggest celebration of the year – it was one of two days (Christmas being the other one) when the mines shut down. There were picnics, firefighter competitions, and a parade. May had enjoyed the day but was exhausted by its end.

She had given notice at the Opera House on July 5th but gave Mrs. Montgomery as long as she needed to find a replacement. Mrs. Montgomery was still there; a grand jury had taken up the case last month and determined her shooting of Againsky was in self-defense.

Leishke's injury had helped convince the grand jury members that Againsky's death was justified. Thinking of that injury, May was again filled with gratitude for his recovery. Frank was just now returning to work himself; his recovery had been a long one, and he was supposed to try to take it easy now he was back at work. May doubted that was possible for Frank, but planned to help ensure he got enough rest.

He was still suffering from headaches, but his mental acuity didn't seem to be affected. At times, May joked with him that she was almost sorry it wasn't – she could not hide anything from the man. Just this morning, as they rose from bed and prepared for work, Frank had asked her about her courses. He had noticed they were supposed to have started a week ago. May was very regular and suspected that she may be pregnant. Now, it appeared that Frank did also. She really couldn't hide a thing.

They had married the first week in May; Frank had just been released from the hospital, and May had wanted to wait until he was more fully recovered. Frank was determined; he told May that coming so close to death had convinced him that he didn't want a life without her in it. Commissioner Hensen had performed the ceremony since Frank wasn't strong enough for a church service. He had promised May, however, that he would come to church for a blessing whenever she chose.

That would need to be soon, she thought, before she began showing. They were living in Frank's house in Juneau, which was another reason that May needed to quit work at the Opera House. Traveling via the ferry each day to and from work was time consuming and meant an extra early rising time for May. That was an extra inconvenience for the newly married couple.

Today, she and Frank would be helping bring Rhys Davies back to his home from the hospital. He had been moved to St. Ann's in Juneau several weeks ago, to be closer to his work and to make it more convenient for friends to visit. His recuperation had been a long and difficult one. There were several times when the staff at the hospital had believed he would be lost, but his youth and strong constitution had seen him past the infections, fevers and even pneumonia.

He would continue to need some care and would not be returning to work at all for at least another few months, but he was looking forward to leaving the hospital.

Fannie had left Juneau after the grand jury met; she was moving up to Cordova for work, she told May. Cordova was another Alaska boom town, with a nearby railroad camp and lots of mining activity. May and she had exchanged a couple of letters, and Fannie said the money was good. She was hoping to make enough to establish a brothel, perhaps in Cordova or even back in Juneau or Douglas. Before she left, she had given, as promised, all the details she could recall of the Warsaw Club, and Frank had sent the information to San Francisco authorities.

Andersen had been charged with assaulting Davies and was to go to trial in a month's time. It was expected it would be an easy conviction. Kilburn had also been charged with assault and sentenced to one year and one day in federal prison. The sentence tipped the conviction into a felony, and it was likely it would be easier to convict him in the future. Although he was a suspect in the Petersburg assault, and in the attacks on the Douglas Opera women, none of his victims would testify against him. May just hoped he would be arrested quickly after his next release from prison.

Selena Dowling had also recovered, but was expected to have weak lungs, possibly for the remainder of her life. Her benefactor, Max Whelan, had continued to woo her. Frank had been asked to attend their wedding at Whelan's home the following week. There was certainly gossip about the relationship, but Whelan continued to prosper and May thought they would be happy.

She knew she was. She had left work after the dinner hour and caught the ferry for the short trip to Juneau. The steep mountains of Gastineau Channel still had some snow on the peaks, and she saw that reflected in the flat calm water of the channel. The sun was warm, and none of the boat's occupants wore jackets; even the men carried them, although all still wore their hats. After all, that was a matter of propriety, not comfort.

As they approached the Juneau dock, May heard a whoosh, and looked next to the boat. A humpback whale had sounded its blowhole a few feet away, before leisurely lifting its hump from the water of the channel and diving, waving a large tail as it went into the depths.

Frank was waiting for her as she stepped off the Juneau dock. She often found him there, and wondered how many ferries he greeted each evening before finding her. She didn't ask him; she was just always so happy he was there.

He reached to take her hand and guided it to the crook of his elbow. They began walking up the street together.

"How was your day?" he asked her. "Are you feeling well?"

"Yes," said May. "I am feeling well. And I had a good day. Right now, it's the best part of my day." She looked at him. "I do love you, you know," she said. "Thank you for being here."

He smiled and patted her hand. "I feel the same," he said. "And I'm glad to be here."

The End

Acknowledgments

This book is based on a real murder in Douglas, Alaska. The victim called herself Babe Brown, and the man suspected of her death was named Harry Againsky. He had an alibi for the murder, so ended up being charged with violating the federal White Slave Traffic Act. He served one year in federal prison.

The story of Babe Brown's background as part of the Warsaw Club is based on interviews of her friends at the time, and contemporary accounts of a sex trafficking cabal that worked out of Buenos Aires for decades. Babe was almost certainly a victim of this notorious ring. Her friend, Fannie Miller, was also a real person of the time – another prostitute whom federal marshals charged with perjury after she lied to them about Againsky.

Frank Leishke is also a real person – and the story of his capture of the notorious killer Edward Slompke is also true. Although he was probably with the federal marshal service at the time of Babe's murder, he was not involved in the investigation.

So, this book is a mix of fiction and nonfiction, and it's my attempt to create a fictional end that is more satisfying than the one that really occurred.

My husband, Ed Schoenfeld, and my aunt, Cathy Bagley, were instrumental in my writing this book with their enthusiasm and support. I also want to thank beta readers Elizabeth Schoenfeld, Joy Lyon, Dee Ellen Grubbs, Anitra and Tom Waldo, Laury Scandling, Larry Persily, and Laura Lucas for their comments and suggestions.

I want to end this acknowledgement by recognizing the real victims of the Warsaw Club, as well as Babe Brown and Fannie Miller. These women's names were not the ones given to them as birth, but their suffering at the hands of men was very real. May they rest in peace.

About the Author

Betsy Longenbaugh is a life-long Alaskan who is a former newspaper writer and social worker. She now researches historic murders in her hometown of Juneau, Alaska. In 2022, Epicenter Press published Forgotten Murders from Alaska's Capital, featuring ten of the stories her research uncovered.

With her husband, retired journalist Ed Schoenfeld, Betsy has presented more than a dozen programs on historic murder cases. The couple also created two walks featuring historic murders in Juneau and its neighboring town of Douglas. These events benefit the Juneau Douglas City Museum and the Episcopal Church of the Holy Trinity in Juneau.

Information on new cases and upcoming events is on Betsy Longenbaugh's author Facebook page and at www.truecrimealaska.org.

About the Author

Emily Longenbaugh is a for long Alaskan who is a former Anchorage writer, and social worker. She did on research in Juneau middens in her hometown of Juneau, Alaska. In 2022, Epicenter Press published, *Forgotten Murders from Alaska Capital*, featuring ten of the stories he researched in journals. With her husband, retired historian Ed Schoenfeld, Beecha presented non-fiction book programs on historic murder cases. The couple also created two walk-through Haunted museums in Juneau and as neighborhood feat of Douglas. These took are behind the Juneau-Douglas City Museum, and the Juneau Arts and much of the Hill of fame in Juneau.

For information or new cases inducing on line, go work to res.alaskr-Longenbaugh author Facebook page and at emailemsaac.alaskr.org